THE
COLOUR OF
FOOTBALL

STEVE STACEY

Bristol Books CIC
The Courtyard, Wraxall Hill, Wraxall, Bristol, BS48 1NA

The Colour of Football
by Steve Stacey
Edited by Martin Powell

Published by Bristol Books 2019

ISBN: 9781909446199

Copyright: Steve Stacey/Bristol Books

Design: Joe Burt

Printed by: Short Run Press, Exeter

Cover photograph: Courtesy of *The West Australian*.

A CIP record for this book is available from the British Library.

Every effort has been made to trace the copyright holders and obtain permission to reproduce the photographs within this book.

DEDICATION AND THANKS

The Colour of Football is dedicated to my wife, Dorothy May Stacey. In those early years, when I had little faith or confidence, she took my hands and guided me through untold teenage turmoils. She followed me wherever this great game took me and cared for myself and our children without any complaints… Bristol, Wrexham, Ipswich, Exeter and finally to Australia, for a 'holiday' that has lasted 40-odd years, from Geelong and Melbourne and back to Perth, and here we are still in this great country which has been so kind to us.

I can hear her now, the plaintive call from the kitchen. "Steve where are you? Still on that book? She has been a real treasure and without her patience, fortitude and support there would be no book at all. This story belongs as much to her as it does to myself. During my career she has never once complained about moving house, meeting new neighbours, or of her husband missing every other weekend in the search for glory on some far flung fields.

I have met some interesting people on the journey. From Bobby Robson, the late England and Ipswich manager, to the Floreat Athena Committee in Perth, Western Australia, to my American family and the truth about Black African-Americans in Kemper County, Mississippi, and last but not least meeting my American father Clarence Lee Sims his family and siblings.

All in some way have contributed to my life in the world of football. I'd like to thank the Professional Footballers' Association for helping me overcome a recent health problem and for sponsoring this book. Much appreciated.

Finally, to Bristol Books and to Clive Burlton who has patiently guided me through the many paths that has led to this book and these memories, some of them stored in my consciousness for many years. Thank you Clive.

It has been an interesting experience about life and living.

CONTENTS

FOREWORD
BY GORDON TAYLOR OBE

Football is not just about the big name stars, who gain fame and fortune around the world. It touches every aspect of life and is a great leveller. People of all backgrounds, races, religions and cultures can come together through football.

Steve Stacey is not one of the big stars. But, as the son of a black American GI and a white English woman, he was a pioneer

Professional football is all about the Steve Stacey's of this world, climbing the ladder from playing in the street, school, through non-league to some of the less glamourous venues of league football. Playing in the rain at Newport, struggling against hamstring strains, and dressing room high-jinx are what the great game is all about.

The Professional Footballer's Association is proud to have helped Steve tell his story. It is one that will resonate with football lovers everywhere and is a great insight into what it was like to be a professional footballer in Steve's time.

Gordon Taylor OBE
Chief Executive
Professional Footballers' Association

 **THE PFA**

SIGN-ON DAY – IS THE PRESS COLOUR BLIND?

9am, Monday, November 27, 1961
Manager's Office
Bristol City FC
Ashton Gate

T he message had been clear. 'Fred's office at 9am sharp. Don't be late'. Fred Ford was the manager of Bristol City.

Tony Ford, (who was no relation to the manager), and I were both excited. After all, it wasn't every day that you got to sign the prized contract that was the dream of so many young boys.

Tony and I had joined the club at the same time. We had worked as ground staff together, swept the endless terraces more times than we cared to remember, had played in the youth team, Colts and reserves together. We had taken girlfriends on dates together, washed the team socks, cleaned the senior players' boots and talked over our football ambitions together.

We had been talking about a professional contract for the last month. How signing that piece of paper would change our lives.

Fred Ford had talked to me about this day. My 17th birthday was in August and Tony's was November. "We will sign you both on Tony's birthday", Fred had said.

I can only assume that my skills sweeping the terraces clear of paper and cigarette butts twice a week were exemplary and would be sorely missed.

I could not wait for the three months from my birthday until Tony's to pass. I was so focused on signing that piece of paper that I never did ask Fred to up my wages from ground staff to professional during the waiting period. No wonder agents are in high demand today!

Les Bardsley was the club's physio; he was also the apprentice footballers' guardian, and it was a relief that he was also there that morning.

Les guided the ground staff down the narrow path to professionalism on a daily basis. A hard but fair hand, kind, considerate, and tough when he had to be, Les was ruthless in his dedication to guide his young prodigies through the gates to the prize of a professional contract.

Les was also a counsellor. Trouble at home? Talk to Les, a caring father figure; at least, he was to me. Many days were spent on the physio's bench trying to fix all kinds of injuries, particularly my hamstring, which would plague me for my entire football career. Les would offer advice, both on playing and personal. Always positive, Les conjured up my nickname, 'Flash'. He reckoned I was the quickest thing on two legs over short distances in the club.

Lemmo Southway was the type of man every club needs. He was 'the Grandfather' of the Colts and junior sides, bootman and storeman. Whenever anyone had a question at the club they would ask Lemmo. Everyone who played for Bristol City crossed paths with Lemmo daily. He was a World War 1 warrior and had lost several fingers to prove it. He always wore a flat cap and had a distinctive gait. The ground staff loved him. He was honest and friendly. When Dot and I got married Lemmo sold us - well he gave really, it was that kind of bargain - our first three-piece suite.

Club Manager Fred Ford was tall, silver-haired, often wearing his grey tracksuit, with the FA badge on the breast pocket. Fred was an FA Staff coach and had been in charge of the England 'B' and Under 23 teams. He was well liked and considered by all to be a fair man, someone you could talk to. Fred was a World War 2 veteran.

Fred had more than one fatherly talk with me about growing up in a difficult world. He was a true father figure and the kind of man that you wanted to play football for. When we arrived at his office there he was, smiling, "Come in, lads."

Fred's office was small. There was barely room for the seven of us to stand, let alone sit, but sit we did for the photos. Fred introduced us to the cameraman and the reporter from the Bristol Evening Post.

"We're going to do the photographs for tonight's edition of the Post," declared the reporter, clearly the leader.

Restlessness and excitement filled the room. The silent pieces of paper on Fred's desk spoke to Tony and I. 'Come on sign me! Give me those names! Scrawl here, so they last an eternity. Who will forget the day Steve Stacey and Tony Ford signed their first professional football contract? Are your hands twitching Steve and Tony? Is it all too late for changing one's mind? Would Fred even contemplate that?'

I hadn't thought about how much I would be getting from now on in a brown folded envelope every Friday. Must be more than the fiver I was getting on the ground staff. What does the contract say, I wondered? I don't know, and I don't care. In five short minutes, I'm going to be a professional footballer. That means more than anything to me.

I hadn't talked to Lemmo, Les, any of the other staff, or my stepfather about my contract. My stepfather wouldn't know and probably would care even less. I hadn't spoken to any of my fellow professionals about how much they earned. They were unlikely to walk around the dressing room telling you what they earn. I hadn't discussed it with the manager. I hadn't negotiated a deal.

I thought it worked along the lines of "we are going to sign you" and I say "thank you, thank you". The club decided your fiscal fate. I was just happy to be a professional footballer, which meant more to me than the money I might make.

I would soon learn the folly of this kind of thinking. You can play football but you can also negotiate outcomes as a footballer even though you're a 17-years-old.

Where's my agent?

"Fred, who's who?" asked the reporter.

Silence.

Silence lingers, the kind of silence you know when the mind is sorting out a question that no one thought would be asked.

I'm staring at this idiot, along with Fred, Les, Lemmo and Tony, none of us uttering a word.

It is not because I'm black and Tony is white, or that we had a high opinion of ourselves, thinking we were superstars. It was the expectation. We are Bristol City; you are supposed to know us, like the girls did on Saturday nights.

"I'm Steve, I score goals; you know, the things that win matches. Currently I'm pinging them in on a regular basis for the youth and reserve teams and you don't know me?" is what I wanted to say. I'm outraged, like professional players are supposed to be when their status is challenged! "Tony saves goals; he kicks wingers. Haven't you done your homework?"

The silence is broken.

"Tony Ford's the white one," said Fred, hardly able to contain his laughter.

We laughed, smiled, tried to look serious, happy, nonchalant, with a pen, without a pen, looking at the camera, looking at the contracts, signing the contracts and variations on a theme. The cameras clicked.

This was the first case of every man for himself. It should have alerted me as to what was to come.

"How much did you get?" I asked Tony as we walked down the tunnel to training the next day.

"11 quid."

"11 quid? I only got ten."

I started making enquiries. The answers elicited the fact that because Tony lived in Thornbury, a bit of an outpost north of Bristol, he got another pound for bus fares! His father must have proposed the deal!

The next thing I know he turned up for training in a Ford Cortina!

However, I wasn't going to argue. The week after I got married, Fred put another two pounds on my wages and I didn't even ask. That's the kind of man he was.

On that day in November, 1961, I woke up as I had for years dreaming of the day I could say I was a professional footballer. By midday it was official. My boyhood dream had become a reality.

Were there better players than me that I met growing up? In those formative years can I remember anyone, when we played under the gaslight on Horfield Common, Muller Road, at Fairfield, on Highridge Playing Fields and for Sneyd Park on the Downs, was there anyone?

Yes, without a doubt. Did they eat, breathe and live every moment for the game? No. Did they want it bad enough that sometimes it hurt? Not as badly as I did. How do I know? Well, where are they?

I was the professional footballer now.

JOE AND CLARENCE

I was a professional footballer. It was all I had ever dreamed of being. At the time I never realised how lucky I was, how many people dream of playing football for a living and never make it.

The odds on being offered a professional contract as a footballer are incredibly slim when you consider how many people play the game and how few are given the chance to play for a living.

I did not know it at the time, but my genes were all about going against the odds. I never realized how fortunate I was to actually be here, or how miraculous it was that my parents were here, let alone me.

My ancestral roots are linked to the two world wars that engulfed humanity during the 20th century, and to two men who fought for the armies of their respective countries. One man was white and the other was black; my English grandfather, Edward Joseph Stacey, and my American father, Clarence Sims.

Ultimately these two men sealed my life and the joy and happiness that has come to my family and I. There are also some very brave and loving women who have played their part; my mother, Evelyn, grandmother, Edith Emily, and my mother's sisters, Edie, Beryl, Eileen and Mavis.

My father and my grandfather came from two different worlds, and I reflect on the circumstances of their lives often.

EDWARD (Joseph)

My maternal grandfather, Edward Joseph Stacey (known as Joe), was born on August 4, 1888. He served in the British Army, both in India and during the Great War. Private EJ Stacey. 8086 1st Battalion

Gloucestershire Regiment.

Joe and my gran lived in close proximity before they married. It is certain that they grew up together despite a five-year age difference.

I recall Gran telling me that the soldiers had left for the Far East in their red tunics and returned in the familiar khaki of the British Army.

On December 1, 1905, aged just 17, Grandad enlisted in the British Army, with the Gloucestershire Regiment at its HQ on Horfield Common, just a short walk from the Wellington Arms pub, where years later he was to tragically enjoy his last pint of ale, collapse, and die.

He served in India and Malta and qualified in ambulance duties.

In 1912, he had completed the standard seven years in the army and returned home. The usual lot of a serving soldier was seven years as a regular and five years as a reservist.

By August 1914, the dark clouds of war hung over Europe like a hungry beast waiting for the slaughter to begin. Edward had been courting my gran for two years but the rumblings of war had cast doubts upon life and living.

They married on Saturday, August 1, 1914, the same day that Germany declared war on Russia. The German invasion of Belgium on August 4, sealed the fate of a generation of young men and women. Britain declared war.

The Gloucestershire Regiment was mobilised at Bordon on August 7. Edward left less than a week after marrying.

I can say with some certainty that, during the retreat from Mons and onward to the Marne and the first Battle of the Aisne, the old warrior suffered a wound, serious enough to have him evacuated to England. The official reports list the Gloucester's in action in the Aisne region between September 5 and October 7. At least, that's where they draw the line under the engagement in their casualty lists.

The War Diaries cite September 18 as the actual last day of the battle.

The Gloucestershire Echo and the London Times of November 3 both reported Grandad in the American Women's Hospital at Paignton, Devon, on September 27, 1914.

Indeed, the London Times had him listed as not previously reported as wounded but admitted to hospital. I read this to mean that perhaps he had recently been wounded, within the last few days. We have to consider that, from receiving a wound, getting initial treatment at the Aid Station, evacuation from the front, transfer to La Havre, loading onto the boat and sailing back to England, and then the journey from Southampton to Paignton in Devon, it may have taken a week at least.

It was further reported in the Times and the Gloucester Echo newspapers that Joe had been wounded in France, probably during the retreat from Mons. He was in and out of the war in less than six weeks. To be evacuated from the front line back to 'Blighty', the injury must have been fairly serious. I cannot discover when or whether he returned to the Regiment, or for how long the wound kept him out of the fight. We do know that, at some point, he was transferred to the Labour Corps, designated no 453438.

The Labour Corps was formed in 1917 and essentially was responsible for the building and maintenance of a vast array of 'the works of war'; roads, railways, military buildings and camps. The Corps accepted officers and men not rated as A1 for front line duty and they were often posted within range of enemy guns. If this was the case then the possibility of injury from gas, particularly in 1917 through 1918, was high.

In March and April 1918, during the German Spring offensive on the Somme, The Western Front, some Labour Corps units were used as infantry.

In later years growing up, Gran showed me Edward's medals. The Mons Star was awarded to those that served in that theatre between August and November 1914, and Edward certainly did that. In addition he would have been entitled to the British War Medal 1914-1920 and the Victory Medal 1914-1919.

As war-ravaged Britain struggled to recover from this conflict, and as jobs became harder to find, and money even more so, personal belongings were sold to those who would profit from the war. It is sad to think that many of the medals for which men and women died were sold for the value of their silver content. We need to ask ourselves are or were heroics and countless lives wasted on the Somme any kind of substitute for family hunger? The old warriors' most precious moments sold, to buy bread and milk for his family.

In hindsight, with the number of lives lost, Joe was lucky. I was lucky. My family and I were lucky, and grateful. Would Joe and Gran have married had there been no war? No war, no marriage, then no Evelyn, no Steve.

CLARENCE

My father and his family faced battles of a different kind.

He came from a country that had grown rich on the back of slavery, and that had treated those with skin of a different colour as less than equal, far less equal. Here, the life of a black person was worth no more than the paper it cost to buy him or her at an auction. No second thought was given before they tore him or her away from their family and set them to work in a life of abject poverty and degradation for the rest of their days.

It was a country where governments made laws that prohibited people of colour from marrying a white person. Or, as I came to learn, from assuming positions of authority in an army that was fighting a war to set the whole world free. Except of course that the war was not fought to set black people, including my father, free from anything.

In his book 'The Land Where the Blues Began', Alan Lomax describes the fate of black Americans in the state of Mississippi, where my father was born, a state in the very Deep South of America.

Lomax says that, despite the whole world experiencing and singing and dancing to that famous bluesy music, blacks were experiencing a 'feeling of melancholy dissatisfaction that weighed upon all their hearts. Feelings of anomie and alienation, of orphaning and rootlessness, the sense of being a commodity rather than a person; the loss of love and of family and of place.'

Blacks were 'excluded from public facilities, were poorly paid, badly housed, constantly insulted and bullied, and were without equal rights before the law.'

Clarence Sims was my father, although his name does not appear on my birth certificate. I don't know why.

My mother was not yet 20 when she gave birth to me. Was it her choice not to name Clarence as my father? Who knows? I never asked. There is a great deal of mystery surrounding Clarence.

On the October 8, 1945, we do know that he lodged an Application for a Social Security Account Number (SSA), and I think we can be pretty sure that this was his first SSA application. SSA's are the American version of personal identification numbers that stay with a person on a lifetime basis.

Clarence had crossed with an 'x' the box that asks whether he had ever applied for an SSA before, indicating he had not. This was the time of his demobilisation from the army.

Clarence was not registered for social security prior to this date, which I find interesting. The reason being that the United States could send young men overseas to fight in a war, but had previously denied or failed to register them for any kind of social security. In effect this means that, for 20 or more years, the United States Government did not even know of his existence!

Did he act out of national pride by enlisting? Could he have chosen not to go to war? If he had made that decision who would have known? After all, he did not exist. Did the recruiters simply drive through the area and rope in every young black man that they could find?

The 'Kemper County Messenger' was the local newspaper of the time, published in De Kalb, the County Seat of Mississippi. In the issue of Thursday, February 12, 1942, the paper tells us that; 'Monday (February 16) is the date of the Third Selective Service Registration'… 'Nine Kemper County boys left for Camp Shelby' and that… 'all men between the ages of 20 and 44 are required to sign for service.'

In the Thursday, April 2, 1942, edition the report indicates that the 'Local Board is seeking Negro draft evaders' and that the Board is unable to locate the whereabouts of 13 Negro residents.'

Clearly even second, third and fourth-class citizens were needed for the war effort.

The criteria for service, it appears, was birthdays, rather than American citizenship, or voter rolls. The Selective Service Registration meant that all persons who celebrated their 20th birthday before December 1941, and who had not reached their 45th birthday before February 16, 1942, must register for duty.

If we applied those criteria through to the end of the war, then my father's story becomes problematic. Clarence never reached the age of 20 until 1945, according to his headstone at the Veterans Cemetery, where he is buried.

A search of Clarence's war record has thus far turned up nothing. It's as though he was never in the army. There is no record, not even a name. So how did Clarence end up in Bristol, England?

There is a limited amount of information available even to next of kin when seeking answers to these questions, about black America during the pre-war period.

The blacks had no rights, so there was no documentation (or if there was, it was limited). For instance, birth, death and marriage was, to a large extent, only provided by an oral record. Much of black American history is simply a recollection of the memory.

So, the question is, if you were black and had no social support from the government, how would they find you during a crisis like the Second World War?

The local county sheriff would round you up. If you did not want to fight the white man's war there was only one option you had, and that was to run away.

For one brief moment in time, put yourself in Clarence's, or any other black man's, shoes. You are in the Deep South of the United States. White people are still hanging blacks for no particular reason. Blacks would disappear, never to be seen again. There is no government support for you and your family. You totally depend on the people around you. The white population needs your labour, but you have no bargaining power. No work equals no money; if you didn't work then there were plenty who would. It was a case of take it, leave it or starve.

Suddenly the army needs you; to fight for a society that is built around the total degradation of the Negro race. It's not as though they need you at home. You will need to work on a battlefield thousands of miles away. You have no radio or television. You are cocooned in a small town in Mississippi, a world war? The south is your world, Mississippi is your world, Kemper County is your world, Scooba is your world, and a small wooden house in the backwoods is your world. So why would you sign up?

However, given the Selective Service Registration that all people attaining the age of 20 by December 1941 need to register, we know the following about Clarence. According to his death certificate he was born in September, 1925. Providing that the record of his birth is correct, he was 16 years and three months at the time of his signing up. I was born on August 27, 1944, and at that time Clarence was just short of his 19th birthday. Clarence had to have been in the UK in November 1943 and had to be just a shade over 18.

This scenario means that Clarence was probably roped into the enlistment process and sent overseas when he may not have been of eligible age, and that's why he has no army record.

The record shows that a fire in a building in St Louis, Missouri, just after the war destroyed many army records. Conspiracy theories abound. No record equals no service pensions, no black heroes, no medals, no martyrs, no retributions.

The strange thing is that there is, however, a record of his re-enlistment in 1946, an attempt, I believe, to use the army to get back to see my mother. This enlistment is for a year only and the record is carried on his gravestone at the Veterans Cemetery.

Yet for some reason there is no record on the headstone of his service prior to 1946. So, did he get a war veteran's pension or benefits?

Social security records show various changing details of Clarence's birth. The initial application, his own application for a social Ssecurity number dated October 8, 1945, says he was born in Jackson (the State Capital), Mississippi, Hind County on September 23, 1923.

In December 1941, the United States entered World War II. They had expected a quick finish, but that wasn't to be the case.

One of the many parts of the war that is rarely discussed concerned the presence of the segregated US army in Britain. Keen not to risk antagonising an important ally, the British Government took no stand against segregation. Separate accommodation and canteen facilities were provided for the American military where requested. Efforts to keep personnel of different races apart when outside the camps in pubs, dancehalls, clubs and the like were rarely formally challenged. Yet nor were they entirely successful as the protests of black GIs and friendliness of local civilians suggest.

As a result of the prolonged action in the Pacific and Asia, the US Army needed to fill as many regiments of fighting men as it could. As the number of troops grew, so too did the logistics arm. I can sense that a decision was made to use the black folk, the darkies, in this field. They wouldn't be trained to use weapons – who would want that when the war is over and there might be a revolt? No, they can be drivers, and cooks – as long as their hands are clean – hole-diggers, latrine-cleaners and any other dirty job that the real army needs doing.

There are a few odd tantalising details on his initial application. He lives at 122 West 131 St, New York City. He didn't return to good old Mississippi. He's 'unemployered.'

On his Social Security Application, (SSA) he spells his first name in three different ways.

First he's 'Clarance'. Then he's 'Clarens'. Perhaps then the clerk gave him some help and he became 'Clarence?'

What kind of inequality leads a young man, fighting for his country, to be unable to spell his name when he's over 20-years-old, and to not know where he was born?

Having established a place of birth you would have thought that he would have simply stuck with Jackson, as suggested, but the next SSA account, completed in 1985, has him born on the same day and month, but this time the year of his birth is given as 1925, and the birth place as Electric Mills.

The mystery deepens as a 1992 document gives the same date and year of birth, but in that he was born in Meridian.

A year, in 1993, another report has him born in 1922, but this time the place of birth is not noted. This registration that was made with the SSA was on April 18, 1993, the day Clarence died.

So we can agree on my father's date of birth being the September 23, but not on the year or place of his birth.

My mother, Evelyn, always told me that Clarence was from Electric Mills. She also said that Clarence was older than her. Evelyn was born late in 1924.

When he died his wife, Daisy, must have filled in his death certificate. One might assume, over the years and a hundred family discussions, that the year of his birth had been worked out. Daisy says that it was 1922. Maybe Daisy was being stubborn. Clarence himself claimed 1923, on his first SSA application on discharge from the military. Perhaps Daisy never filled in the year of his birth on the SSA, simply because no one knew for sure. Memory lapse, bureaucracy, clerical error, administrative convenience, it all seems very strange. As for his place of birth, it is probable that Clarence himself did not know.

The truth of the matter is Clarence was probably born in some shack in Electric Mills, where his father was working. The black community would have known the details of his birth. There was no need to register it, no family allowance, or child support or any other kind of support, so what good would it do anyway?

Is it important where Clarence was born? Meridian, Jackson or Electric Mills?

Perhaps it's typical of the time. Clarence was a Negro. Did it matter that the record was right or wrong?

Who cares what year he was born? You live, you die. That's it.

No. That's not it. It's important to me.

I need to know about my father.

My mother Evelyn had always told me that Clarence had said he was born in Electric Mills, Mississippi. So, if it was good enough for Eve, it must be good enough for her son. The truth will never be known.

In later years Clarence would say that his birth was in Kemper County in Mississippi (Burning).

The records show that some 6,500 African-Americans died in some form of racial violence between 1865 and 1965. Some 2,400 were lynched, hung, roped, strung up, dangled from a tree.

Mississippi lays claim to 500 of these blacks. Men, women, children, reverends, preachers and anyone else who happened to get in the way, from the mid-19th century through to the mid-1960's.

I have tried to imagine being a young black person growing up in Mississippi, as Clarence would have been. Tales of wild lynchings on the lips of everyone, of midnight knocks on shanty doors and a sense of helplessness, an endless burning desire for freedom, wondering if you could ever forgive.

Hate is a cheap commodity to pass down the ages.

Do not look me in the eye, do not drink from the same water fountain, careful on that word emphasis, and do not disagree, either by looks, talk or facial expression.

Whatever you do, do not think for one moment that you are any part white, in reality or in pretense. Understand, take your place, know where you stand, be careful, be very careful, in wherever you go, whatever you do, and whatever you feel. Tread lightly. Do not disturb the flowers. Leave no footprints.

Kemper County, where Clarence's family, Bill and Mary, my grandparents, lived out their lives and where, 'Aunt Curry Sims' was to tell me years later, as I munched her southern fried chicken and black eye peas, "We Sims go back a long way round here."

In Meridian, just down the road from Electric Mills and Scooba, where I was later to meet Clarence's schoolboy friends, where one of his SSA's records his birth, and where the trial of the three young freedom riders, murdered by the Klan depicted in 'Mississippi Burning' took place, 29 blacks were murdered, 14 of them on Christmas Day and Christmas Eve, 1906. All of them were unidentified. Not much to be said for the spirit of Christmas.

There is a lack of dignity and worth when one reads the term 'an unidentified black person, a nobody.' The value of life has been stripped away.

The callousness never ended; interminable, everlasting, constant, forever and unforgivable.

Two pregnant women at Shubuth, two 14-year-old boys, nine members of the Tapin family in Centreville in 1956, and three members of the McCray's. Then there were the two Stanford brothers in Hazlehurst, and the Reverend TA Allen in Hernando. Some remembered by name, some merely a grim statistic.

What about the trials, and bringing these people to justice? Don't hold your breath.

The Reverend Allen was explaining, telling and preaching to those that listened, that killing people because their skin colour was black was wrong. Did he contemplate the irony as they strung him up? Did he know what he was dying for?

Clarence, his immediate family, and their kin, lived in this world. That his father and his father's father, and that his father's father's father, and those before them, survived this travesty of life and death, that a war was fought in the cause and yet, after the end of that war in 1865, the killing still went on relentlessly, is incomprehensible.

However, I am here because of them, and all the pain, the agony and the horror of it all. Through all of this I was born to a black American soldier whose roots were in Mississippi, and a white mother whose family roots were in Ireland, and whose family had emigrated to England years before, to escape famine, and whose early relative died in the workhouse at Stapleton, a district of Bristol.

This was the environment my father grew up in. The fact that he survived it was a miracle.

Nat, my youngest daughter, was born on March 26, 1966, the same day that, in 1944, the Reverend Simmons died.

My brother Ken's birthday is January 9, 1950, the same day that the three children of Thomas Harris were killed at Kosciusko.

My eldest daughter, Michele, was born on October 28, 1963. On the same date in 1909, when four unidentified blacks were strung up in Kemper County.

People that perhaps my grandparents knew? Do I remember these coincidences? How do we celebrate birthdays?

Do I tell Nat that, on her birthday, I played for Wrexham and we squeezed out a 2-2 draw against Aldershot on Grand National day? Or do I tell her that some rednecks down in Kemper County murdered a preacher just because he was black?

Which is the most important story? Generic, the killing and hate message goes through the family. What do you see when you look at a black person? What do you feel? Why can you not see a person, not the colour of the skin?

They don't have a football team in Kemper County, Mississippi, but perhaps if they did, black and white may well have enjoyed a game or two together. Maybe, just maybe, all of this would have been different. Friendships would have been born, relationships established, trust given, lives saved.

Perhaps.

AUGUST 27, 1944

*A few minutes past 2am,
Sunday August 27, 1944,
Bristol, England.*

The conflict now known as World War Two is drawing to a close. Only hours earlier the French army had marched into Paris and were on the verge of accepting the German surrender. It is the beginning of the end.

Several miles north of the bomb-ravaged Bristol city centre is the district of Southmead. Here was located one of the hospitals that was the home of the maternity wing of the local health system.

'B' Ward is where most of the young children born during this conflict drew their first breaths, where admiring mothers proudly regarded their loved ones and knew that here was the secret of life. Here lay a part of them and a part of a brighter future.

My mother was a young, unmarried, teenage girl, still four months short of her 20th birthday when she gave birth to me.

She wished for a boy, if only for her own sake, having five sisters and a lone brother.

She wished for a boy for the sake of the boy's father. She had loved him from the moment they first met in the Royal Oak pub. The pub was just five minutes from where she lived in the family home, a short bus ride away from the hospital bed at Southmead.

He wasn't there. She needed him. But so, too, did the army.

Evelyn's mother, Edith, had supported her through her pregnancy, as had her sisters. Indeed, if it had not been for them, it was unlikely there would have been a birth, no new life, no memories and no first breaths.

After much trepidation, Evelyn's father came around to loving this unborn baby, his first grandchild. This was a moment to savour. After a war that had stretched on longer than many cared to remember, a birth provided the chance to celebrate life.

Forgotten now were the strong words he had spoken to her, as he cast her adrift from the house where they had all lived, in Horfield, away from the family roots in the small nearby village of Westbury-on-Trym.

He was a soldier. He had seen death. Had witnessed first-hand the waste of life, and had seen minds and limbs shattered. This helped him realise that life is too short. Life and all that she throws at us is to be embraced. All of this is confirmed with that first breath. This baby was, after all, his flesh and blood.

There were several concerns, though, which he knew needed to be faced. How will we deal with the social issues? His wife assured him that there was no need for concern. It's war and things are different. Society is changing, as is the way people think and act.

But his daughter is not married. Many couples are facing the same dilemma, the world will understand. His wife was again the voice of reassurance.

The father is a foreigner. Yes, one of those sent from overseas to help save us. There are thousands of these young men all over England. "They are our allies", is her measured response.

He is a soldier, too; he will need to return to his own country eventually. He will take the baby and Evelyn with him. Perhaps, but we will cross that bridge when we come to it.

The Americans have said that he will not be allowed to marry Evelyn. Why?

The father, he's a Negro, a black American soldier.

Through all the uncertainty, Edith was the calming influence.

She was the rock, the glue that kept that family together.

On Sunday, August 27, 1944, at 02.11am, I took my first breaths outside of the womb. Sister Stephens wrapped me in a blanket and lay me gently in my mother's arms.

My father was driving a truck to East Anglia with supplies for the build up to the allied assault after the Normandy invasion six weeks before. My grandparents were asleep at Oak Road, Horfield. I was not expected for a day or two.

It must have been hard for my mother. Sister Stephens again is the one who calmed her fears.

Although there was something about her demeanor that told my mother that something was not right. Her face was taut, her brow furrowed, and her usually smiling eyes were drawn tight, her smile forced.

Sister had grown fond of Eve. In two or three short days she had felt some compassion for this young girl caught in the throes of war, pregnant and unmarried to some soldier or serviceman.

Eve had already made one decision although she had told no one. The baby, her son, will be called Stephen after her friend, the kindly nurse, Sister Stephens.

She told my father when he arrived and he told her how he was named after Clarence Darrow, a civil rights lawyer. They decided my middle name would be Darrow.

So, I am named after Clarence Darrow a civil rights lawyer from Chicago, who is best known for the Scopes Case and The Monkey Trial.

The Monkey Trial revolved around the teaching of Darwin's theories in Tennessee when High School Teacher John T. Scopes was prosecuted for teaching evolution.

In 1925, Clarence Darrow defended Dr Ossian Sweet, a black medical practitioner who wanted to make a home in an all-white neighbourhood of Detroit.

On September 8, 1925, Sweet and his wife moved into their house. A crowd of close to a 1,000 people gathered outside. A larger crowd gathers the day after and this time rocks are thrown and the mob are baying for blood.

At about 8.25pm a shot is fired from an upstairs window in the house. It hits and kills Leon Breiner, one of the white crowd that was about to rip Sweet, his family and his house apart.

Of the 12 occupants in the house, 11 are arrested, jailed and charged with first-degree murder. The exception is a 12-month-old baby.

The National Association for the Advancement of Coloured People (NAACP) contacted Darrow and asked him to represent the Sweets.

The case went to trial in October of the same year, shortly after the Klu Klux Klan nominee in the mayoral election failed to get elected - perhaps the beginning of black bloc voting in America.

On November 24, 1925, Clarence Darrow said during the Sweet trial:

"If I thought any of you had any opinion about the guilt of the clients, I wouldn't worry because that might be changed. What I am worried about is prejudice. They are harder to change. They come with your mother's milk and stick like the color of skin. I know that if any of these defendants had been a white group defending themselves from a colored mob, they never would have been arrested or tried. My clients are charged with murder, but they are really charged with being black."

Then, in his closing statement, he reminded the jury of their duty to justice.

"Gentlemen, I ask you to use all of your judgment, all of your understanding, all of your sympathy in the decision of this case. I speak not only for these 11 people, but for a race that in spite of what you may do will go on and on and on to heights that it has never known before. I speak to you not only on behalf of them, but on behalf of the millions of blacks who look to these 12 white faces for confidence and trust and hope in the institutions of our land, and in the guarantees that the laws have made to them, those blacks who all up and down the length and breadth of our land, and whose ancestors we brought here in chains…"

The jury listened to the evidence presented and considered everything and pronounced they are unable to give a verdict.

Judge Murphy orders a miss-trial. In December, 1925, all the defendants were released on bail. In April, 1926, the second trial began, but not before the Sweet home was torched, fortunately without much damage.

Henry Sweet, Ossian's brother, is one of the occupants of the house that fateful day and was, indeed, the person that fired the fatal shot at Leon Breiner.

This time the defence has chosen to have all of the 11 people initially charged in the first trial to be charged separately in the second trial.

Clarence Darrow delivers a seven-hour closing argument in defence of Henry Sweet. Part of that closing speech saw him state:

"I would like to see a time when man loves his fellow-man, and forgets his color or his creed. We will never be civilised until that time comes. I know the Negro race has a long road to go. I believe the life of the Negro race has been a life of tragedy, of injustice, of oppression. The law had made him equal, but man has not. And, after all, the last analysis is, what has man done? - And not what has the law done?"

The all-white jury deliberated for four hours before they delivered a 'not guilty' verdict. This was unprecedented. A black man kills a white man, albeit in self-defence, and lives to tell the tale!

In July the following year, the prosecutor finally dismissed all charges against the remaining ten defendants.

Soon after the trial, Sweet's two-year-old daughter and his wife both died of tuberculosis, contracted in prison by Gladys. After failing to find a buyer, Sweet moves back into his home, in the all-white neighbourhood, and stays there until 1944. In March, 1960, Dr Ossian Sweet committed suicide.

This is the man I was named after; Clarence Darrow, a poet, a lawyer, and an orator. I can't do him justice. I cannot find the words to try and explain the impact he had on so many lives in his life. For me there is a lifetime of injustice that this man fought for on behalf of both black and white, and who either could not, or would not, fight for themselves.

It's interesting that the word of mouth handed down to me by my mother, as to her young child's name, quoted the Scopes trial and not that of Ossian Sweet as a naming reason. I am convinced though that both of these trials would have been part of Clarence's growing up.

I am further convinced that Bill Sims, Clarence's father, and my grandfather, had passed these oral messages of Scopes, Sweet and others, on to his son.

EVELYN

My mother, Evelyn, was the one of six children born to Joseph and Edith Stacey.

I have no idea what my grandfather, Joe, thought about black people.

At that time, most English people would have believed in the superiority of the Empire. But whether they viewed the black Americans as they did the Indians, or other dark members of the Empire, good for service and all that, who can tell.

Although anecdotal evidence suggests that the black troops were well thought of by the English, subsequent riots in Bristol between black and white American soldiers were caused in a large part by the refusal of English women to treat the black Americans any different than the white ones!

Evelyn and Clarence had discussed the pregnancy. Evelyn had told Gran and her sisters, Edie, Beryl, Eileen, Mavis and brother George. The defensive lines were drawn. The critical conversation was between Gran and her husband Joe. Granddad had already thrown his daughter out of the house. He knew his daughter was pregnant. He knew that Clarence was the father.

"The army wouldn't let them marry, Joe."

Gran always called him Joe.

"Evelyn will be alone when he goes back stateside. They love each other. It's the Army to blame, not Clarence.

"Let her come home. It's our daughter and grandchild."

I don't know when Joe and Clarence sat down and talked about Eve and the baby, but I wish I had been a fly on the wall.

At some point Joe relented and my mother was brought back to number 58.

I grew up in a world that was far different than today's. It had no computers, jet aircraft, or electric trains. Woodstock, the Beatles and the Rolling Stones were something that a generation that had fought two murderous global conflicts would find hard to understand.

It was a world where not being married and pregnant was a far bigger social crime than marrying a black man.

The US Army refused my father permission to marry my mother because he was black. Mixed race marriages in many American states were illegal, unwanted and, in the eyes of white America, scary.

America is often thought of as the 'land of the free', forged in the main by Europeans seeking escape from tyranny perceived or otherwise.

Boy meets girl, they fall in love, they wish to marry. There are no objections from the family.

What's the military got to do with it?

Black and white or any such mixed race affair?

If marriage is a private contract, then if both parties agree and their parents do not object, surely no one should stand in the way of a union between black and white or of any mix-race marriage.

At 21 years of age, it doesn't matter anymore, people make their own decisions no matter how controversial.

This kind of argument was too simplistic for the American military.

As was common at that time, my father's unit, made up of black soldiers and non-commissioned officers, was led by white American Officers. Lt Schumaker was the man who refused Clarence Sims permission to marry Evelyn Mary Stacey. Why, and on what grounds? If one searches army regulations, will you find any that say that serving soldiers in the United States Army cannot marry?

Will one find a more specific army regulation that states that serving black soldiers in the United States Army cannot marry? Is there a difference? should there be?

Over the years I have considered this decision by Lt Schumaker. How can anyone legally entitled to marry be denied that right, simply because they they're black?

In a civil world, getting married, having babies, and an entitlement to state benefits is taken as read. How do you justify refusing, limiting, denying civil liberties?

How can an instrument of the state, the armed forces, justify this and how do the politicians explain it to the civil world unless, of course, those politicians concurred? Perhaps the young couple could have simply met at the church and organised their own ceremony. The consequences, court martial for Clarence, and being sent stateside? Evelyn would have had to go against the wishes of her father. Perhaps not wanting to act without his permission, which she knew would not be forthcoming, she decided to accept the circumstances.

She was prepared to lay her future with the black man she loved in fate's hands, and more importantly where she would continue to love him, than in an America that was clearly a nation that seemed to care little about its black population. Perhaps the thought of leaving her own comfort zone swayed her.

Maybe she wasn't that much in love. I never asked. It was not an easy situation when you consider that in many American states the union of black and white by law was illegal.

The US Army took Clarence from my mother and I after WW2 ended, and they sent him home. I was another insignificant black child without a father.

I know that my mother and I were not the only ones to suffer such prejudice from the military.

Hundreds of black babies were left in the UK and Europe after the war as fatherless children, while many, many, more white children returned to the States with their American fathers and mothers.

Looking back at Clarence and my mother meeting in Bristol, I cannot help feeling that there is a great irony in their story. 'Goodnight Irene' was the theme tune of my first love in football, Bristol Rovers.

In those days, every football team had a song. The whole Bristol Rovers crowd would be singing this tune 'Goodnight Irene' as the lads ran onto the pitch. These were the days when a crowd of less than 30,000 was considered below par!

Huddie Leadbetter, a black American blues singer, better known as 'Leadbelly', developed this song, although the actual author is unknown. Others who have shared their version with the public include The Weavers, Johnny Cash, Jerry Lee Lewis, Little Richard and Peter, Paul and Mary. Which is some testament.

The ongoing argument is about the lyrics, changed by some to fit the mood and the audience. Leadbelly's original version contains a reference to his lost love Irene, and to drugs and suicide. Lyrics clearly unsuitable to a Saturday afternoon football game, in a land thousands of miles away. It has been said that black music tells the real story, the real truth, and we all know that some can't handle the truth!

It is The Weavers' version that was generally sung on the terraces.

To me it seems a huge coincidence that a song sung in the Deep South, and probably known to my father to express the helplessness of black American life, and a love lost, a loss that he would experience himself, as if in a movie script, should become the theme tune of my favourite football team, playing at a venue within walking distance of the Royal Oak public house in Bristol where he and Eve met. Yet in some way this irony broke the shackles of hate and intolerance and led a young boy onto the playing fields of England where he would be accepted as a football player, for his skill with a ball, and not the colour of his skin.

I do ponder how the Rovers came to adopt this song. Did these lyrics from the Deep South arrive with the black American troops stationed in Bristol?

Clarence's unit, stationed at Muller Road barracks, was just a short walk from the Rovers ground at Eastville Stadium. There is nothing like a sporting event to bring people together. Did these black troops sing of their anguish at the local stadium? Did Clarence express his own hopelessness of living in the Deep South here, at what would have been a very foreign game to black Americans?

The strange twist of fate that, years later, the son he never knew would stand, never realising that this was his father's history being chanted by thousands of people, who thought only that dear old Irene was their lost love. Or that I would stand there never knowing that my father had led the way years before, stood on these terraces, singing the same song.

The reality as to how the song became a Rovers anthem is very different. Plymouth Argyle came to Bristol to play in what was almost a local derby in those days; Plymouth being the city in which my wife Dorothy was born. The date was November 4, 1950.

Innovation was the key in that era and the visiting team had brought with them an accordion player, strolling the boundaries of the hallowed Eastville ground playing songs.

Why did he play 'Irene?' Well, The Weavers, an American group that included Pete Seeger had, in late May of that year, sung a version of Irene that had leapt to the top of the charts.

At half-time, the visiting supporters taunted the Gasheads all around the ground singing "Goodnight Irene". Ergo for the home fans, it was all over; Rovers were two goals down and might as well go home, goodnight and goodnight again.

Three Rovers goals in quick succession in the second half settled the issue, and the stadium dominated by the giant gasholder and the greyhound Tote betting board rang to the tune of 'Goodnight (Plymouth) Argyle', sung by the mass of Rovers supporters, to the tune of 'Goodnight Irene'. The rest as they say is history, real Gashead history.

[Thanks are extended to the Fans Forum at the Bristol Rovers Football Club, particularly Stephen Byrne, for the information on Irene].

White and black relations have changed considerably since WW2. How do people feel and treat others of different skin colour? Today people would hardly blink at the thought of an inter-racial marriage. Football teams are full of black, brown, dark and every shade in between players from every corner of the globe.

Having said this, I think my grandparents were exceptional people. In the end they saw two young people in love and that was enough to convince them to act in their children's best interest.

I regret not being able to talk to Edward Joseph Stacey about this.

When the Second World War ended, my father returned to America. Growing up I wasn't alone in not having a father. Many other families had lost loved ones too. At least I had the knowledge that my father was still alive. Muller Road Orphanage, just a short walk away, was full of fatherless, family-less, lonely children.

As I grew up, all of my friends and those I played football with were white. I'm ever grateful to them, all of them. I knew friendship, admiration and companionship.

As I turned professional, and signed that prized professional contract, I was admired for my skill with the ball, not for the colour of my skin. It was an easy transition.

It was a lonely existence at the time being a black footballer. I can recall only two instances in my career where, in a senior professional football league team, there was another black player.

These were rare exceptions over almost two decades in the game. In the Bristol City youth team, there was a young guy called 'John White', who played a couple of games as a winger. There is certainly some irony there. Then there was John 'Dusty' Miller, who played during my time in the youth and reserve teams at Ipswich Town. He was also a forward.

There was no one to share feelings and experiences with and compare. You had to hold it within yourself and make your own judgments.

Being 'black,' 'dark' or 'coloured' in those early years was lonely. Sure, my fellow professionals were supportive, always. But inside, this feeling of loneliness, questioning your self-worth, being conscious of failure, but most important that you were different, was always there.

No matter what I did, or how I played, I always feared that someone would judge me for being different. Waiting for that first failure to be followed up with a comment along the lines of "told you so, hopeless these darkies."

This was a lack of confidence on my part. In time, I began to understand that to know that I was alone with nowhere to go became a different and lonely part of my character.

There was little, nothing in fact, to share with those like myself. In the dressing room, on the pitch, on the long journeys on the coach or train, there was only the game. There were no others.

There was no sharing of thoughts, ambitions, or failures. There was no family around to talk of forgotten fathers, and share strategies. I admit I struggled with the realisation of colour, of being different.

People would talk of families, fathers and mothers, brothers and sisters. I could not share their experiences. My life was guided by what little knowledge I possessed while growing up, from what I had observed of others, and what I had experienced. I learned on the run. I enjoyed my successes, but I wallowed in my failures, and often repeated my mistakes.

I rarely led, and often followed. I was always conscious that I was different. Caution, wait and see, tomorrow things will be different, I told myself. I could only rely on myself. Where could I seek advice?

In my early teenage years, I began to question my place in the world. Every slight became a personal affront. Once I became aware that I was different, that a person's response reflected their attitude to a different persona, I started to believe that everyone was watching and judging me because I was what I was, black.

My confidence plummeted. I would not act, I would not do anything, I froze. I froze because of the fear of failure. I suspected that all eyes were upon me, awaiting that failure, and then would follow the knowing nods and winks, and then the 'I told you so.'

I had a recurring image in my head. I'm stood on the kick-off spot in a huge stadium. The crowd is in the stands and on the pitch too, filling every foot of space between myself and the four corner flags. If there's anyone out there like me, come and hold my hand. My hand is still outstretched. I'm still waiting…

Today in the English Premiership, indeed the whole of the English Football League, teams are brimming with players of different nationalities and colour.

Black, brown, coffee, and all shades in between. They are British, French, Ghanaian, Portuguese, Brazilian, American, Canadian, and this is the way it should be.

Football is played in every corner, every nook and cranny, of the globe. There are 240 million players playing in more than 200 countries. Others had gone before me and many have followed. However, now in the twilight of my life, I like to think that, in some small way, I was part of the beginning.

OAK ROAD, HORFIELD

I missed the advice and friendship of a father, someone whom I could confide in. I made some bad decisions. I should have known better. The literature on fatherless children is profuse. Yes, there is a danger of running off the tracks, alcohol and drug abuse, and emotional and other issues. However, I was in good hands. Gran and the girls, and later my wife, Dot, kept me on the straight and narrow. However, at times – like Wellington at Waterloo – it was a near run thing.

My mother married and I spent a great deal of my childhood with my grandmother and my aunties, and I think it fair to say that they had the greatest influence on my life. My stepfather was a non-event in terms of guidance, support or advice either in life, playing football or anything else.

So I was brought up by a bunch of loving, caring, women, including, time to time, my mother, grandmother, Auntie Edie and a younger aunt, Beryl. I love them all, and always will.

Gran was one of the loves of my life. She was always there when I was growing up. I probably spent more time in my formative years at Gran's with Beryl and Edie, than I did at home, where Mum, in the clear and certain knowledge that my father was gone forever, had remarried Hector Bruce Gunstone and was bringing up her other family.

Gran was born on December 14, 1894, and brought up in Hotwells, a suburb of Bristol down by the docks, ironically where the slave ships tied up.

Mum and I lived with my grandparents until my granddad died. After some time he forgave and took Eve and I back into his home, his life, and his family. Maybe, after all, he never ever saw black or white, just his daughter, his own flesh and blood.

I do think that my mother made a conscious decision that her son would not be leaving England under any circumstances. Clarence wanted Eve to let his 'sister', who lived in Little Rock, Arkansas, adopt me. At 19, maybe 20, Eve wasn't having any of that and apparently said so.

Mum knew well enough what life was like in America for the black man. She wasn't about to give up her son for that. I'm glad.

Whether Clarence had any intention of returning to Mississippi is unknown, but it is doubtful. Would he have returned to Arkansas to live with his 'sister' and bring me up there? Eve always maintained that she never contemplated joining him and returning to America to live anywhere with Clarence; Mississippi, Arkansas or New York.

I believe that they both knew that this was the last resort. The issue of the black/white relations was too difficult in the USA. They were not easy in England, either. There was family shame, a white mother and a black father. Stories, whispers, innuendo, sniggering, and jokes; she was undoubtedly subjected to some of these, perhaps even all.

Thousands of white British GI brides made the trip back to the United States after the war's end. In excess of one million Americans called Britain home in the years preceding D-Day. Of those, 130,000 were black. Estimates put the figure of war bride marriage in the UK during the war as high as 65,000. Brides came from 50 European countries and may well have totaled 200,000.

Evelyn wasn't one of them.

It was at 58 Oak Road, Horfield, Bristol, that my childhood hopes and ambitions flowered, where I first dreamed of being a professional footballer.

Football, yes football. It was in the street we started playing. It truly was the working man's game back then. Yet strangely, I can never remember any of the kids saying, "it's Saturday my dad is going to see the Rovers play and I'm going with him". There was never this early connection of Saturday afternoon and off to the Rovers ground. The reason was we were too busy playing ourselves.

Traditionally, Horfield belonged to the Rovers. The Pirates. They were the only professional team in the league to play in the blue and white quartered shirts. The greyhound track surrounding the pitch and the large gasometer rising above the Greyhound Totaliser board dominated the southern part of the Eastville ground.

The north of Bristol was generally accepted to be over the Bedminster Bridge, past St Mary Redcliffe Church and further on, sweeping beyond Temple Meads Station, the centre and Broadmead.

The south side of this bridge and the River Avon was all City, Bristol City, the Robins. The disdain between rival supporters was plain for all to see and hear, hung out like last week's washing.

We kids transformed this rivalry in all its forms to the streets. Imagination was the key. The drive to win, not play, but to win, was evident only among the few. As a result, the few always won.

We invented calendars of our own, featuring what the draw was for the next round of football, the prestigious Football Association Cup, for instance. The names of the mighty were scribbled on pieces of scrap paper and carefully drawn from someone's hat, a box or simply from the pavement.

Why was it that all the young men wanted the best players to be on the worst team, bottom of the Third Division (South) as it was then, and be drawn against the kings of the country, Arsenal or Newcastle? It was because we were dreamers with lively imaginations.

Oak Road turned into a stadium, Eastville or Wembley. Thousands called your name. You score the winner in the very last minute and Arsenal are out, eliminated, finished, and you, the local boy, administered the coup de grace. Yes, dare to dream young man.

I have been told that my father Clarence was the first black man that anybody in Oak Road had ever seen. That maybe puts it all into context. I bet mum didn't think then that, year's later, her son would be playing football in the same streets with a tennis ball, kicking everyone and everything in sight.

I often think of that link I share with my father. Clarence was the first black man that some of the residents of Oak Road had ever seen and I would have been the first black boy that their own children played football and dreamt dreams with.

Clarence visited Oak Road several times to see Eve. Mum told me of his coming to tea, fish being served and Clarence getting one of the bones stuck in his throat. This would have been around a crowded table in the dining room.

Clarence wheeled his son in the pram down Oak Road. Out for a walk with the proud mum. Showing all that he was happy taking responsibility. Perhaps they walked around the common, arm in arm, with Steve gurgling away in the pram. Did they talk the talk, plan the future? Did Clarence consider Evelyn living in Harlem? I was too young to remember, but had I understood the conversation…?

Here's how I do remember those days and times.

Mum and I lived with Gran and Grandad Stacey, and Mum's sisters, Edie, the eldest, Eileen, Beryl and Mavis, the youngest.

George, the only son, and the second eldest child, had married Doris and moved away to Southmead, a suburb of Bristol a little further north than Horfield.

Doris ran a 'club', essentially a mail order home business. Order whatever the provider marketed, mainly clothes, and pay the sixpence or a shilling a week until the account was paid. Edie and I used to travel up to Southmead most weeks, 30 or so minutes on a bus and a short walk, to pay the money back to Doris. I was a major beneficiary of this club on the Stacey account!

Edie took over the motherly duties. She cared for me as f I was her own son. She made sure I went to school, went to the parents meetings, cuddled me when I was hurt, admonished me when she had to, and gave me advice on the joys and the sorrows of growing up. I fell asleep in her arms on Sunday nights listening to 'Journey Into Space'.

When I was ill, the measles or the mumps or some other childhood illness, I would be lying on the sofa in Gran's front room, a fire burning merrily away in the grate and the curtains would be closed. Edie would fuss around as always, feeding the fire, boiling cups of tea, but most of all caring for her nephew.

When I went to school, the change to my life came in like a stiff southwesterly. I was called names. There were different faces than those on the street at Oak Road.

When it became clear that I was blessed with the genes that would propel me into a professional football career, the issue of a father receded

Then there was Gran. My grandmother was a treasure. I owe her my life. I can never remember Gran as any kind of young person. She was always old, with her little stoop, her hair in a bun, the crinkles on her face, her crooked smile and the Woodbine hanging from her mouth.

She was always the last to go to bed, but would be up at 5am every morning to light the fire. She would stir it late at night to catch the last of the dying embers until all light had faded. I never heard her raise her voice. I never saw any kind of temper from her. However, it was very clear that she ran the show.

When my mother married Ted, for a short while we all lived at Oak Road. We then moved out to Paulton and Radstock and such places, closer to Ted's family, before taking a country cottage at

Kilmersden, and then a brand new council house at Peasedown St John.

It wasn't long before we all moved back into a council house in South Bristol, first at 26 Goulston Road, and then, a short time, 1 Derham Road, Bishopsworth, where the family was to stay for a good number of years.

I was coming up to the 11-plus exam at this time, which determined whether you would pursue an education that could take you on to university, or whether you would pursue an education in a comprehensive School.

I didn't get on with Ted. Mum had given me a couple of my siblings by this time, Ken and Vanessa, and I felt left out. I got spoiled at Gran's, so it was a better proposition for me to move back in with her, no matter how much I loved Mum.

One moment that changed my life forever was when my mum, or it may have been Auntie Beryl, took me to the pictures, downstairs in 'The Premier' on Gloucester Road and a short five minute walk from home.

On the Movietone news they showed clips of the 1952 FA Cup Final, which had seen Newcastle United play Arsenal.

When the movie was over I wanted to stay and see the clips again. No way. In those days you went to the pictures at any time. There were no set session times. You would go to the movie and arrive maybe half way through the film. You would watch the end, watch the feature and see the start of the 'B' film until you got to the place where you came in. Then you left!

As soon as we arrived home I pulled out my drawing book and started to draw all the bits from the game I could remember.

The film was in black and white, of course, but I rightly drew Newcastle in black and white stripes; but as far as I knew, Arsenal played in grey shirts with white sleeves. I was then unaware of the famous red and white. For the record, the final score was Newcastle 1 Arsenal 0.

I kept on and on all week to get Mum, Edie or Beryl to take me back to see the same film again, just so I could watch the football. All my childhood pleadings were to no avail. Next week was a different film and, alas, no football.

There were some good players in that final. Joe Mercer at Arsenal and 'Wor' Jackie Milburn, probably the most famous face to wear the black and white striped shirt of Newcastle United.

A couple of things came out of those first glimpses of football. It does one well to remember how life is linked and football experiences just keep going round and round.

Some 16 years later I would meet Joe Mercer, the Arsenal half-back, at, of all places, Ellesmere Port.

Joe had become the manager of Manchester City and he was introduced to the teams at a charity game played by Wrexham at Ellesmere Port. Joe shook me by the hand when he was introduced to the players. With a twinkle in his eye he said to me, "Anyone looking for a full-back?"

One night, after leaving the cinema, I walked on the edge of the pavement and scanned the gutters, as was the usual practice. Might find something there, a marble or a penny.

It was winter and the water in the gutter had frozen. I spied a sixpence encased in ice. Now, sixpence was a lot of dough back then. It was a seat upstairs in the cinema, or a trip to the City ground on the bus, and a train ride to Temple Meads Station or two pockets full of sweets or three Woodbines at the local café, on the common.

On my hands and knees, on the main road through town, the Gloucester Road, I was scraping the ice away for this precious find. That was when I heard a voice above me. "What's up, young 'un?"

A youthful policeman stood looking down at me.

"I, er, found this sixpence," I said.

My immediate thought was that the policeman would keep the money and hand it in at the station. Goodbye to my plans of bulging sweet pockets.

But this young copper bent down, pulled out his penknife and, in a jiffy, as we both knelt in the gutter of the A38, had the tanner in his hand. He held it out to me.

"Here you go," he said, and handed it to me.

I looked. He smiled. "Thank you."

I skipped and danced up Gloucester Road. I looked back a couple of times. The first time he was watching and smiling, the second he had his back to me proceeding on his beat. Moments like these you never forget.

Often we would venture up over the common to the main road that led to the Downs, Kellaway Avenue. In later years we would congregate here at one of the cafes.

One summer afternoon, I ventured up to the café alone, and was surprised to find that none of my usual comrades were there. Across the road was a lane that ran up behind the sports field of the then premier school in Bristol, the aptly-named Bristol Grammar School.

I noticed a group of people congregated around the playing field and most noticeably around the cricket nets. I went through the hedge and approached them on what was technically private property. There were a couple of kids in the nets and an older bloke. As was usual then you always enquired whether you could join in. "Yes, son, grab a ball." They were clearly impressed as I did my best impersonation of a medium paced seam bowler, and were even more impressed when I took the bat. Stuart Allan, the young lad who had first noticed me, was the son of the older bloke who was bowling. Stuart and I would go on to become good friends as we shared a love of cricket. So too did Stuart's old man. I was invited for tea and watched a couple of FA Cup Finals in the family home, which was on the same land as the large playing fields. Stuart's dad was the groundsman and caretaker.

I asked Stuart on that first night when they would be back in the nets again.

He mentioned the days, say twice a week, for an hour or so. Paradise! All the gear, flat wicket, proper nets.

I spent a great deal of that summer playing cricket. We enjoyed ourselves, until one night I was there and I had a red shirt on. There was a school game in progress.

Suddenly a call came from the middle. "Who is that person in the red shirt. Get him out of there."

What difference did it make what colour shirt you batted or bowled in, providing you were in the nets? Only later did I realise that these were the Grammar School playing fields and elitism reigned. Stuart's old man said something we weren't supposed to hear and was back in two minutes flat with an old white shirt. There were no more complaints and we were never again interrupted.

Stuart's parents asked about my family. I told them that I didn't have a father, that my mum was away at some other locale, that I lived with my grandparents, and that I wandered the streets looking for sporting opportunities! They took to me.

Stuart and I lost contact when I went to Fairfield Grammar School, but we met years later, while I was indulging in my other love, at Temple Meads Station, trainspotting. He and a few other people were on their way somewhere. I often ask myself that, why in your life, when you have met hundreds and thousands of people, why do I remember Stuart and his family so well?

GASLIGHT FOOTBALL

T he FA Cup, some would argue, is the greatest cup competition ever, and in 1956 it had thrown the Pirates, Bristol Rovers, against Manchester United at Eastville.

Manchester United would win the English First Division title in 1955/56 and 1956/57, just prior to that fateful night in Germany in February, 1958, when the team was decimated in a dreadful air disaster. United would seal the First Division championship with 60 points, a massive 11 points from Blackpool and Wolves, who both finished with 49; there were only two points for a win in those days.

Rovers were an ordinary mid-table Second Division team. Tickets were like gold dust. Rovers' ground capacity then was about 38,000. Apart from the regular Rovers fans wanting to see the game, everyone from the surrounding towns and villages suddenly wanted to be there for the big match, scheduled for January 7, 1956.

Rovers had played four games in seven days, away to Doncaster Rovers on December 24, where they lost 2-1, a 2-1 home win against Leicester City on Boxing Day, and then, as was the custom, a 2-4 loss to the same team the day after! Four days later, on December 31, Rovers thrashed Sheffield Wednesday 4-2 at Eastville. This was a great result, as Sheffield Wednesday would win promotion to the First Division that year and Rovers and Leicester would both finish a few points short of second place.

I badgered my aunts, telling them that I had to go to the game.

"I'll get tickets," said Beryl. In those days there was always someone who knew someone, who had a brother whose aunties cousin knew a relative, a distant relative, who knew someone close to the staff, who was friendly with a player who could get tickets.

I relaxed. I was going to the game. Alas, there was simply too strong a demand for tickets. Beryl didn't get a sniff. I played up. I threatened to throw myself down the stairs but all I did was jump off the bottom step, making as loud a noise as I could, moaning, screaming of an injury, trying to win sympathy.

No one came. "I'm really doing it this time," I yelled and off I went again and again. This was a new tactic. It was one I was not used to; how could they ignore 'the chosen one'! I even tried to change the angle of my fall, and tumbled down the stair at a right angle and rolled next to the parlour door.

"Steve, stop it. We can't get any tickets."

Eventually the big day arrived. I went to the pictures to drown my miseries. All of a sudden, the message came up on the screen, Bristol Rovers 4, Manchester United 0.

The whole cinema burst into applause. People celebrated, bought ice creams, and sang 'Goodnight Irene'.

As is the case with football success, it is often short-lived. In the next round Rovers were held to a draw at home by Doncaster Rovers - who finished close to the foot of the second division that year – and lost the replay.

I saw my first professional match. It was on February 21, 1953. The Rovers beat Coventry City 5-2 at Eastville Stadium.

I remember it clearly as though it was stenciled in my mind. It will never be forgotten. I was eight-years-old and was alone!

There were no adults, although I cannot remember if any of the Oak Road lads had come with me. Today, that would be unthinkable but then, a short while after the war, this was a real community. People would pick you up and put you on their shoulders; if they had to move for any reason, they would pass you on to the next bloke. Crowds were in excess of 30,000.

I watched in wonder. I don't know whether Gran and the girls knew. The next game was the 3-1 win against the cross-channel rivals Newport County, on April 25. I was hooked.

I wanted to be a professional footballer. I wanted the prestige and the glory. I wanted everyone to see me play. I needed the arena, the stage. I wanted to be someone.

My home city, Bristol, and its surrounding districts, was home to around 350,000 people, half of whom would be male, so the chance of playing professional football was slim. Assuming that both English League teams, City and Rovers, carried a professional list of 40 players, your bare numerical chances of achieving a professional football career comes out at something like 0.046 percent.

First you needed the genes. If you had them, then you needed luck. You needed the ambition, the drive, the will, and the opportunity. In my case, I felt this as I grew. You can't acquire it, you either have it or you don't.

Five yards or so along the pavement from our front door in Oak Road was a street lamp. It was gas. Somebody must have lit the light and someone must have snuffed it out. I never saw him or her light the lamp or snuff it out.

Gas lighting had been used in Bristol since 1811, long before football was declared a legitimate sport. The Bristol Coal Gas Company was the instigator of the birth of football in Oak Road.

I never noticed, or have no recollection of, the change to electricity, just this vague memory of the power that the gaslight held over us all. The gaslight never knew us, but it watched over us protectively. It controlled our hopes, and our dreams. No gaslight, no game, which meant no dreams, no future.

In Oak Road, the game ended only when we couldn't see the ball anymore. The power of the gaslight was limited. Our daylight pitch condensed to that power. A big pitch with many kids during the day became a small pitch in crowded roads, eventually emptying into dark shadows.

This was where size overcame ability. Around 20, maybe 30 or more, kids on a road ten yards wide and a gaslight that gave us maybe another ten yards. Consider the density of bodies, consider the skill needed, consider the learning experience, consider the transfer of skill to brawn, and then back to skill!

The pitch was the road. Good old English tarmac. There were lots of kids. This was big time baby boomer country. On Cup Final night there would be maybe 15-20 on the tarmac.

The captains could always choose who they wanted to be and they could nominate their mates to be other players. I would be Jackie Milburn at Newcastle, Geoff Bradford at Bristol Rovers, or Doug Lishman at Arsenal. I always scored goals.

If you had another pretender to your status as the whiz kid of Oak Road, you put the pretender in at centre-half. "You stay there by the corner and feed the balls to the forwards. We'll do the rest." Cruel it may have been. Unsporting it was, for sure. Brazen it definitely was, along with extreme selfishness. You will receive no apologies. Everybody wanted to score goals. There was no glory in being a centre-half or a full-back. The headlines belonged to forwards, and centre forwards in particular. We wanted to be in the headlines.

Scoring goals changed your status and gave you privileges otherwise unknown. Did all the kids respect you and ask your advice at school? Yes. Do your homework for you if asked? Oh, Yes.

We created our own FA Cup draw. Everybody got a chance to nominate a team that was put in the hat. We started at the fifth or sixth round so we could get to the final quicker. The draw was always held outside the off-license on the corner of Oak and Ash Roads. We choose this spot because, being on the corner, there was enough room for all the players to gather and be heard.

We would then play out the entire draw over the next week or so, which meant multiple games on the weekends. My favourite fixture was when my team would be Bristol Rovers and we would be playing Arsenal or Newcastle. I would sit around the tea table and tell Mum that Rovers beat Newcastle tonight and that they had drawn Arsenal in the next round. Even with her limited interest in football, Mum said the Rovers could never win the cup. Well, in Oak Road, they always won it!

When I first started playing, there were rules. The goal was as wide as the street, maybe ten yards. We had one goal and both sides attacked and defended that same goal. The game tended to be compressed. You had to have eyes in the back of your head, to know what was going on. Everybody followed the ball, a tennis ball. You had to be good.

The goal was so wide that almost every decent shot went in, often taking a ricochet off three or four legs. If you hit a cracker from ten yards, and some lucky sod from the other side got a touch, no matter how faint, it was the other side's goal. The keeper couldn't see anything and was on a hiding to nothing. It was too crowded in front of him. We spent hours parleying who had managed the last, faintest, unnoticeable touch. It didn't have to be the touch of the body. A shirt, sleeve, or trouser-leg was enough. Someone once claimed it hit his shoelace. The height of the crossbar varied, depending on who talked the talk.

You could have rebounds off the gutter, off the wall, off the house and off the windows, if it bounced far enough back, and always providing the ball never went through the window! You tried to play on the side of the kids who had shoes, not 'daps'. When you got clobbered on the shin by a shoe, it hurt. You didn't feel the little poke from a dap.

You either had the kids who could afford shoes and daps, or the kids whose parents had spent money on shoes that you wore to school and played in. To maintain the longevity of the shoes, these kids' parents would often have steel caps fitted to the toes and heels, and sometimes even steel studs on the shoe bottom, to prolong wear on the leather sole. A tap on the lower leg area with a shoe like this really hurt.

You had to negotiate with the kids that could play and those who owned shoes only to play on your side. The key was making sure that they 'appeared' at just the right time, to be selected for your team. Timing was everything.

Both captains tried to get Jeff Dent to act as the keeper. It's fair to say that Jeff was one of the least athletic of the group. When we played cricket he would use the bat like a shovel, and hit everything sideways and skywards. He spent 99% of his time fielding! The major point is we didn't care, and neither did Jeff. He was part of the scene. When he played in goal on our tarmac version of Highbury, sometimes he would dive!

Jeff was the bravest of the brave.

He proved that there is a niche for everybody. We, the knowledgeable leaders, saw Jeff as an asset, definitely not a liability.

Control of the game was, shall we say, tenuous. There was no referee. Usually the loudest mouth won the day, or the captains decided, except that in my case, when I was captain, I was often the offender and therefore in the wrong.

Even if a free kick was awarded, there was absolutely no chance of a sight of the goal. All of the opposition players would form a semi-circle around the ball, two or three deep. It was an impenetrable wall. Some claimed the wall should retreat ten yards as in the real game. It never did.

Mothers would call their kids for tea or supper.

"I can't come now. This is Highbury and Rovers are winning 23-17."

"You're playing for Rovers?"

"Yes, mum."

"How do you know who's on your team, they all look the same?"

"Because we know."

"Your time's up."

Disgraced, called to the tea table when your side is so close to snatching victory!

The thought rushing through your mind is "who is going to pick me if I have to go to tea at half-past eight every night?"

We had meetings to affect a strategy to counter the maternal call. Nothing worked. We figured mums would never venture onto the pitch to frog-march their precious siblings to the tea table. We were wrong. We tried the group approach: "Mrs Sheppard, can't David play a little longer? He's Don Roper and we, ahh, I mean, Arsenal, need him." Arsenal sounded more impressive.

An icy stare followed and then the words. "David, or Don, whatever your name is, in now!"

How the hell are we going to counter the fact we now have only two left-wingers? Mothers just didn't understand.

I outshone everyone, which meant I was regularly Captain. We all knew that the best players got to be the leader. Who would be the first to say, "Steve can be captain tonight?" Was it just a "Who gets first pick, Steve or Billy?" How did it occur? I cannot recall. It happened seamlessly. A whole bunch of white young English boys decided that a young, black, Afro–American lad would lead them. Where I go, you follow, where you go, I lead.

This was an important first revelation about the power of ability in sport. Funnily enough, it didn't surprise me, I expected it. These were the rules. The best player gets to be the captain.

This was my realisation, that colour played no part in street football. No matter what had happened in the past, name-calling, being ignored, I never felt I was less worthy than anyone else on the street again, ever. I have considered this often on my journey. With all the glamour of a professional football career, perhaps being captain of the street team was the most important and crucial appointment of my whole life.

The transition from the gaslight to Horfield Common was an easy one. It was a natural progression. More and more kids from outside of our patch were turning up for the 'gaslight games', and soon it became too many. "Let's go to the common", someone said and so we went. The gaslight would be fondly remembered, but it was time to grow.

Sliding tackles were suddenly in vogue. No more scraped knees for Jeff. The bigger pitches would mean the big lads would dominate, so there was some opposition. The move was obvious as we grew bigger and stronger; we needed more room.

The favorite pitch was surrounded on three sides by houses with the back gates facing the pitch. This created a stadium feel for us young dreamers. Alas, the noise and the inability to keep the ball out of the back gardens, vegetable patches and pigeon coops cost us, and we had to move. Even the fact that some of the players lived in houses that backed on to the pitch couldn't save us.

We shifted to the area just beyond the oak trees; it was not a big move, only 100 yards further up the common. Here we created a pitch with the trees as our imaginary stand. One lesson we had learned from our move was the importance of keeping the ball on the ground.

One day I was up on Horfield Common practicing my football skills on my own.

The ball I was using was a real football; Gran had spoiled me and bought it for me. A ball this size would attract the most dedicated of aspiring young hopefuls.

Two older lads approached me and, as was the polite thing to do in those days, asked whether they could have a kick. Of course they could.

In those days after the war had ended, following the carnage on far-flung battlefields, and with fathers, mothers, sons and daughters that would never return, people learned to share. If there was anything at all that came from the killing fields in distant places that some could not even pronounce, it was the awareness that everyone had suffered a great tragedy. We were all poor and we all knew that it would take perhaps many lifetimes to have this country of ours back to where it rightfully belonged. Sharing a football on the common was part of the recovery. We played 'keep ball,' a favourite pastime, and that evolved into a two-on-one game.

All went well for a while, until one of bigger kids became upset. Maybe he was annoyed that the young black kid is a little too football smart for him. The game rules were simple. A small square was marked out. Within the agreed area, two players attempted to keep possession of the ball away from the single player. If you were the last player to touch or play the ball, and the lone ranger intercepted it, then you replaced the lone ranger. Sometimes you could be running around for ages unable to get a touch.

Suddenly, out of nowhere this boy used his bulk to flatten me. I complained, to no avail. Then his friend joined in as well. They grabbed my arms and legs and dragged me to the edge of the common and threw me into a bed of stinging nettles alongside the hedgerow.

They laughed while I cried. What had I done to deserve this? The two boys ran off up the common, laughing. I picked up my ball, put it under may arm, and trudged home shedding tears.

It's October, 1955. I was 11-years-old. Was this an early brush with racism? Did they think I was different, or was it jealousy? Was it simply a young, smaller boy baffling two older and bigger boys with his football skills?

There was nothing to say that this had anything to do with race or the colour of my skin; they never called me blackie, darkie or the 'n' word. Maybe they just thought the colour thing, he's different.

The gaslight started our dreams. Now on the common, our games were more organised. If we couldn't manage a team with two different sets of shirts, grey or white say, then one team took their shirts off. Our games included spectacular diving saves, sliding tackles, and colossal airborne heading duels. Our games were more sophisticated and our dreams became bigger as a result.

A friend of someone knew this team in Fishponds or Westbury-on-Trym that wanted to play us. The question was when and where? Saturday two weeks from now, on a patch of ground just like ours, but a few miles away, was the answer.

We still only had shoes or daps, no boots. The only choice of identification left was to wear the standard issue grey school shirt. Our mode of travel was walking.

Team selection, as always, was controversial. Six players picked themselves. Whoever owned the ball was also in. Sometimes we did the blade of grass in the hand trick to decide who played. It was all very democratic. Jeff was always picked to play in goal. Kick off was 3pm and we were all ready to go.

Of course, things could and did go wrong. Players wouldn't turn up. Maybe they had upset mum or dad, or both, and so wouldn't be allowed to wear the school shirt. If it was raining they may have decided to go trainspotting instead. Others moaned because it was too far to walk and went home. Some simply couldn't find the ground or they got the dates, place, park or time wrong.

It was a disaster. It rained. We all got soaked and walked miles for nothing. All those who had not been picked for this very important event now had to be placated. If not, they would sulk for a week.

Another organised game was just down the road, only a short distance from school, against the Muller Road Orphanage. The orphanage was opposite the barracks where Clarence had been stationed during the war. Black troops and white paratroops had been stationed close together for a while on the old orphanage site and this had inevitably led to high racial tensions.

The day of the game was bright and sunny. The orphanage kids wore a quartered shirt, red and dark blue. Some of their dads had been killed during the war, or, like me, they were children left behind by soldier fathers.

This was the first time I questioned the whereabouts of my own father, and that night, after the game, I recall talking to my mother on the subject. I remember one of the kids told me that his dad had been killed in Italy. I really did not have the heart to ask about his mother or any other relations. He asked me whether I had a father. I didn't know what to say. Instead, we talked football, and he said I was a very good player.

We had tea, cakes and biscuits after the game. I left feeling something I had not felt before. It was like a great sorrow. This game made an impression on me that I would never forget. We won easily, but that was irrelevant compared to learning a sad lesson about life. Here I was, I had lost a father, but I thought then that perhaps I would see him one day. That he may return. These boys would never see their fathers. There was no hope for them, none at all.

These were wonderful days. The sun always shone, the 'stadiums' were always full, and there was always joy and happiness. We were just a bunch of kids having the time of our lives.

SCHOOL DAYS

The playground at Ashley Down Primary School became an extension of the gaslight. There were more players, and a different shaped pitch, but essentially the stage was the same. The difference was that here there were two goals, and balls could be thrown from one end of the play area to the other. This was a step up the ladder.

Our playground was anything but the rectangular shape of a football field. It sloped considerably, contained the bicycle shed and the 'goals' – well, brick walls – were at right angles.

Amazingly, we never had a school team.

I remember writing my English exam essay on, of all things, a football match. It was a game between Earth and Mars!

As the game progressed I clearly remember that Ron Nicholls, the Bristol Rovers goalkeeper, was in goal for Earth. At that time in my life I was living with Gran at Horfield, and every Saturday I would traipse down to the Rovers ground to worship their heroes. Ron was one of them.

When I heard that I had passed my 11-plus exam I was astounded. Perhaps it was the innovation of an interstellar game between Earth and Mars that did it.

I was definitely not the brightest lamp in the street. I was even more astounded when I found out that no one from my class would accompany me to Fairfield Grammar School.

When I got to Fairfield, I was the only coloured bloke in the place. A young lad called Saeed Ahmed came later, and I believe his family fled India after the partition.

Five years later, when I took the General Certificate of Education

(GCE) exams, my two passes comprised English Language and English Literature. Justification perhaps for the educator who read the inter-planetary game plans!

Around the time of the change of schools, a major transition occurred. Muller Road was a short hop from Ashley Down Primary School. Across Muller Road was a large grassed playing area that was big enough to harbour five or six full-size football fields. Physical Education was just a glimmer in educator's eyes back then, but occasionally we were taken to the playing fields at Muller Road.

This gave us an insight into the real game. This was different. We had two goals. We had lots of space to move and play. The ball was bigger and heavier and you were expected to pass it further. You certainly couldn't keep up the same levels of energy that you could on a compressed road or similar sort of pitch. The hackers and the pushers were being weeded out.

This represented a fundamental change in the way we understood, appreciated and played the game

It must have inspired someone. A birthday perhaps, because the word got round that, after school, the game was on at Muller Road with a 'proper' ball. Half the school was there. Same school clothes, same shoes, and same enthusiasm. In fact, the same disorganised bunch, with the same boundless energy.

Now we were falling down in our enthusiasm and getting dirty and wet. Sliding tackles were all the rage. Jeff was understandably in his element.

However, there was a price to pay. All this enthusiasm and commitment incurred the wrath of the people who had to wash 'the Arsenal' shirts. Numbers started to dwindle. Clearly the maternal word was still a powerful response to our visions of glory.

So, a solution had to be found; bring any old clothes you can to school and we'll change at Muller Road. Granddad's old shirt, things that looked like modified towels, brother's shirts three sizes too big and even the odd sister's blouse was worn. We weren't proud. What a sight we must have been!

One day, we were arriving for the game and there's this young kid with a new football. Not any new ball. The new super plastic coated white ball used for the new-fangled floodlit game. This was an exhibition of serious money flaunted before us. He was not one of us either. This boy did not go to our school. However, rules are there to be broken. Of course he was welcome to play.

His mother was standing over by the gate, the back gate of the house that led straight onto the field. Her arms were folded, apron on and turban wrapped around her head. Once the game started she was gone, satisfied her child would be among friends. He couldn't play, but we ignored that; after all, he had the latest ball, a proper ball.

Now with that ball, we, too, were playing under lights. We were superior. The ball had made sure of that. This ball travelled so easily. It never got wet and heavy, and you could really hammer the thing from 15 yards. It transformed our game. The gaslight had vanished.

After a while I became curious as to who played at this venue on Saturdays. The next Saturday I walked down from Oak Road in time for the 3pm kick off. One team played in an orange shirt that, for the time, was exceptionally bright to say the least. They had black collars and black on the end of their sleeves, and black shorts. This was Eden Grove Old Boys.

Eden Grove Old Boys became my favourite team and the goalkeeper and I would chat away about football forever.

Eden Grove were in the Bristol and District League.

Their goalkeeper pointed out to me some of the requirements of being a 'keeper, the importance of angles for instance. He didn't seem to mind that he was keeping goal and advising a budding future goalkeeper at the same time.

He had been good enough to warrant a trial with West Bromwich Albion so the papers said. I'm not sure how he finished up, but I don't think he earned a contract.

I guess I watched the team for six or seven games until my curiosity was satisfied and other things assumed importance.

I used to think of him though, when we kids were up playing on our pitch, with the coats for goals, and I imagined that I was in between the 'big' goalpost on a Saturday.

My good-natured goalkeeping friend, whether he knew it or not, had placed a thought, a mission maybe, in my mind. I had wondered how easy or difficult it was to play in goal, the last line of defence. As much as I liked being the hero winning a game, scoring the winner in the last minute, the idea of being the team's saviour also had a great deal of appeal.

When mum and Ted moved us to Peasedown St John, Ted took me to watch football on Saturday afternoons. He had an old Norton motorbike and a sidecar. I loved it. If Peasedown, in their red and yellow quartered shirts, were playing away, we'd go to Radstock, Clandown, Welton or Paulton.

Funny how you remember colours. Welton played in a crappy green shirt while Paulton had this purple concoction. Radstock wore red and black while Clandown played in black and white stripes. As I was to learn, it's not about how you look. It's how you play that counts.

One evening I remember Bristol City Colts were playing the locals. Tony Cook, who was to play in the same team as I at Bristol City several years later, was in goal. I was fascinated. I had never been this close to the real action before. Up close and personal to all the players. I heard everything, even the heartbeat of the crowd. It was another step up the ladder for me. I held the players in awe.

Soon, we were on the move again. Probably Eve needed to be closer to Gran and the girls. We were moving to the south Bristol council estate at Bishopsworth, close to the massive post-war development at Hartcliffe and Withywood, an hour on the bus across the city from Gran's place. I didn't want to leave my football family again so I pondered staying with Gran and Mum's sisters for a while.

In Goulston Road, just before we moved to the life-long habitat around the corner in Derham Road, I was drawing planes and boats on the inside of a frosty window. Ted flipped me around the ear: "Don't do that", or something similar.

It evoked a tirade of pent up passion, grief, and virulence. "Hope you fall down the pit shaft and never come up from the pit again, stay down their forever," I shouted.

I remember Eve holding me to her bosom as I sobbed my heart out.

He said: "It was a flick not a slap. It didn't hurt."

I answered: "Don't touch me you're not my real father."

I was growing up and I hadn't yet realised the fact.

From then on my time was split between Gran's and Eve's new council house at Bishopsworth, on the other side of town.

I came of age at Derham Road. Made friends, kissed the girls, drank alcohol and smoked cigarettes, went to the youth club, put snow through Jack Locke's letterbox, and used an air rifle to put a slug in all the apples on the neighbour's tree.

I played cricket, walked Whitchurch Lane, went mushrooming on the Dundry slopes, strolled the lakes at Chew Magna, joined the St Peters Church film night, went to the dance there and at Headley Park, fell in love and out again, knew loneliness and heartbreak.

FAIRFIELD

At Fairfield Grammar School, my favourite teacher was Mr. Roy Edwards, the PE teacher. He was a young bloke, not long out of university. He rode a BSA Golden Flash 500 motorbike.

He was enthusiastic. His physical education lessons were always interesting and he had that youthful outlook that was important to us younger kids. Roy was a new breed of the Physical Education, PE that was sweeping schools.

The playing fields of Fairfield were a long, long way from school, up over the Downs and on the way down to Westbury and the Portway. I had missed the transport, the bus that used to deliver the believers or non-believers, of whom there were many, and along with those that had been delayed in some way, usually of their own volition, and was lingering around the play area when Mr. Edwards came along.

"What's up Stacey?"

"Can't get to sport sir, I missed the bus." This was serious; there was no way that I would intentionally miss a sports period He looked at his watch.

"Come on," he said. He rolled out the 500cc monster and motioned me to get on the back and off we went.

Mr. Edwards let me know that I had a football talent. He was in touch with us kids, nearer our age group, and talked the lingo. He was one of the first Physical Education specialists to be placed into schools as opposed to the usual 'Sports Master' who could be anyone interested in sport.

We played regular games against rival schools. There was no league like the comprehensive schools system, just friendlies. I had no idea what 'friendly' meant. School sport meant that you couldn't play on Saturday mornings with your mates or for anyone else any more. You had to play for the school. If you got picked and did not play then you did an essay or something similar on whatever afternoon school sport was. They had you.

Mr. Sissons, 'The Cisco Kid', was a kind, gentle man who, besides being responsible for bringing the common game back to Fairfield, ran the science class with flair and support that made it all good fun. I cannot recall anyone who had a bad word to say about Cisco.

Cisco was well past 50 I would have guessed. He was never without his pipe and thin, wire-rim glasses, which added to the distinguished look of his silver grey receding hair. When he supervised us - coached is too strong a word - and it was wet, he tucked his trousers into his socks.

He was a kind man. Always ready to give advice. I'm not sure he knew much about coaching young boys, but he loved the game of football and was responsible for reintroducing it to Fairfield after an absence of ten years. It was almost a class thing. The rugby master was Mr. Jones, who came from the Welsh valleys. Mr. Jones was the complete opposite of Cisco. He was always smartly dressed, wore proper sports togs, shirt, shorts, socks and expensive boots.

His black hair was always brushed, he had glasses and he spoke with a refined accent. We were frightened to speak to him.

If you were selected for the rugby team and didn't play, then you didn't play football in the second term either. There must have been some wrangling over this in the staff room, I can tell you.

So I played one year of rugby. I played in the position where you got the ball from the lad who got it out of the scrum. I infuriated Mr. Jones. A couple of us larger and quicker lads would run through the opposition. This was a sports day of our own. Fellow pupils and classmates were the opposition. There weren't enough kids with enough ball skills to make one rugby team, never mind two.

Yellow shirts, white collar, navy blue shorts, yellow and navy hooped socks. That was Fairfield Grammar School's football kit. My first pair of real football boots.

In those days you had to nail the studs in, and take out or put on a layer or two, depending on the conditions. Mine were all purpose. The studs stayed long.

My gran, God bless her, used to iron, starch, press and crease my football gear just like my school clothes. The collar would be crisp, my shorts had a crease down the front and sometimes Gran even bleached the laces of my boots white.

I played centre forward and was appointed Captain by Cisco. Cisco thought he had struck gold. We smacked Portway, a local comprehensive school. It must have been the first win for a while because even Cisco was overcome. We did them again next week and the platitudes flowed. But then the reality set in.

Maybe last year they were really good and Fairfield had been worse. St George, another grammar school, belted us. It took about four games for us to realise that we were not invincible. It was a bitter pill to swallow.

In my first year as captain of the junior team I made some kind of history by playing for the Intermediates as well. This, as I understood it, was unheard of.

It was one of those issues that was to follow me in my early years. If you're good enough, you get a game. If you can care for yourself on the park in a physical sense, then go to it. None of this under 12 and under 15 stuff, or 'when's your birthday?'

Here's what Cisco wrote about me: "The human dynamo from the first year plays equally well with head or feet." Cisco, bless him. Thank you, Mr. Sissions, wherever you may be.

I got admiration from the teaching staff. They were blown away with the fact that, almost single-handedly, I would win games. I was making my mark. It didn't go unnoticed.

The Bristol Boys selection committee advised the school that I had been selected for the Bristol Boys Intermediate team trials, to play Newport at St Phillips Marsh park.

I suspect that Mr. Edwards had led the charge and called whomever he had to call to get someone to have a look at his talented lad. Grammar school people never ever got to play at the top levels of the working man's game, they all played rugby. The pathway to professional football was virtually erased at a grammar school; this was the pathway to Oxford and Cambridge.

In those days, luckily for me, scouts were crawling all over the place. I was notified that I would need a pair of black football shorts and a pair of specified colour socks. Gran and the girls duly obliged.

I turned up for the first training session. My shorts were of the latest style.

I made the cut for the Bristol Boys Intermediate team selection. The day was wet and the ground hard, with little grass. We played Newport Boys. There were no coaching sessions, just a group of kids who could play thrown together for the day. Soon, it was all over. It finished in a draw as I far as I can recollect.

Sometime later, there was a game held just up the road from Gran's at Kellaway Avenue. This may have been for the senior Bristol Boys team, as I clearly recall Fred Ford and a couple of other people, I assume from Bristol City, being present.

I scored a goal or two, and chased a lost ball to the touchline to prevent a throw in, right in front of the great man. I stepped on the ball, carried on past the touchline and looked to see that none of my colleagues were within ten yards.

Fred and the crew were excited. "Well done, son," they said.

Cricket at Fairfield was run very much along the same lines as football. House teams, and a first and second XI. My performance with the bat and ball quickly elevated me to the first XI. Cisco, Mr. Edwards, and Ross Gilkes were usually in attendance at these games, and like football, they were played on a Saturday morning. These were more serious affairs. A lot of the older boys were members of the cricket team, including our two table prefects, Kerry Woodward and John Sherrington. So here was I, 11 or 12-year's-old, facing up to these 16, 17 and sometimes 18-year-olds. Quite intimidating.

From what proved to be a very inauspicious start, I was invited to join training sessions for the Bristol Boys Cricket Intermediate team. We had several sessions up at the indoor nets with George Emmett, the Gloucestershire skipper, and former England player, as well as other senior players.

I played three or four games, a couple at the County Ground, Nevil Road, home of Gloucestershire County Cricket Club, and travelled to Southampton, Taunton and Gloucester.

Even at cricket the masters wanted to run the show. I remember we were playing the most celebrated school in Bristol at their ground, Clifton College. This is one of the great public schools. Clifton is generally known as an extremely wealthy and affluent suburb, founded by the excesses of the slave and tobacco trade. The grounds are known as 'the Close', and WG Grace, the great man of English cricket and of Gloucestershire CCC, scored 13 of his many centuries on these hallowed grounds.

We were taking their cricket team apart. We had batted first and reached an impressive score. Now we were bowling and I had opened, along with a tall, gangly dark haired lad, who was not as quick as I was, but moved and swung the ball a fair bit. They were not very much at all for five or six wickets, and the master, in his wisdom, informed my opening partner and I that the next over would be our last.

We questioned the wisdom of such a decision. "Yes, old boy, but if we leave you two on they'll be gone for 40 or so. Can't have that, need to make a game of it. Don't want to embarrass them, do we?"

Talk about pissed off. I couldn't stand all this gentleman stuff and said so in no uncertain terms. "More to the game than winning, Stacey," was their response.

One Saturday morning we were playing Cotham Grammar School on our home turf. I might have been three or four in the batting order, no lower, when my turn came to bat. A lad called Glynn Hughes was batting at the other end, going along nicely. We were well placed when he got out for 30-odd, and I took on the responsibility of pushing the innings ahead.

I could do no wrong, as I belted the attack with what Cisco said was 'a savage well-coordinated innings.' Our allotted time, or overs, were coming to an end and I was informed that if I wanted a century I had six balls to get it. I was quite flabbergasted. The lads had let me know loud and clear that I had got my 50, but that seemed like only an over or two ago. I was enjoying my domination of the bowling so much that I had lost count of where I was. I was in the early 80's apparently. So the question was to slog it out through an over or just go on playing. I went on playing and ended the innings with 87 not out which, as I understood at the time, was a school record. Sadly, we couldn't bowl out the opposition and so had to settle for a draw.

The innings was the talk of the town after the game and on into the next week.

JP BSc, Fairfield's headmaster, read the sports results to the whole school at assemblies.

"Now, the cricket team drew with Cotham. Our top scorer was Stacey with 87 not out." Gasps around the hall and swiveled heads, as my chest swelled a bit.

On the Monday Mr. Gilkes sought me out.

Down we went to the cricket storeroom and he asked me to pick a bat. I picked a bat that had clearly been used a bit with ball marks and nicks on it.

I couldn't believe that someone would give me a brand new, unused bat. He said something along the lines of, "A first rate innings like that deserves more than a second rate bat." He picked an unused brand new bat and said: "This is the best bat in the storeroom", and handed it to me. I took a stance and practiced a forward defensive.

The next morning assembly was almost over.

JP suddenly started up again. "You will recall that last weekend one of our outstanding cricketers scored 87 not out against Cotham Grammar School. This is in the true tradition of Fairfield's sporting history. Would Mr. Stacey please come forward."

So I edged along the row of songsters into the aisle that led to the front of the hall, turned right and walked below the stage, left up several steps onto the stage and approached JP.

I was alone on the stage with the headmaster. The whole school was peering upwards toward us. Of all the pupils in school, several hundred, maybe more, in celebratory circumstances, perhaps half a dozen would greet the great man in similar circumstances.

To look out from that stage across a sea of faces, to hear first of all the sound of one hand clapping, smiles, looks of admiration and then, through the hubbub of noise here and there, they call your name, was incredible.

As I approached the headmaster, the noise and the calling began to fade. I gazed again across the now vast expanse of the assembly hall. These faces still holding their admiration. "You can take this anywhere. In a game played on a summer's morning in beautiful surroundings, where, apart from the two teams, the spectators could be counted on the fingers of two hands, you achieved something that will last in the memories of students, teachers and parents for weeks, months or years perhaps."

I realised then that they would not remember me for the 'D's on my report sheets. They would remember me for this moment. This is the meaning of success.

He met me and extended his hand, a smile on his face.

"Well done, young man, well done, an excellent achievement."

"Thank you, headmaster."

He then presented the willow to me and the whole school burst into applause.

When I was at Fairfield Grammar School, Sheila Anne Clarke was my schoolboy romance. I loved Sheila in a puppy dog, first love kind of way. Sheila was in my year at school. We used to do things together, pictures, concerts and sports events.

She would turn up at school football and cricket games. I never tired of those looks of admiration. I used to belt 'em in the 'net', although we never actually had netting - turn and run toward the touchline just to see that smile. Boy oh boy, 12-years-old and steaming.

We would go to the cinema or Cliff Richard concerts together. Sometimes Sheila paid. We would sneak a drink down at the centre centre. Best of all though, Sheila always said yes when I wanted to go to the County Ground to watch the cricket.

We used to sneak the odd kiss and Sheila sometimes did my homework. Yes, did my homework!

This masterpiece of writing is from the Fairfield Grammar School Summer Magazine. The notation says that, "It's written by Stephen Stacey class of 2B", folks. The summer of 1957 makes me 13-years-old.

Small big round and fat,
Purple, grey, blue and black,

As big as an elephant
As small as a gnat,
Long and thin with hunched up back—
Now the dramatic, the second verse of 'The Sea Creatures' goes:
Some swim the oceans of the west
Others think the north is best,
The mystic waters of the blue
Pacific is others dreams come true,
Where there are wondrous rainbow hues—
The Sea Creatures.

OK, which verse did I write? Sheila wrote another three verses and the whole poem got published in the school magazine under my name. Now this was no small event. The school magazine was the essence of intellectual property. This was big time notation.

There goes Steve Stacey. Do you know he plays football, rugby and cricket for the school? He writes too. He was published in the school mag. A conspiracy? Yes, Did we have a laugh? Oh yes, plenty; the joys of young love.

LOCAL FOOTBALL

While playing football at school, aged around 14 I noticed an advertisement in the local Evening Post for training sessions conducted by a local Downs League team, Sneyd Park.

Why did I choose Sneyd Park? The training venue was just down the road. It was close, convenient. Secondly, all the games were played on the Downs, so there was no particular hassle of travelling all over Bristol in the Suburban or District Leagues. From Gran's, it was a ten-minute walk over the common, and a six-stop bus trip to the Downs, easy. At that time, the team changing rooms were a pub at the top of Whitehorse Road.

That is my version of events, although I have been told another version as to how I ended up at Sneyd Park. Old friends from the club that I met years later say that John Coomb, a veteran of Sneyd Park as a player, committee member and an executive of the club, met me while I was playing cricket for Bishopsworth or football at Highridge United.

I don't recall it after all these years, but the story is that John discovered that I flitted between Bishopsworth and Horfield and invited me to the training sessions at Zetland Road.

I had played for St Peters Youth Club in Bishopsworth. We youngsters had joined because, on a Monday night, they held film nights or dances mainly. The main attraction was girls.

I'm not sure whether, or how, St Peters football team melded into Highridge United.

Mike Tudor, a friend that I had gone on holiday with, played for them and suggested that I do the same. Mike Stitfall and a guy called Keith (who's surname I can't remember) ran the show. We just had to turn up with boots, shorts and socks, and they did the rest. We owe these guys big time. They made it so easy for us.

They still play behind where the Golden Cockerel pub used to stand in Lakemead Grove, Highridge.

Years later I visited the UK and popped into the Cockerel to refresh old memories, and there on the wall was the picture of the team. A couple of blokes walked over and a conversation started up.

"Good team that, was probably our best."

"Yea, I know. I played in it. That's me," I said, pointing to myself with a big grin on my face.

"Is that you?"

"Yep. Steve Stacey," I said and then added, "I played for the City."

"We've been wondering for years who that was!"

The photo and this incident occurred at least 40-odd years apart. These lads wouldn't have been born when the photo was taken!

My rise up the local football ladder had been rather quick, from Hartcliffe Boys club to Highridge United and then on to Sneyd Park, all in a season or two.

At Highridge I played two different roles, that of goalkeeper and goal scorer. It was while at Highridge that I was chosen to participate in the 'County' trials at Mangotsfield in the role of goalkeeper. I had a fairly successful evening, but I believed that my real place was goal scoring and not goalkeeping.

Sneyd Park was my first experience of all kit being provided. Shirts, darkish red and blue squares, blue shorts and red and blue-hooped socks. Just bring your boots.

The first week, I was chosen to play centre forward in the fourth team and scored two goals. A week later I was in the third team and scored two goals. The next week I was in the first team.

I never got to play for the reserves! In my first team debut it was another case of bang, bang, and another couple of goals.

At that time Sneyd Park was a high class, old and well renowned (1897) club. This wasn't a 'working mans' club. There was more of a professional leaning amongst the players and committee, I recall. Tony Brown, the Gloucestershire cricketer, and one time captain, played there. Tony later went on to be the Secretary of Somerset County Cricket Club and England team Manager.

As a measure of my ability, Tony was moved to outside left to facilitate my inclusion at centre forward. I continued to score goals freely and, even though I say so myself, became something of a legend. We swept aside the local competition, the renowned Clifton St Vincent's club, and trashed team after team.

I went on scoring goals. We finished third in the league and we went on to the final of the prestigious Norman Hardy Cup. I got the first goal against Phildown Rovers in the cup final, which we eventually won 3-0. The crowds were large, at the final for instance. They were all standing and they would have been five or six deep all around the pitch.

It's clear now that Bristol City were keeping tabs on me. People that I would later recognise as Fred Ford, the City manager, Alfie Rowles, Cliff Duffin and Cliff Morgan, who were all part of the city scouting system, appeared at our games on a regular basis.

My stint with Sneyd Park was short. It lasted a season at most before City paid £100 to the club for my services, a considerable sum for a small club in those days.

The fact was that I was a 15-year-old kid, pumping in goals wherever I played. I had been told that, at the end of the season, Bristol City wanted to sign me as an amateur. I was still living at Gran's and attending Fairfield.

The word was that Bristol City's Chief Scout would be calling at Gran's with the forms for signing as an amateur.

Things were so different back then; there were no academies for talented players to attend. It was all done by word of mouth and remembering that someone was always watching.

Back then, a young boy's dream was to play for either the City or the Rovers. We wanted to play for our local teams, not the teams in cities we knew nothing about.

I had grown up a Rovers fan, but I wanted to play football and City, arch-rivals or not, had come knocking when my team hadn't. I remember one day Roy Edwards (PE teacher) called me over in the playground at Fairfield and told me that Bristol Rovers wanted to sign me. I was dumbfounded. I thought that the Rovers had no interest at all. I had not seen anybody that I recognised, neither had any kind of approach been made.

Roy was shattered when I told him I had already signed for City, although he hid it well. The City may have jumped the gun. In those days, professional clubs, when signing young players, had to notify the parents, which they did, and the player's school, which they did not.

My day had come. This was the culmination of the dream. I had seen the scouts, at school matches, Bristol Boys trials and on the Downs.

Cliff Duffin was the chief Scout. He came to City with the previous manager, Peter Docherty, from Doncaster Rovers. He had a reputation as a discoverer of young talent, and between them had brought several young players to the City from the Yorkshire area. I thought Cliff a bit of a dandy. He was always immaculately dressed and, like all Chief Scouts, couldn't stop talking and had an opinion on everyone and everything!

It was Cliff Duffin who called that night at 1 Derham Road, Bishopsworth, Bristol.

Dead on the dot, knock, knock. There stood the great man. Eve showed him into the front room. The coats, which were usually left hanging on the banister, had been removed to the back dining room. The china cabinet had been polished up, and Eve had given the old front room the VIP treatment.

We had an old three-piece suite, one of the large ones with big arm rests. The fireplace was laid, but there was no fire. The curtains were drawn. This was important business, and not for prying eyes. The give away would have been the car. It would have stood out like a dog's dinner that something was on at the corner house that night. We only ever used the front room on special occasions, and believe me, this was special.

After all these years of watching, praying and dreaming, I had no hesitation in signing the first professional contract laid in front of me. I had broken a promise I had made to myself, but I justified that by thinking "if the Rovers weren't interested, well then, why not sign for the City?" It's the same game, just a different colour shirt.

What a great moment for a kid, not yet 16, signing for one of the Bristol professional clubs.

Eve spoke to Mr Duffin first, alone in the front room. I was told that they would call me when they were ready.

It felt like an age before the door opened and I was called in.

"Stephen." Eve always used my full name when she was serious. "This is Mr Duffin."

He wore a suit, tie, shirt, and had shiny clean shoes, I still wonder why did I look at his shoes? As he stood, I saw his camel hair coat with velvet on the collar draped over the arm of the chair, along with his hat. It was not a trilby but one of those that was a bit truncated. People didn't dress like that where we came from.

Although I had seen him before at school matches and on the Downs watching our games, I had never heard him speak, and his first words in a strong Northern accent were, "So, you would like to come and play for City, eh?"

Before I could find my voice, the question was answered for me. "Yes, he would, Mr. Duffin." It was my agent, or rather, my mother, who then added for safe measure, "You know the Rovers have been asking, too?"

Cliff knew that Bristol Rovers, had been sniffing around and watching my games.

I looked at my mum, pleading with her with my eyes and not saying a word. "Please shut up." I winced.

"Yes I do. But we're just down the road, and we will look after your son like he's one of the family," he answered. Smooth, silky smooth, I thought.

"Who pays for his boots?"

"We do. Look, I've brought a couple of pairs with me." He bent down to a bag alongside the chair and pulled out a couple of pairs that he passed in my direction. "Here son, try em on."

My mind was made up. New boots meant goodbye Fairfield, goodbye school. I tried them on. They came up just over the ankle and were a bit low cut compared to what I was used to, but this was the best of the best, crème de la crème of boots, I'm sure they'll do.

I ran round the living room with a big grin on my face. "Mum, look at these." The look that returned my excitement and joy made it quite clear that I was diminishing Eve's bargaining power.

Before she could speak, Mr. Duffin continued, "Shirts, socks, shorts, all paid for, won't cost a thing."

"Bus fares?" Eve countered.

"We pay 'em well."

"How well?"

"The ground staff get four quid a week at the moment."

"Is that all?" says Eve.

Take it! Take it! My eyes are saying to her, if she would only look my way.

"I know that we're considering putting it up this year to a fiver," Mr. Duffin replied.

I almost squealed out loud in delight. Hallelujah!

"Do we (note the phrasing and the royal 'we') get anything for signing on?" Eve asked, still as calm as if she entered such negotiations on a daily basis.

"What do you mean?" It was the first time Mr. Duffin looked ruffled.

"Oh, the man at the Rovers…" Eve went on.

I was desperately trying to get her attention. "Mum! Are you trying to finish my career before it's started?" However, her eyes were fixed on Mr. Duffin. Suddenly, he spoke.

"Oh, you mean a signing on fee, that bonus?"

"Yes, a bonus."

Mr. Duffin reached into his inside pocket and pulled out of his wallet five quid and handed it to Mum.

It was five individual one-pound notes. She took it, counted it, one, two, three, four, five. She then held it up and said, "Ummm, hmmm." Her look then returned to our visitor.

Without a word being spoken they both knew it wasn't enough.

Back he went again to his inside pocket and presented my mum with five more crisp one pound notes.

"And he gets five pound a week?" she asked.

"Yeah, ok," Mr Duffin replied after a slight moment's hesitation.

Mum put the ten quid into her purse, and then stuffed the purse down the front of her bra, along with her packet of Woodbines and a box of matches. Now she turned to me.

"Stephen. You can sign the forms now. That is, if you want to play for the City?"

I frowned at her thinking to myself, "If I want to play for the City? Mum, get real! I would have signed without boots, for four quid a week and no signing on fee. Great job, Eve!"

Cliff was true to his word. My first wage packet was five pounds less a National Health Stamp contribution of five shillings and five pence. This meant that my take home pay was four pounds 14 shillings and seven pence. I gave Eve 30 bob a week.

After my first week, Eve was in the kitchen washing up the dishes, cigarette dangling from the corner of her mouth, pinny round her waist and scarf wrapped round her head turban style.

"Mum, that ten quid that Cliff gave you?"

"What about it?"

"Just wondered mum…" I never finished the sentence.

"What did you wonder about, my love?" said my agent.

"Where's my ten quid, Eve?" I thought, but quickly abbreviated it to, "how much can I expect of my ten quid?" But before I uttered those words I abbreviated it further. I suddenly thought, "come on, Eve's fed, housed and clothed you for 15 years give her a break." A meek, "Nothing" came out of my mouth.

"Are you going out tonight?" she asked without batting an eyelid. "Any money?"

"No."

"Want a loan 'til pay day?"

I was stunned. I could not believe it! My self-appointed agent was about to lend me a portion of my own signing on fee. Eve was a natural-made agent for sure! Eve had received a premium for delivering the goods. In truth, she deserved it a million times over.

I was ready to take on the world. I had signed as a fully-fledged amateur, soon, if good enough, to become an apprentice professional, and then the gold pass, a fully-fledged professional contract.

I couldn't wait. I had to show that I could play.

DOT

I met Dot one afternoon at a friend's house. Our meeting was quite by chance, as love is wont to be. Boy meets girl and they fall in love.

We met in June, 1960. I was 15, I would be 16 in a couple of months, and Dot was just 14-and-a-half. Little did we know then that, in a few years, it would be off to court to get married, too young for her father's liking.

I was playing professional football and whether this cushioned us from the usual everyday issues of race and colour, which is problematical, I am not sure.

There were a few snide remarks growing up and, Dot tells me, later on sometimes aimed at the children. I often think of a life as a plumber or a brickie, would it all have been different? Who knows? England, I think, was more tolerant then.

So what did Dot see?

A shy boy? Handsome, maybe, but very shy.

Colour?

What colour?

Dot and I have been married now for over 50 years

It was Monday, June 6, 1960, when we met in Bristol. I met her while doing an errand and we arranged our first date for the following Sunday.

Sunday came and I was early. Time slowly dragged by. I was wearing a royal blue knitted sweater, collar, long sleeved, white shirt, and black trousers. You could say an early John Travolta, smart, and unable to be missed. I wanted to be unforgettable. It was a nervous wait. Only then did I realised how much I cared about this meeting and this girl.

I needn't have worried. We walked up onto Bedminster Down to look over Bristol. We held hands. The day made an impression on both of us. Two young people, both hardly old enough to know anything about life, let alone fall in love. We met here and here to some extent, we will spend our eternity together. Our ashes, both of our remains, we decided, are to be scattered here, to lie where we fell in love on that day, and where we will love each other for the rest of our time and beyond.

When we did eventually move on, we found ourselves walking across a field until an irate farmer chased us off.

The rest, as they say, is history.

Dot's dad, Bert, was an old sea dog. He was in the Royal Navy and did his bit from 1934 to 1956, serving throughout WW2.

He knew his way around. He had seen plenty of dying. All that took a lot of storytelling. In time, I heard all of it.

In 1956, he returned home to his wife, Elsie, and (then) five children, all girls.

When Dot was 11 or 12, the family moved to Bristol.

The prospects were better.

When I met Dot in June, 1960, Bert was four years out of the navy. Dot's fifth sister, Carolyn, a late thought, had been born in September, 1959. Bert had secured an executive position at Linfoods a large grocery company, headquartered in Bristol.

This was the man I had to deal with during my relationship with his daughter.

It wasn't easy. With six daughters, he was very protective.

All the girls had trouble marrying. No one was good enough for Bert, and I had a 'sun tan' to boot. Barbara and Colin, in fact, actually ran away to Gretna Green, just over the border in Scotland, to marry. One other sister had to visit the doctors before she married.

Another of the sisters married a Merchant Navy officer and so was untroubled by the scrutiny that Bert put his other children through. The eldest daughter escaped any scrutiny.

Carolyn, the last-born, was sadly involved in a car accident that kept her in a coma for three months and in a wheelchair for the rest of her life. She married Terry when all the other girls had well and truly left the roost, so escaped Bert's wrath.

Negotiations were carried out for our marriage through sisters and Elsie, Dot's mum. Elsie and Eve became friends and remained so for the rest of their lives.

Despite being just kids, Dot and I wanted to marry. I was 18 and Dot pregnant and 17. I called on her house, at 27 Manor Road, to talk to Bert.

I knocked on the door and after what seemed like an interminable length of time, it opened. There stood Bert, in his trousers, shirt and braces.

"Mr. Jones, may I have a moment to talk to you?"

He said nothing. Looked at me briefly and slammed the door.

I thought to myself, "I think that means no."

Bert slammed the door on me once, but my bet is he did that to all of the eventual son's in law.

Elsie was OK with us wanting to marry and had no problems. Like Eve, she thought only of what was best for her child. I'm not sure whose call it was, but we decided to go to court in front of the magistrate and get permission to marry.

Bert, however, was determined that his daughter was not going to marry this young, coloured upstart of a professional footballer.

This was when I learned never to underestimate the power of women in relationships. My own mother had suffered having me during the war to a black American soldier. What pressures did she face? I knew that Grandad threw her out of home for a while, but she had Gran, Edie, Beryl, Eileen and Mavis for support. There must have been some powerful arguments around the kitchen table. Did Grandad swallow his pride? What did his mates say? How did he handle it? I'll never know.

Bert got the same treatment as Grandad. All the older sisters would come to the wedding and support the relationship between Dot and I. Also there, lending her support, was Elsie, Dot's mum, in defiance of Bert and in support of her daughter.

We went to court. Eve, Ted and Dot's sister, Kathleen, accompanied us to the place where our young futures would be decided.

Fred Ford, the City manager, gave me a letter saying I had a two year contract, was responsible, had a future with Bristol City, and that, if need be, the club would find us a flat to live in. Bert was outgunned.

The three judges in the (private) magistrates' court asked if we went to youth clubs and if we generally met with other young people and had a life. The City gave us cinema tickets and put on ancillary activities, cricket and supporters club nights to keep the social wheel rolling. We went to St Peters Church Hall on film and dance nights, and to Headley Park Club for a Friday rock'n'roll session. There was no reason not to let us marry.

Elsie had refused to go to court and speak against her daughter's marriage. At the end of the hearing, the Chief Magistrate asked me for my autograph for his son, who was a Bristol City fan!

Bert's brief, in his immaculately cut suit, dark of course, tie shirt and leather shoes, never had a chance. "We see no reason why these young people should not get married," said the Chief Magistrate. Bert and the brief are gob struck.

Let me get this straight, this may well have had a little bit to do with my 'sun tan.'

To this day, I think not. Bert, I believe, was concerned that his daughter was young, pregnant, and that she was marrying a young professional footballer in his prime. That, I think, was his concern.

In all the years I knew him, I never, even when the beer was flowing and the jokes were tumbling, heard him say anything disparaging against or about people of colour.

Years later, he would tell Kathleen and Dot that his opposition was not about Dot and I, but about the prejudice that the children would suffer. Mixed marriages were most uncommon at that time and perhaps Bert shared the same fear for his daughter that Eve had feared if her son had left with Clarence for Alabama or Mississippi. Bert had seen the treatment of people in many distant countries during his time at sea.

I am pleased to say that Bert became my best friend.

APPRENTICE PROFESSIONAL

At 16 the club could sign you on as an 'apprentice professional'. They could keep you as an apprentice for a period of two years, or up until your 18th birthday.

As soon as you reached that age they could either sign you on as a full-time professional, retain you as an amateur or let you go. What they could not do is to keep you as an apprentice.

The danger of being an amateur, of course, is that you were free to change your mind. You could walk over to the Rovers or anyone else and ask, "What's in it for me"?

I signed as an apprentice professional just after my 16th birthday, August 27, 1960. As soon as I had left school I was invited to join the City as an amateur, working on the ground staff.

The way I saw it, I was three steps away from stardom. The next step was the Colts team; the third team, in effect, playing in the Western League. They would play on hallowed ground that I trod before at Peasedown St John. I would be playing against the likes of Clandown, Radstock, Welton and Paulton as well as a little farther afield at Taunton, Barnstable, Weston, Bridgwater, and Bideford.

The next step was the reserve team. This was every young boys dream. It was 'Roy of the Rovers,' as you could end up playing against the superstars of the day that might be on their way out or recovering from injury. Not only that, but unlike now, the games were played on the actual club grounds, places I had only ever imagined playing at: Highbury, Stamford Bridge, White Hart Lane or Upton Park.

Then it would be the big boys, and I would be helping City to get promotion to the First Division, playing on the same grounds, first team, First Division. Point me in the right direction, wind me up and let me go.

The first game of the 1960/61 season for me, the pulling on of a Bristol City shirt, with unimaginable pride, was playing for Bristol City 'A' in the Suburban League. The same level as my friend, the goalkeeper at Muller Road. I clearly remember playing in the change strip, white shirts and black shorts. This was effectively Bristol City's fifth ranked team, and the Bristol Suburban league was a real tough amateur league.

We had all young kids playing against these hardened grown men. I had been playing in a similar league on the Downs, although it was not as tough as this. That experience gave me confidence, as I knew I had proved that a 15-year-old kid, if skillful and tough enough, could do the business in a no-age-limit league.

I'm not bragging here but I could see what I had to do and where I had to be to find the net. I guess I had been given a natural gift, something that couldn't be coached. It was so natural and I really didn't find it too difficult at all. I scored a hat trick.

After only one match, I was promoted to the strange sounding Bristol City United in the District League. Things were getting tougher. This was a move up the ladder to City's fourth-ranked side.

I must have set the tongues wagging. Cliff Duffin, Cliff Morgan, Alfie Rowles and Lemmo were all in attendance.

Alfie Rowles, an old City stalwart, was in charge. Alf had been a promising player but had his career cut short by injury. Dark Brylcreamed hair, Alfie was a straight shooter. He didn't say a lot, but what he did say made sense. I liked Alfie, and it appeared he liked what he saw in me. At Bristol City United, I added two more goals to my name. I felt unstoppable.

Fred Ford was City's manager and had signed on a three-year contract. This infuriated the Rovers supporters across town as Fred had done the unthinkable. He had left them after five years as their manager to join their biggest rivals.

Fred was a firm friend of the soon-to-be-great Liverpool manager Bill Shankly. He had made a name for himself as a coach, having managed the England under 23 team in Italy in 1958. He was a trusted, caring and compassionate man.

Bill Harvey was Fred's number two. Bill was a no nonsense individual. Bill ran the reserve team and sat with Fred sometimes at the first team games. Bill was nearly always dressed the same way, football boots and socks, tracksuit bottoms and a Bristol City playing shirt. He rarely ever wore a tracksuit top, no matter what the weather was. He offered quick, uncomplicated, straightforward advice. Bill and Lemmo Southway had overlapping responsibilities for the Wessex youth team.

Len 'Lemmo' Southway, was a highly regarded City player of yesteryear. Lemmo played 27 games for the City at full back between 1919 and 1922. He was approaching 70 when I joined and was in charge of the third team, the Western League side, and, along with Bill Harvey, the soon to be created Wessex League youth team. Lemmo ran the ground staff with a gentle but iron hand.

The ground staff loved Lemmo. He was in charge of our daily tasks. Training and washing the kit, cleaning the stands and terraces. He was a father figure and confidant to us all. He was held in high regard and was universally respected. A World War 1 warrior, he had lost fingers on both hands. He had no hair, a gnarled face, and was easily recognised from a distance by his distinctive gait and the flat cap always perched on his head.

Les Bardsley, City's physio, was instantly recognisable by his long white coat. He sat next to Fred at all the first team games along with his buckets and sponges ready in a flash to administer the magic sponge and satisfy the players in times of need. He had a distinctive bow-legged running style.

After dealing with the players' injuries on a Monday morning, he would come looking for the ground staff, but we were always too quick. If Les had taken off his long white coat, he may have caught us lounging in the stands, both hands on our brushes, but with that white coat we could spot him from a long way off.

Les nicknamed me 'Flash' because of my fleetness of foot. He was a genuine man and could always be relied upon to give you a straight answer. He was always there for the players and would take patients at a moment's notice.

Every Monday, after a home game, the ground was a mess, as were the terraces. It would take all the ground staff recruits all day Monday to wash the socks, three sets of them. The shirts and shorts are sent to the laundry. However, we had to clean and polish the playing boots, clean the dressing rooms and sweep, sweep and sweep more cigarette ends, bits of paper and all the other debris left from over 20,000 fans from the terraces. As if that wasn't enough, out would come the garden forks, and then we would have to help the groundsman replace and flatten the divots on the pitch. If there was a midweek game scheduled, and these were almost always played on a Tuesday, the workload was desperate.

Sweeping the terraces bored us youngsters and a knock, no matter how minor, had to be attended to by Les on Mondays. Just to delay the inevitable sweeping.

One morning, Fred called an early meeting of the coaching staff in his office for a very specific and important reason. Apprentice professional contracts may have to be offered to several players, all of them on the ground staff. Stacey, Ford, Bryant and Pratt. The last thing he wanted was the rumour mill starting to turn based on some scrap of a conversation heard in a dressing room.

Did my colour come into consideration? These old pros knew

that there were very few coloured players in the league. They would have known it was going to be lonely, but I believe their attitude was that they could keep an eye on me as I travelled the path. There would be no favours, but they would be aware of my circumstances.

Two weeks into the season and they reached a decision to throw me into the Colts. The next Colts match was on Saturday, August 27 – my birthday – at Minehead. It was agreed I would play as centre forward. In the meantime, little did I know that apprentice contracts were being drawn up for Tony Ford and I.

It was on Alf and Lemmo's say so I got this first big promotion.

This was my toughest assignment so far, by a long way. These teams were made up of old pros and players that didn't quite make it further. Believe me when I say this was a giant step up from the Bristol Suburban or District Leagues. These players wouldn't think twice about putting young upstarts like me over the fence.

I don't remember being nervous. I'd been a kid playing against men for the last 12 months. It was nothing different for me, but these were part-time professionals. They all had statements to make, on the back of your leg if you weren't careful.

I ran all day on that wet rainy afternoon. I hit a couple of hopeful shots whenever I got the chance; I kept trying to make myself available for the ball. I flashed a header over the bar, and smacked the keeper once or twice. I also got flattened a couple of times, too, for my trouble. We lost two-nil. But I had lived the dream, survived and done OK.

I would be an ever present in the Colts for the rest of the season, scoring a hatful of goals.

Tony Ford was a tall gangly right back. Over six feet tall, he went on to play almost 200 games for the City. Tony was probably my best mate. We talked a lot about tactics and developed some interesting plays in the youth team, particularly from free kicks on the right hand side.

Tony was not particularly quick but was deceptive on account of the long strides he took. He had a good sense of position and, at six foot plus, was good in the air.

So Tony and I were to sign apprentice professional forms together. Whereas we were over the moon, there are always those who miss out, and Geoff Bryant and David Pratt were two players on the ground staff with us who suffered that disappointment.

As a rule back then, City, like all clubs, ran three professional teams. The first team, that played in the English Football League, the reserves, which played in the London Football Combination, and the third team or Colts, that played in the Western League.

The London Football Combination comprised two divisions and was made up of the reserve teams from all major south of England and London clubs, and a smattering from the midlands, Birmingham City and Nottingham Forest, for instance.

So you could easily find yourself, as a young apprentice professional, playing Arsenal reserves at Highbury, Chelsea at Stamford Bridge, and Tottenham Hotspur at White Hart Lane, against the superstars of yesterday or the young guns yet to come. Some reserve team matches attracted crowds of close to 10,000.

You could find ex or even current international players, recovering from injury, perhaps, in the reserves. It was a period when ticket prices were extremely low, as were the player's salaries. This was how some clubs could afford to run a professional staff of some 40 players.

In the 1960s, the club, in its wisdom, and to cut costs, left the Football Combination and chose to play its reserve side in the Western League

Here, the opposition came from some beautiful English towns: Bideford, Barnstaple, Glastonbury, Minehead, Dorchester, Portland

and Poole, to name a few. But if you were an older pro seeking to break into the first team, or a young kid seeking to be tested week after week, this level of competition was not likely to help your cause.

It meant for young kids that did gain a first team call up that you were being asked to make the jump from Western League competition direct to the second or third division of the English Football League. In many cases, it was too big an assignment.

At the end of the 1960/61 season, City withdrew their Colts team from the Western League, and for four seasons, from 1961/62 until 1964/65, the reserve team played in the Western League.

The figures tell the tale: Champions in 61/62 and 62/63, runners up in 63/64, ninth in 64/65, and over 100 goals scored in the first three of those seasons, with the magic target being missed by a mere four goals in 64/65.

This is where I spent the best playing years of my career, from 17 through to 21 years of age. From that day to this, I believe that this decision probably cost me a raft of second and third division games that may have accelerated my own personal career.

Rumour has it that Harry Dolman, City's chairman and owner, made the cut in order to build the Dolman Stand.

In the 1965/66 season, common sense prevailed over other priorities and the reserve team returned to the London Combination.

We apprentices knew that Lemmo kept a book in which he reported on how we played on a Saturday. One day, as we carried out our ground staff duties, we happened to lay our hands on it. We found it in a cupboard in the kit/boot room.

This room held all the playing boots for the staff, numbered and named for convenience. In a cupboard on the right hand side of the room were shelves, which held the playing shirts, socks and shorts, including the so-called change kit.

We were rarely given access to this spot. Lemmo generally

organised the kit distribution. He had the key and would often, on a match day, simply leave all the gear in a pile in the home dressing room, or Fridays for a Saturday game, for us to hang on the appropriate peg.

On this particular day, Lem had left the door unlocked and was down in the away dressing room. Geoff Bryant was being nosey, rummaging through the shirts.

"What's this then, Stace?" Geoff said, emerging with a book in his hand.

"It's the frigging match reports! Give it here," I said, and Geoff duly obliged.

The last report was a match against Weymouth in which 'Stace had played enthusiastically, scored two goals but was generally quiet although he was up against their best player.'

"Put the book back where you found it, quick," I said and handed it back to Geoff. Geoff dug into the pile of shirts and then innocently emerged to stand with me alongside the boot bench and continued busily cleaning the first team boots.

"Hurry up," said Lem, "you need to get out on the terraces with your mates as soon as you've finished."

"Yes, Lem," we replied in unison. We couldn't wait to share our little secret.

Further access to the little book required planning. As you walked in the main entrance to the ground, past the stairs that led to the grandstand and to the Robins, or Supporters Club, past the manager's office on the right, you came to a pair of double doors. Walk a step past these doors, and directly in front of you, was the players' 'race' leading directly to the field of play. To your right was a corridor leading to the visiting team's changing room. To your left was a similar corridor leading to the home team changing room. With the double doors open, as they often were, this couple of square yards gave you a 360-degree view of anyone coming or going. This was the key position to be in.

The two ground staff washing socks and cleaning boots would need time in the boot room. The plan was to the socks to soak and clean the boots. The two sweeping terraces would have to come in for their morning cup of tea. There would have to be a home game of some sort on a Tuesday or Lemmo would be collecting the laundry delivery on a Thursday. In other words, the kit room would have to be open, as we had no key.

One of us needed to be stationed in the key position. One outside the kit room, monitoring the home team dressing room, one in the kit room reading the report, and one tracking Lemmo or engaging him in a serious conversation about football. If ever anyone asked what we were up to, we were on our break.

Then came the inquisition, "What did he say?" The usual response was, "I was the best player, you played like a pratt, Geoff's lazy and Fordy's got too much mouth."

"Don't believe you."

"Go and look for yourself."

We didn't like mid-week games. First team mid-week games consigned us to a double dose of terrace work in one week, severely limiting time with the precious ball. What usually happened was that we worked in the morning and trained in the afternoon. Sometimes, if Fred wanted numbers, you would train with the pros and work in the afternoon.

With a mid-week game, we would get the brushes out on Monday and there would be no training morning or afternoon because the ground had to be clean for Tuesday night. Then we were back on the brushes first thing Wednesday. It seemed as if Tony and I had been washing socks and sweeping terraces forever.

A year or so into my apprenticeship, City drew Aston Villa, then

Friday November 6, 1942. The First Lady, Eleanor Roosevelt, meeting black GIs at the American Red Cross 'coloured club' at St Brendans School, St George Street, Bristol. Afterwards she visited white GIs at the 'white club' in Berkeley Square, Clifton. (Bristol Archives RefNo PicBox/7A/WW2/6)

Muller's No.5 Orphanage that was used as a base for black African-American GIs based in Bristol, including my father, Clarence Sims. (John Penny Collection)

The Royal Oak public house in Horfield, Bristol, where Clarence Sims met 19-year-old Evelyn Stacey. (John Penny Collection)

Evelyn Stacey with me around 1946.

(Stacey family collection)

I passed the 11+ examinations and attended Fairfield Grammar School, Bristol, from 1955 to 1960. (Bristol Archives RefNo 45212/Of/11/144)

1956 and Fairfield's 1st XI school cricket team. Back L/R: Risdale and Bridges. Middle L/R: Meisbiser (scorer), Williams, Woodward, Whittaker, Totterdell, Mr Ross Gilkes (teacher). Front: Wring, me, John Sherrington (capt), Upward, Hambly. (Bristol Archives RefNo 21131/SC/FAI/HM/1/13)

Fairfield Grammar School photograph from May 1956. I am in the second row at the back and eighth in from the left. (Bristol Archives RefNo 21131/SC/FAI/HM/1)

Highbridge United FC at Lakemead Grove. Believed to be the 1st team in the 1960/61 season, when they won the Bristol & District Division 6 title. Standing L/R: Ron, Keith, Mike Stitfall, Mike Sully, unknown, unknown, John Cryer, Pete Kew, Roy Packer, Kenny Laken. Seated L/R: Me, Terry Slocombe, Mike Tudor, John Shore and Dave Rowett (Stacey family collection)

Dot and I at our wedding at St Peter's Church hall in Bristol in 1959 with family members. (Stacey family collection)

My favourite lady. Granny Stacey. (Stacey family collection)

Our wedding day, Bristol, June 1, 1963. (Stacey family collection)

The 1964-65 promotion winners. Back row (left to right): Brian Thurlow, Jack Connor, Mike Gibson, 'Chuck' Drury, Gordon Low. 2nd row (left to right): Les Bardsley, Harry Dolman, Alec Briggs, me, Terry Bush, Bobby Etheridge, Mike Thresher, Tony Ford, Fred Ford (Manager), Arthur Proudler. 3rd row (left to right): Jantzen Derrick, Brian Clarke, John Ateyo, Bobby Williams, Ray Savino, Peter Hooper. Front row (left to right): 'Lou' Peters, Gerry Sharpe, Gordon Parr.

Wrexham FC Welsh Cup Final team 1966/67. I am seated second left. Manager Alvan Williams, seated centre, and coach John Neal, standing far right middle row. Wrexham lost to Cardiff City over two legs.

1970/71 season. Back playing for Bristol City against QPR at Loftus Road.

September 9, 1968. Blackpool v Wrexham, League Cup replay at Bloomfield Road. I just beat former Bristol City team mate Alan Skirton to the ball, but we lost 3-0.

Bristol City first team squad 1970/71. Back L/R: Alan Dicks (manager), Gordon Parr, Chris Garland, Ken Wimshurst, Ian Broomfield, Mike Gibson, John Galley, Alan Skirton, me, David Rogers. Front L/R: Geoff Merrick, Gerry Sharpe, Brian Drysdale, Danny Bartley, Trevor Jacobs, Dickie Rooks, Gerry Gow, Trevor Tainton.

Exeter City 1971 to 1973. Dot, myself and the kids
loved the far West especially the beaches.

Bath City team from 1973/74. I am kneeling third from right. (Stacey Family Collection)

CASC NEWS

The official newsletter of
Charlton Athletic Supporters Club

WINTER 1998/99

**CHARLTON
ATHLETIC**
SUPPORTERS CLUB

PROUD TO BE CHARLTON

In this special edition, how the anti-racism campaign is helping Charlton to become one of the country's most respected clubs on and off the field

Who is this player and why does he have a special place in Charlton's history?

Read Mick Everett on Page 3

This newsletter is free to all members of
Charlton Athletic Supporters Club

SPECIAL EDITION ON OUR ANTI-RACISM CAMPAIGN

Price £1

On loan to Charlton from Ipswich in 1970. I scored a rare goal on debut at the Valley.

Steve Stacey scores in the 70th minute against Huddersfield Town at The Valley on February 2, 1970, to level the score at 1-1. Alas, Frank Worthington scored a winner for Town a minute from the end.

STEVE STACEY, OUR FIRST BLACK PLAYER
- HE CAME, SCORED AND WAS GONE

So who was the first black player to represent Charlton Athletic at first team level?

The breakthrough came in January 1970 in the form of Steve Stacey, a Bristol-born centre half who came to Charlton on loan from Ipswich Town.

Steve played just one game for us and actually scored - against Huddersfield Town in a Division 2 match. He never appeared again.

Another nine years was to elapse before black players appeared in the first team, two arriving together on August 11, 1979, in Charlton's League Cup tie against Peterborough United.

The players were Leroy Ambrose and Phil Walker, with Phil scoring in a 3-1 defeat.

Leroy went on to appear 34 times for Charlton, scoring one goal before joining Hvidore IF of Denmark. In later years, he became a familiar figure in local non-League football with both Fisher Athletic and Dover Athletic.

Phil was bought from Millwall in July 1979 for £120,000. He made 91 appearances and scored 17 goals before leaving at the end of the 1982-83 season.

A gifted midfielder, Phil suffered a pelvic injury and his career faltered. He then joined Gillingham on loan in November 1982 before playing with some success for Boavista in Portugal.

Blackheath Bluecoat old boy Paul Elliott was the next black player to appear, making his debut against Crystal Palace in September 1981 and going on to a distinguished career with Chelsea, Aston Villa, Pisa and Celtic.

In the 30 years since Steve Stacey made his appearance, the football landscape has changed. Over the past 10 years especially, black players, many of them local, have regularly come through the ranks, and it now virtually impossible to imagine a Charlton side without them.

They have become an integral part of the club.

by MICK EVERETT, Charlton's Club Development Manager

A rare photo of my goal scoring abilities!

Back home in Nailsea. I was transferred from Ipswich to the Robins for the 1970/71 season and made nine appearances for my home-town club. Myself, Dot, Michele (R) and Natalie.

1974 and my first Australian team, Floreat Athena. Ken Sandercock, the former Torquay player, 3rd right front row kneeling. Ken and I became good friends.

No wonder I chose this photo as the cover for 'The Colour of Football'. The game is at the Velodrome, the home of Athena, and our opponents are Ascot. Memory tells me that the photo won a Sports Picture of the year award with the West Australian newspaper.

Floreat Athena team, 1975, in our new strip.

Team talk in the dressing room at the Velodrome, home of Floreat Athena. Yes, I did take my watch off before entering the field of play!

Our Greek-based team always had a tough time against the Italians, in this case Perth Azzurri. Having said this, Azzurri was one of the best organised and supported teams in Western Australia.

The Velodrome was the home of Floreat Athena and was somewhat restricted in supporter comfort as shown here. Where's the ball?

OK, he finally got a cross in!

Western Australia state team, 1975. This photo may have been prior to the fixture with Manchester United. Football was finally beginning to become a major sport in Australia and, besides United, we also played Glasgow Rangers, Middlesborough, Legia Warsaw and Toronto Metro, the Canadian champions.

After exchanging pennants with visiting team captains it became a struggle to hang on to it. This Glasgow Rangers pennant is a symbol of the capacity of the underdog to roll the giants of the game. We beat the Scottish champions and were the first Aussie team to beat overseas opposition!

in the First Division, in the FA Cup. The television cameras came to Ashton Gate. Les had us in our training gear and there we were, proudly doing our sprints on the red gravel track, trying hard not to smile at the camera.

I told Dot that I was going to be on the TV that night. We gathered the family, and all my mates and hangers on. The broadcast started and the opening shot was a vista of the ground and then a shot of the players training. Next was an interview with Fred who was saying how great it was having Villa come to Bristol and, not surprisingly, saying we could beat them.

Next was a shot of Fordy, Pratty, Geoff and I leaning on our brushes, laughing and smiling. The backdrop was our workplace, the main stand terracing. We thought at least they would have featured us training, running round the track. Suddenly we faced a serious identity crisis. How could we live with the fact that we were supposed to be superstars, at least in our neck of the woods, and now all and sundry had seen us with the tools of our trade? Not boots but, instead, brushes; it was shameful!!!!

A memorable draw was secured with the replay narrowly lost away at Villa Park. Tony and I were to become regular members of the Western League side.

Weston-super-Mare was the playground of most Bristolians, little more than 20 miles down the road, an easy trip.

We were getting changed in the rooms at Weston, a real hot day for the early season fixture.

"This will make you feel good," said Lem. I have a quick look. The boys are passing round and swigging from a bottle, a quart of White Horse scotch. This must be new, I thought. Then my turn came.

"Thanks, Lem." I swig back a mouthful.

The poor old full back that day, I tore him to pieces. Lem's little book said I was a real handful all afternoon!

At that time, our major rivals were Bideford, a lovely little town on the west Devon coast.

Both sides had reached the Western League Cup Final, which was a two-legged affair. We narrowly lost the first leg at Bideford by a single goal. So Fred strengthened the side for the return leg. Gordon Parr, Tony Cook, Jantzen Derrick, Peter McCall, Alex Tait, David Noakes, Gordon Low – all players with considerable first team experience – were brought in. We thrashed them, and scored five goals, of which I got three. A cup final hat trick, the stuff that dreams are made of!

Bideford were seriously pissed off. But this was the core of the problem of playing the reserve team in the Western League, and not the London Combination. Often against the better sides like Bideford, it was a tough assignment for up and coming ground staff, but a walk in the park for seasoned pros.

At some point wisdom dictated that the Western League team would no longer play their games at Ashton Gate, but at the County Ground, the home of the Gloucestershire County Cricket Club. Not on the main cricket wicket pitch of course, but on the area behind it.

It was here on one momentous day I scored the quickest goal of my entire career.

I was at centre forward; Brian 'Nobby' Clark, was at inside right and Adrian Williams - my daughter Michele's God parent – was at inside left.

I kicked off to 'Willy,' he played it back to the half back, who may have been Peter McCall. He played an inch-perfect through ball to Nobby, who squared it first time in front of goal, I eluded the centre-half and knocked the ball in from all of six yards. This all happened in the space of ten seconds and the opposition had yet to touch the ball. Sadly we did not build on this and my memory tells me that it ended as a two-all draw.

There were no stands here, and no seating. Everyone stood along the touchline. What a transition if, next week, you were playing in the first team and had to front 20,000 at Ashton Gate.

In a game against Weymouth, I had a little tussle over by the touchline with a defender. It became a little heated.

There was this older gent on the sideline, flat cap and gumboots. He looked every part a country 'gent,' farmer perhaps, but very recognisable as a man from outside the city.

"Oi!" he said, in his best West Country accent, "what's thy game then, young en?"

I reply in my best West Country accent, "Football, what's thee think it is?"

Here I was, this little coloured bloke running around causing all sorts of hassle, speaking with an accent like a Dorset farmer. The supporters on the touchline, most of them Weymouth supporters, erupted in laughter and my farmer friend retired looking a little sheepish. All good fun.

The role of the manager has evolved over a number of years. Fred, like many in that era, was a hands-on manager.

I had been married a few months and we were due to leave Ashton Gate for a game down south, in the Western League. It was early on a Saturday morning, say 10am. The coach was waiting in the car park outside the main entrance to Ashton Gate to take us to the game. Stragglers were arriving. To some, 10am meant 10am on the dot and not 9.45.

I was playing at centre forward, or at least that was what the team sheet said. I was waiting patiently for the rest of the team to arrive. Most of us are there with our new coach, Arthur Proudler, who had recently arrived from Aston Villa.

Then Fred appears. He's got on his gray tracksuit and in his hand he's got a garden fork. He's deep in to conversation with Arthur.

Next thing I know, they wave me over.

"How do you feel about sitting on the bench for the first team?"

Now this was in the days before substitutes, so effectively it meant that I was to be deprived of a game. Not only that, but if we won I would miss out on another two quid win bonus.

I looked at Arthur. He shrugged.

"First team appearance money and win bonus," says Fred.

Well that was ten quid up front and another four quid if the boys win or two quid if they draw. Bottom line was if they lose I'm still ten quid in front.

"If you say so, Fred." I replied nonchalantly.

"Right," he says. "Go and get changed into training gear and get a fork. I'll see you on the pitch."

There had been a mid-week game and Fred was concerned that all the divots had not been flattened properly. "Our job," said Fred "is to find all the divots that 'Chinny' - the groundsman - has missed."

Fred and I had a good old chat. I think this is what he wanted. He knew, of course, that I had just been married, also that Dot was expecting Michele, and that the club had done all they could to persuade the court to let us get married, by providing a letter of intent to guarantee not only employment for two years, but a club flat if necessary. There was a kind of bond. That day on the pitch I got some fatherly advice about marriage and some further managerial advice about my career.

That afternoon I duly sat on the bench and watched the boys do their stuff, ten quid extra first team appearance and the four quid win bonus. I couldn't wait for the next weekly wage packet.

I told myself, "I must get into this first team stuff somehow!"

FOOTBALL LIFE

F red Ford and Harry Dolman wanted Second Division football. City had lingered too long in the old Third Division (South). They believed that new faces, experienced players Jack Connor, Mike Gibson, Gordon Low, Tommy Casey, Alex Tait and others, could do it for them, together with an outstanding group of youngsters who had gone to the semi-finals of the English Youth Cup, Brian Clark, Jantzen Derrick, Adrian Williams, Alan Williams, and Terry Bush, to name a few. Things were looking good.

Add to this the experience of the likes of John Atyeo, Tony Cook, Mike Thresher and Derek Virgin and the outlook was bright, very bright indeed.

The realisation then came that to sustain this advancement in strategy one needed the basis of youth development.

Hence the Wessex Youth League, Stacey, Peters, Bush, Ford, Macey, Bartley, Sharp and others, all who went on to play first team league football for the Robins during that period…all, that is, except the dark, prolific goal scorer Steve Stacey.

I remember, prior to my signing for Bristol City, going to Ashton Gate and watching the youth team play West Ham and Chelsea in the quarter and semi-finals of the Youth Cup.

West Ham and Chelsea were First Division (equivalent to Premier League) outfits at the time, but City won a two-legged quarter final 6-5 over West Ham, only to get dumped by a classy Chelsea outfit 3-0 in each of the home and away legs in the semis. This was the 59/60 season.

A few months later, I was on the ground staff. The guys from that year's youth team, Janzten Derrick, Terry Bush, Adrian Williams and Brian Clark, were now full-time pros. This time around we drew Swindon Town away in the first round of the youth cup, in the 60-61 season. Rather than watching, I was playing.

There was a bit of history in this match. Not only were Swindon and Bristol City local rivals, but also Fred and Bert Head were old mates and a keen personal rivalry existed between them. It went a lot further than, "Done you today Fred," it was like a proof as to who was the best manager.

Swindon and Bristol are a bare 40 miles apart. Bert had his own young stars, including Ernie Hunt and Mike Summerbee. In terms of local youth football, it was a titanic showdown.

I started at outside-right, and Terry Bush at centre forward. It was a wet night, control was difficult and there was a bit of mud around. There was always this dilemma at the City about playing me at outside-right. There was a prodigious amount of talent at the club that could play up front and score goals. I was talented, but was untried in the first team and frankly wasn't ever going to get a game with the likes of Atyeo, Bush, Tait, Barry Meyer and even Alan 'Rhino' Williams, who was a centre-half playing in the number nine shirt.

I hated playing out wide, I much preferred the action in the middle, in the goal mouth where a single mistake could cost the opposition the game and where the odds were, in my view, always on my side. One mistake and I would pounce and it would be all over.

Fred swapped Terry and I at half-time, position for position. Terry reverted to out wide and I went to centre forward, and we almost cracked it. I hit the post, Terry hit a few crackers but it wasn't enough. We lost 3-1. Fred was angry, no disappointed, but hid it well.

Bert did the, "Well played lads, always a killer when that happens."

Go and gloat in your own time, were my thoughts as I despondently sat in the dressing room.

It's always the same. No matter how well you or anybody else thinks you played, it's not worth a cracker unless the game is won.

The Wessex Youth League had just been created in which the youth teams of, among others, Bristol City and Bristol Rovers, Swindon Town, Oxford United, Newport County, Plymouth Argyle and Bournemouth all played.

Playing as a centre forward and being appointed captain was a little unusual. The precedent had been set however. Big John Atyeo, City's favourite son, also played up front and captained the league side for what seemed forever.

We beat Newport one afternoon at Ashton Gate 11-0, and I remember I scored seven. One was my first really memorable left-footed goal. I admit thinking people must have been saying 'gotta watch this guy, he hits them with both feet.' Was this to be the birth of a legend? My first goal-scoring photo in the local paper, Evening Post, certainly had me believing.

Then it was back to Swindon and the resumption of Fred and Bert's rivalry. Swindon in a Wessex Youth League match, played at our place, Ashton Gate. The 'old guard' have gone, they have passed 18 years of age and are now playing in more dynamic environments.

Fred is deadly serious in the dressing room. He wants to beat Swindon badly. More precisely, he wants to hang it on Bert Head that his kids are better. Swindon had a couple of young lads in this game who had already played in the first team, including a young 'keeper, Tony Hicks. They also had Ernie Hunt, Mike Summerbee and Don Rogers. It was a powerful side indeed.

It was a perfect night. Playing towards the covered end, I got the ball rolling. I was 35 yards out to the right of the penalty area. 'What do I do now?' I started to think when I heard someone shout 'Hit it Steve!' I pushed the ball forward onto my right foot and then, whack. I struck it well. It was soaring towards the goal and it beat the dive, to his right, of the keeper, and continued on its merry way into the far corner.

"One of the best goals ever scored at Ashton Gate," raved the Evening News the next day. So it was. The crowd erupted. All 1,500 of them! They buzzed for another 20 minutes. Every time I got the ball the expectation was there. I could feel it. No matter how many games you play, you can't explain in words written or spoken what that kind of feeling does to you. You suddenly know that every eye is on you every time you touch the ball. You can do no wrong. You feel invincible.

We won 5-0. Bert didn't take it well. Fred was understandably ecstatic. "We done 'em. We done 'em," he kept saying. I had a bigger smile than most as I had bagged another hat trick.

Swindon strengthened their side and beat us at the County Ground 3-0. Fred was disappointed but had won the two-legged tie 5-3. He was ecstatic.

It was during the second season that we started to play with lots of purpose. We drew our cross-city rivals, Bristol Rovers, at home in the first round of the Football Association Youth Cup. There was a good crowd, as there always was when any kind of team from these two clubs met.

As usual, it was a lively affair, but towards half-time, a young lad who was playing left-back and held a place in the Rovers first team at that time, Lindsay Parsons, put in a high tackle, deliberate in my view, just under my right armpit. It was very high up. Down I went, torn shirt and a bit of scratch and blood seeping from his stud marks. It was extremely painful. Out came Les and Lemmo onto the pitch. It was hard for me to stand and so I had to leave the field amid a chorus of booing and shouts for Lindsay's head.

Les got me on the table in the dressing room. It was about ten minutes before half-time. "How is it, Flash?"

"Frigging painful, Les."

"Hmmm. Yes looks a bit nasty."

Les cleaned up the blood and treated the scratches. When he did it hurt almost as much as the crude tackle.

The half-time whistle sounded, and in walks Fred followed by the players. He looks at Les, Les nods in response.

"Sure you're OK, Steve?" he asks me.

"Yep," I replied, still struggling to stand upright. These were the days before substitutes, so I wasn't going to be staying in any dressing room.

The shirt was torn almost in half, so Lemmo found me a new shirt from a different kit. At least its red, but it has a round collar not a V-neck.

We're cruising at half-time, 3-0 and ready to go on pounding the boys from Eastville. The whistle blows in the corridor, "come on, lads" says the ref and out we go.

As I lead the team onto the field, the noise is deafening. No one expected me back on the field. The clapping and the cheers of 'come on lads,' 'good on you Steve' continues for a couple of minutes. At the final whistle I put my arm around Lindsay as we walk off. "Never mind Lindsay, you plonker, there's always next time."

Lindsay says nothing.

The Chairman came into the dressing room, Harry Dolman. This was, let me tell you, an almost unheard of and very rare occurrence. Mr. Dolman was a very rich, and in my view, genuine man who had built a large electrical engineering firm and owned the club outright. He stayed just long enough. "Well done, boys, well done." A special look was followed by a smile and then a pat on the head for me. "Well done, Steve."

Harry Dolman had a big heart for the Robins. It was his wealth that kept the club going. There was nothing Harry liked more than seeing his beloved Robins thrash their cross city rivals at any level of competition. On that night he had his wish, and I was right in the thick of it with another three-goal haul.

In the next round, we beat Dorchester and I scored three more goals. Then we drew Cardiff City away. Cardiff were in the First Division at the time and they, too, had a number of youngsters playing for them that had first team experience, including a young goalkeeper, Dilwyn John. It was going to be tough. To play a First Division club on their home ground was always a challenge.

Fred had not come to Dorchester, but he was fired up for this one. I honestly don't think he expected us to get a result from this game. We played as well as we had all season. The first half was goalless, but that gave us no cause for concern. In the second half we ran over them to win by a solitary goal, 2-1.

I put both goals past young Dilwyn and was really pleased that I had done this against a player who had played in the top league. Proud, there was nothing that could keep me down.

We were going places. The result got us all wondering, just how far could we take this? We were drawn next against Brighton and Hove Albion, a second division club, at home.

Fred had recently signed a full-back from Brighton called David Smith. Smithy said we would have our hands full as Brighton had a well-developed youth policy.

On the night there was quite a reasonable crowd considering the weather. The terracing in front of the main stand was fairly well populated so it appeared that news our fame was spreading.

In the first half, I get a long through ball and it's between the goalkeeper and I. The ball is bouncing and, sure as eggs is eggs, there is going to be a tangle. I get there a split second before the keeper, and nod it past him, but as I do he whacks straight into me and I'm down. I have no idea where I am. I can hear vague background noise that sounds like cheering, Les squeezes a wet, cold sponge over my head and then I hear Fordy saying "great goal, Stace." The boys are all around me and are ecstatic.

Alas, as I slowly regain some kind of coherence, it's clear that the referee has ruled out the goal. He is claiming that there was a handball. Despite the vehement protests, my strike is ruled out. The crowd has come to life, they are baying for blood and questioning the ref's paternity and offering to pay for new glasses.

Despite this setback they did not have long to wait before we did take the lead. I played a one two on the edge of the box with Dave Meacock, our inside-left. This left me one on one with the keeper and, from ten yards out, I side-footed it in to his right.

It is a slender lead to take into the second half against such opposition. At half-time, Fred asked me if I had handled the ball, and I told him honestly that I hadn't.

He nodded and then headed straight away to the ref's room at the bottom of the corridor, next to the visitors dressing room. I don't know what was said but knowing Fred it was a full and frank discussion!

Half way through the second half, and the game is on a knife-edge. A high ball was played into the box and is falling straight down on me. Players, theirs and ours, surrounded me, I had my back to the goal, ten yards out, and so from a defensive point of view was not much of a threat.

Players usually react on instinct. It's one of the differences between street players and fully-fledged professionals. It's not a question of what am I going to do with this, but what do I want to do in this particular circumstance. The options zip through the mind very quickly, in a flash. In this instant I choose the least expected option, the over-head kick. The keeper saw this, but his body movement and positioning shift came too late. Just as I connected, he slammed into me again and down I went for the second time, flat out. One more time and surely the referee stops the bout?

The next thing I know is Les is there again with the trusty magic sponge. "Stace, you brave little bugger," he says. I can hardly stand, but the crowd is cheering, and the boys are dancing. Meanwhile the Brighton defenders are having a right old barney about who should have done this and that. We were 2-0 up and that's how it stayed.

We are now one of the last eight teams left in the cup. It suddenly sinks in, the responsibility we carry on behalf of the club.

This time we drew Portsmouth away. Another First Division club, and at their home, the famous Fratton Park. I was bathing in a bit of glory. We had scored ten goals in four games and I've scored eight of them. I was on cloud nine. The trouble is the clouds are a long way up and it's a long way to fall.

The weather was awful, it was freezing, absolutely freezing, icy in the extreme. The ground was hard and bumpy.

My hands were frozen, as were my feet. It feels like my whole body is in a cold store. I just couldn't seem to get moving, it was hard to get motivated. The eight-goal hero was frozen out. Portsmouth rolled us. They scored three goals before a lone response from Lou Peters.

There wasn't much rejoicing on the way home. Bill wasn't talking much, and we knew we had failed miserably.

So the Wessex Youth League was all we had left to play for and that ran its course. It was my last season, as I became ineligible in 62/63 along with the rest of the survivors. I'm not sure how long it lasted after that, but the league was a great innovation while it lasted.

GOALKEEPING

M y career as a professional footballer could have been vastly different. I was versatile when I was young, and remained versatile throughout my career. Within the scope of professional first or reserve team football, I played in every position on the field. What about goalkeeper you say?

In the early years at Bristol City, I was selected in goal to play in what was then the reserve team.

If we include appearances in the reserve team, and I'm talking about starting games here, not being shuffled during the match, during my professional career, I started in all the 11 positions, from goalkeeper to outside left.

I had no preconceived ideas about where I should play, in the early days. I just enjoyed the game and wanted to be playing. Wherever we had space, whoever was around and whoever had a ball, any kind of ball, off we went. There was some attraction to the lone position between the posts. Isolated, not lost in the jungle of 20-a-side on the tarmac road or the expansive common. The green jersey made the keeper different; so, too, did the gloves and the caps they wore.

Usually, and this was quite common, the keepers wore a different colour pair of shorts during the game. At Eastville, Bert Hoyle and Howard Radford wore black shorts, while the rest of the team wore white. The downside was that while the rest of the mob ran wild on the pitch, mistakes galore, but often salvaged with a goal, there was no such compassion for a keeper. One mistake, a goal that cost the match, and you would know about it, forever.

When we played at the gaslight, no one stuck to a position, it was mob sport. Attackers and defenders weren't defined. It didn't matter that Geoff Bradford was a centre forward and you were busy tackling people all night, and that you had assumed his identity, or that, on the common, you had headed a ball off the goal line, or made that last desperate sliding tackle. You were Geoff Bradford, Rovers centre forward, never mind that Geoff never in his career saved the Rovers with a goal line clearance.

In other games I had been Roland Ugolini, the Middlesborough goalkeeper and a former Italian prisoner of war. I think this was more about his tanned skin than anything else. I'm not sure whether Roland would have been flattered or not.

The first time I played in goal seriously stands out clearly. Gil Merrick played for Birmingham City and England. He was an outstanding custodian. Gil made over 700 appearances for Birmingham, inclusive of war-time games, and won 23 England caps. There is good and bad in every story. He was unfortunately England's keeper when the Old Dart were beaten at Wembley for the first time in 1953, by the great Hungarian side, 6-3, and more importantly was also in goal for the return match, where they went down by a more decisive 7-1 in Hungary.

This era defined a radical change in how professional football would be played for decades on. No longer would the centre half be isolated with two full backs wide, marking two equally isolated wingers. Brawn and hope would be replaced by skill and precision. The Hungarians pushed the one midfielder back into a dual centre half role, with two midfield players to support the front four, or support the back four. The rigidity of the old way of playing was over. The modern game called for better skill definition and fluidity.

For England, being English was now not enough. A new era was upon us. This was all forgotten in April, 1956. Gil Merrick was a schoolboy hero. What's more, Birmingham were in the FA Cup semi-final against Sunderland. The show was on, venue Horfield Common. All those folk turning up at Hillsborough, Sheffield Wednesday's neutral semi-final ground, would be very, very, disappointed!

It was wet, cold and muddy. This never deterred us. I was Gil Merrick. I dived, cut out crosses, picked a dozen balls out of a dozen (imaginary) nets, pushed people out of the way, covered myself in glory and mud. The stuff dripped off me. I only had one lot of clothes for school. I was determined that Birmingham would win this titanic struggle. I left the goal for a while, scored goals, restored the lead and returned to my first love, the goalmouth. Alas, glory is short-lived. Although Birmingham won their way to the cup final, as they would in reality, beating Sunderland 3-0 on the weekend, this version of the semi-final had much more basic consequences.

I rushed in the front door of 58 Oak Road. "Gran, Gran, Birmingham are in the cup final. Gran, we beat Sunderland, we're playing at Wembley!"

Gran looked, looked again, and then raised her eyes to heaven.

It was only then that I looked at myself, and realised what a selfish little boy I had been. From head to toe, I was encased in mud. Shoes, trousers, shirt, pullover, the lot, and I was standing, dripping mud onto the floor in the parlour, never mind the trail I had left behind me from the front door.

Did Gran consider my dreams? She must have. I was never really admonished.

It was at Highridge that I first started to take goalkeeping seriously. After one game at Highridge, I made one 'stupendous' save, two feet or so off the ground, horizontal, diving left, right arm outstretched and tipped the ball over the bar. The opposition coach ran onto the field and told me I was the best goalkeeper he had ever seen! I didn't know how the system worked back then. He claimed he was a scout and that he was going to Bristol City.

Mike Stitfall was a young bloke who ran everywhere and did everything for the club at Highridge. Mike loved the club, like he owned it, and all of us were his children. All we had to do was play.

Mike was beaming when he told me that I had been selected in goal for the County trials. These were generally recognised as the first step to further glory. The game would be played at Mangotsfield, who were then an up and coming team in the County League, or the Bristol Premier Combination, as the top amateur league was then known.

It was a dark chilly night, and the game was played under floodlights. There was a bit of a crowd; no doubt including the scouts. I don't recall the score. I made a couple of saves, but left with the feeling that I was a better centre forward.

Pre-season at Bristol City, Fred was obviously aware of my versatility. For some reason, we were a goalkeeper short. Bob Anderson, a long time City stalwart, had gone in the early 60s. Tony Cook had been at the club for a decade or more, and was into his twilight years. I must say, Tony was a real joker.

My most enduring memory of big Tony is at Torquay's pitch, Plainmoor.

It was a reserve game. Torquay were awarded a penalty. The penalty was well hit. It flashed past Tony to his right, before he had even moved. The ball hit the stanchion at the back of the net and rebounded straight to our man. Tony caught the ball and, being a quick thinker, threw it to Danny Bartley, outside of the penalty area, watching the action like everyone else.

Off goes Danny, the length of the field. He then slots it across the box and one of our guys pops it into the Torquay net. Meanwhile, the Torquay team are celebrating and slowly jogging back to the centre circle. The referee, however, awards us a goal!!

Eventually the game restarts; who scored what, where and when is clarified and, as you can imagine, is played out with a lot of vigour. My memory tells me we won comfortably. Eric Webber, the well-respected manager of Torquay at the time, summed it up like this: "The most remarkable piece of gamesmanship I have ever seen."

Not long after we are at training, Fred calls me.

"Steve, get the keepers' jumper on."

"OK."

The practice matches usually panned out in two ways. Either the first team played the reserves, or the first team forward line joined with the reserve team defence and vice versa. This day, as I took my place between the posts, I faced the first team attack, big John Atyeo and all. We played a full 90 minutes. Big John got a header from close in, but that was it. That was the start.

Even when we had a full complement of keepers, it wasn't unusual for Fred to put me in goal for 30 minutes or so. One day, I remember I had been in goal and cut out a cross from the right, stretching high and grabbing the ball with both hands. Fred was the referee and was a couple of yards away as I grabbed the ball, and I heard him say, "What a player, what a save."

Next it was the newspapers. The photographers came to the County Ground, where we usually trained. Bobby Etheridge stood on the six-yard box and threw me a couple of balls that I dived and saved. It looked quite spectacular in the Green Un that Saturday, with the title: "Look out Gibson and Nichols, here I come." Underneath was a little bit of a write up detailing my career as a goalkeeper. More was to come.

At the end of a light training session, I got a call to go and see Fred. He told me that two of the three regular goalkeepers were injured and I would be playing in goal on Saturday for the reserves at Weymouth.

I have to say I was fearless. I never thought the day would come, but here it was. My own ability had got me to be second choice goalkeeper for Bristol City. I had plenty of advice from Cookie, Ron Nicholls and Mike Gibson about angles and so forth, when to come off my line and when to stay. Go forward with your foot in front of you, be prepared to punch, you have the advantage of height, use both fists if you can. Once your mind is made up, don't change it.

Then it started: "Stace in goal? Could be a record score!", "don't get your hand caught in your jumper", "only side foot the back passes," "how many pages do we need to keep score?" I heard them all.

Then came the game. The first ball that was crossed came from the right. I got a little under it and, in my haste to protect the goal, palmed the ball onto my own crossbar. Good start!

The nerves soon disappeared. I became the model of a competent keeper. I took control of the box, bellowed instructions, and got my body behind every shot. In truth, there weren't many; two or three, and a couple of headers and more back passes rather than attempts at goal!

The final result was a goalless draw. I couldn't complain about that. There were looks of admiration from the boys. I even signed my first autographs as a goalkeeper.

There were no mobile phones then, so on Monday morning, when I showed up for training, Fred approached me as I was jogging on the running track. "Good game Steve, well done. Couldn't wait to get the Green Un," said Fred. He said he saw the result, and thought it was 10-0 not 0-0. But there was a twinkle in his eye. "Well done," he said, and off he went.

Fast forward to Bootham Crescent, home of York City FC, on Friday, April 7, 1967

I have to be honest and say I am not sure what happened at Wrexham. There had never been any great discussion on my career as a goalkeeper. I didn't play in any practice matches, as we always had a full complement of keepers.

After my debut at Southport, Jack Rowley had said that he bought me because I could play anywhere, even in goal. Fred must have told him about my career between the posts.

We were on a good run and had lost only one of the last nine games; but we had drawn five. Despite that we were still well and truly in the promotion race.

On this particular night, we are getting hammered. York City completely have our measure and they're 3-0 up.

John Schofield, our keeper, goes down in a melee. John was wringing his hand, and grimacing in pain. He couldn't go on, not in goal anyway. John Neal is on the field. My goalkeeping activities have been discussed. Jack Rowley has said I can play anywhere, even in goal, that's why he bought me. Alvan Williams, the manager, and his sidekick, John Neal, believe him. I had already worn eight different shirts that season; in those days, teams wore shirts numbered according to their position.

This was totally different though, a different colour jersey, totally different from just a different number! John dutifully went over to outside right. The team was reorganised.

I thought of the common and the garages as I pulled the green shirt over my head. Despite my dreams of saving a penalty and the game in the last minute, I knew that this wasn't going to happen. There were only maybe 15 minutes left at the most. York were well on top, and you could have bet your last penny that they would keep coming at us with our reorganised team and deputy goalkeeper. They didn't take long

The centre forward got in between two players and made it 4-0. Great start, I thought, I haven't touched the ball yet and I'm picking it out of the net.

Next was a fairly weak ground shot, and then a header, and I held both comfortably. Then came a through ball. I raced to the edge of the box and, in a scramble, managed to clear it. Where were our defenders? I gave them a few choice words!

They won a corner. Johnny Schofield knew the score. He ran into the area and held or bumped anybody who looked like a forward or had 'goal' written on his face. It was never going to happen if John could help it.

Last, but not least, and the piece de la resistance, a ball ran loose on the edge of the box. The York player turned and volleyed it. He caught it perfectly. Luckily, I anticipated it and as the ball hurtled towards goal I fell to the right and hugged it close.

"Well done Stace," "Played keeper," from the York players, and applause from the crowd. As much as I enjoyed that moment, my career as a league goalkeeper is over. There won't be another chance.

On the long drive home, I couldn't help thinking about Geoff Dent under the gaslight and that this is where it ends, at York on a misty Friday night. There was no glory here.

BABIES

Michele Lee, our first child ,was born on October 28, 1963. I was 19 years and two months old and Dot was 17 years and 11 months. We were babes ourselves.

The pregnancy had been fairly normal and Dot had sustained herself on Pork pies and Tizer!! We were living with Evelyn at Derham Road, Bishopsworth, on the council housing estate

In those tough times local public transport was the way to travel for 99% of the population. One time, on the bus heading into town, Dot and I sat there minding our own business. Dot was feeling warm and asked me to open the window. I slid the window open and no sooner than I did I drew an instant response from a fellow traveler sitting behind us.

"Would you mind closing the window, it's too cold here?"

"My wife's pregnant and is feeling a little hot," I explained

His response caught me off guard. An expletive was followed by, "why don't you lot go back to where you came from, where you belong, in your own country", or words to that effect. I was stunned.

It probably never occurred to him that my father, just a few years before, fought a vicious war to ensure that this person had the right to air his views on public transport. I looked at him but remained calm, I could sense other passengers were watching.

"My wife is pregnant and she's feeling a bit warm," I repeated making no attempt to close the window. He said nothing.

Maybe he'd had a bad day, problems in the family, lost his job. I think the expletive and the tone and manner of the delivery request, followed up by the "go back to where you came from", said it all.

Dot was a little late, the date we were given for Michele was

October 2, and suddenly we were into the 20's.

We had instructions from the clinic at Bedminster she had been attending regularly that, if labour started at any time, or if nothing has happened by Thursday, October 24, we were to go straight to Mortimer House Clinic in the trendy suburb of Clifton. At that time, the facility was a kind of overflow for Southmead Hospital.

As nothing had happened by the deadline off we went, two teenagers hand in hand on one of life's greatest adventures, to bring our own child into the world. Dot and I caught an early morning bus together up to Mortimer House Clinic. I was receiving treatment for a hamstring injury and needed to be at Ashton Gate for 10.30am. Our first child was due anytime. All looked good and no problems were anticipated. This was soon to change.

I knocked on the door, which was answered by the Matron.

"Oh, hello, Mr. and Mrs. Stacey. Thank you, Mr. Stacey, I'll take the case and your wife's coat." Dot takes off her coat gives it to Matron who hands it straight back to me, and without another word ushers Dot into the hospital and shuts the door.

"I...umm I..." I catch the next bus back to the City ground.

Les Bardsley, the physio, was waiting for me and asked how it was all going.

Les has been trying to get me into a clinic in Bristol, an expensive Catholic place, not far from Mortimer House Clinic. We don't know when the call will come but we know that slots are tight. My hamstring has been playing up and, despite the best endeavors of the medical staff, it wasn't getting better. A new treatment is needed. I will be put under anesthetic and the medical people will pull and stretch the muscle while I'm completely relaxed. The only problem is, when they call I have to go. Waiting could delay my return to the arena for weeks.

After I left Mortimer House, Dot was taken into theatre. She recalls being given a strong relaxant drug. She's so drowsy that when she wakes she thinks that the little one has arrived. No such luck.

There was apparently some concern about the afterbirth arriving before the baby, and decisions were made to transfer her to Southmead Hospital. Dot maintains that she knew nothing of the transfer. She only recalls the ambulance men arriving the next day and wheeling her down two flights of stairs to the ambulance.

In the labour ward at Southmead Hospital, the doctor explained why she was there and the likelihood of a Caesarian.

All Dot was concerned about was whether I knew what was going on.

"He will be informed," she was told.

Dot was just 17. Understandably, she was frightened, scared, apprehensive, and alone. The woman in the bed next to Dot's gave birth to a baby boy. Soon after all the noise had died down, Dot was moved to B Ward, the same ward I was born in!

Meanwhile, after leaving the treatment room, I caught the bus to Mortimer House only to be told Dot had been moved to Southmead. There was no time to head to Southmead, as I had to be back at Ashton Gate. While I sat on the bus at the hospital, Dot had been given another strong pre-med in the theatre. She had just woken up. The doctors had advised her that they had managed to sort out the problem with the placenta and they had induced her. Her waters had broken and the little one should be on its way shortly. Only in later years has Dot told me how frightened she was and how, alone in that room waiting, she vowed never to have another child.

As soon as I arrived at the ground Les came running up to me to tell me I had been booked in on Monday (this was Saturday) for the hamstring procedure and I had been booked in to stay overnight.

This was not good news. I knew that Dot was close to delivery. The good news was City beat Hull 1-0 at home.

In those days the flow of information to the patient, the issues that were important, the future and what your treatment was to be, was rarely given.

There were strict visiting hours. I could never get to hospital in the mornings because I had to be at the City ground twice a day for treatment.

Michele Lee did not arrive as quickly as the doctors expected; she was born on Sunday, October 28, 1963 at about 5.30pm.

In the end, according to Dot, Michele came easily. One big push and it was all over.

Mum, Gran, and the 'girls', Beryl and Edie, had wanted a little boy. They wanted to spoil me all over again. Me, I just wanted Dot to be OK and for our child to have ten fingers and ten toes and all its faculties. I got my wish and have been grateful ever since.

There was no way that I could change the appointment for my hamstring. The club had said jump and I had to jump.

I went to the City ground for treatment and Arthur duly delivered me to the hospital.

It was a Catholic hospital. The nuns had these huge white hats. They wheeled me down to theatre and I heard the doctor discussing my lineage as he put me to sleep. "Yes, I think you're right, he looks like a Negro…"

Out I went and woke up some time later. I was in bed. The nurse was hovering around. My first reaction was, "my wife's in hospital I need to go and see her." I was promptly told I was going nowhere.

I drifted off again but the next time I awoke I was adamant. "I have to see my wife."

Nobody was going to stop me going to see Dot.

I caught a taxi to Southmead Hospital and asked to see Mrs. Stacey. I was heavily under the influence of the anesthetic and, in retrospect, I must have slurred my words. I know that I still had some difficulty in walking and standing up without leaning or grabbing something. I was asked to sit down and wait.

I sat there waiting. An hour passed. There was a new face at the desk, so I asked if there was anything wrong.

"Who are you waiting for?" she asked.

"Mrs. Stacey, I'm her husband."

"Oh, Mr. Stacey, yes, of course, Ward B. Down the passage, turn left and it's on your left." Why didn't they say that an hour ago!

I walked into the room and everyone was there; Mum, the girls, even Ted. Most of all, Dot was there, with this wonderful baby. It must be a boy! Dot's wearing a blue nightdress. We had agreed a blue nightie for a boy, pink for a girl. "Dot, love, can I pick up my son?"

"Steve, it's a girl. The nurse picked up the first nightdress she put her hands on and it was blue," she said, laughing.

I picked my daughter up and knew I would love her forever.

Only later the truth emerged; the first receptionist had thought I was tipsy because of the anesthetic. I had been kept in the waiting room until I 'sobered up'. The circumstances were explained, questions asked, explanations given. But I was furious.

Later, I was shown the way to the nursery. All the babies were in their cots. I had to look at my child through the glass. I had tears in my eyes. I stared in awe at this child part of me, and part of Dot, part of so many people long gone.

Our second daughter, Nat, was born on the Grand National day (won by Anglo at 50-1 and ridden by Fred Winter), March 26, 1966. By then I was 21 years and seven months old, and Dot was 20 years and four months old.

Dot had named our first daughter Michele, now it was my turn, Natalie. Dot thinks it was all about Natalie Wood, but no. I just liked the name. It was to be Natalie for a girl, and Stephen for a boy.

By this time, I have been transferred to Wrexham and we are

playing at Aldershot. Nat is overdue. We are told all would be over by March 16. Dot is in hospital for a few days prior to the birth.

She's keeping her parents waiting. Football kick off times are changed to facilitate the locals watching the Grand National and their favourite football teams. The kick off at Aldershot is put back to 7.30pm.

I was in Bristol at the time, and training at the City ground.

I had to make a separate trip to Aldershot, while the troops travelled from Wrexham.

On the way to Aldershot for the late kick off, I called in to see Dot.

The midwife said not to expect the birth for a day or two. I arranged to call Dot after the game.

The people in the office at Aldershot kindly let me use the office phone.

I was told they 'both' are doing well! Our baby girl had been born at 2.20pm - two hours after I had left with a forecast of nothing happening. I missed both my children being born! They don't let me forget it!!

I stopped at the hospital on the way home. Nat had flecks of blood on her still, and I, well, I fell in love again. My kids are my best friends. Dot and I had them while still quite young and we grew up together.

Father, you abandoned Mum and us just when we needed you most!!, I hear them say.

I can't win this argument against three of nature's finest, two of them Scorpios (ooooh), but they know I love them.

THE POOLS

The English winter of 1962/63 was cold, very cold indeed. After the home fixture at Brighton on December 26, 1962, City did not play again until the 4-2 victory over Bradford at Ashton Gate on February 16, 1963, a period of 52 days over seven weeks.

All this was due to bad weather, snow, frost and ice. Britain shuddered to a halt during one of the worst winters in history, the third coldest, in fact, since record keeping began.

For the first time ever, the Football League asked the Football Association to authorise an extension to the season. This caused the perennial debate about a break in the season to accommodate the notorious English winter raising its head again.

Some areas of the UK experienced continual snow cover during this period.

Severe frost as cold as -16C froze the country solid, causing massive logistical, power and transportation problems. The players used Blackpool's ground, Bloomfield Park, in the nation's North West, as a skating rink.

The dilemma for the managers was how to maintain fitness, when you couldn't get on to a football field. Like many clubs, we played endless five a side games in the car park.

Indoor sports halls, weights, running all morning up and down the steps of the covered stand, count the number of steps, count them again, how many would Fred take us up this time before he changed tack and we headed down; would he go left round the safety barrier or right, would we duck under this one or leap frog over it? We played continual mental gymnastics to relieve the boredom.

Littlewoods and Vernon's ran the football 'Pools'. Forecast eight draws, nine home wins, four away wins, or some other combination, and the rewards were extensive. Enough to buy a house, flash car, rooms of furniture, and a holiday in Europe, depending on how many winners there were. The money was divided into separate pools. The distribution or amount of money depended on how many people participated and, of course, how many had forecast the results correctly. The top dog was the person who predicted the magical eight draws. They would be instant millionaires.

With hardly any games were being played the Pools firms stood to lose literally millions so they came up with the idea of 'the Panel'. This august body of persons would review the form of clubs. If a game was cancelled, then the Panel's recommendation, based on recent past form, would determine the probable result. The pools firms used these results to calculate payouts.

Bobby Etheridge had organised a syndicate and most of the players were in it at two bob each. It's Monday morning. I'm in the dressing room early. Bobby is in the dressing room, waiting. I'm surprised.

"Bob, you're early."

"Won the pools," he answered calmly not even looking up.

"What? We've got 24 points?" I excitedly asked.

"Yeah."

The pools had been known to create millionaires overnight. How many were in the syndicate? I started trying to calculate our winnings, I think maybe there were 20 or so of us. A million divided by 20 is... work it out.

I was on ten quid a week. You could buy a house for two grand and a car for £500. The boys started to filter in. I've never heard the phrase 'twenty four points' uttered so often, so many times in 48 hours as I did that January of 1963.

How much? How many winners? What will you buy? The holiday

in Spain was ordered. The entire team was going. Those few, those merry, now dismal, few who had not contributed their King's or should I say Queen's shilling, were inconsolable. "Don't worry old son, I'll buy you a pint, Mercedes, house, villa, holiday," depending on how deep you wanted the jibes to go.

We couldn't wait 'til Wednesday when the Pools firm revealed how many winners there were, and published the money due to each.

I rushed home to Dot. We were not yet married. But what a start this would be to married life! Plans were made, a house in the country, a car. I had not even got a driving license yet, but that wouldn't be a problem. We would be the first in either family to have an overseas holiday!

The Panel would differ on only minor points of form. There was no recent history to go on. Sure, for two or three weeks after the 'big chill' had set in, the Panel might surprise us with a few differences of opinion on results. But in the end, wouldn't the result on past performances become predictable?

When in doubt, forecast a draw. The number of draws that week was, I think, 11 or 12. Millionaire stuff, well we liked to think so.

The problem was the rest of England agreed with the Panel, or should I say the Panel agreed with the rest of England. It was a dismal dressing room that Wednesday.

We 'band of brothers', adventurers, would-be philanthropists, house hunters, drivers of fast exotic motor vehicles, collectors of suntans in Northern Spain, were shattered.

Those poor souls who had been ribbed mercilessly for their non-contribution to fame and fortune, were vindicated. Saved.

We got a shade over 30 bob (one pound ten shillings each.) So did the other million winners!

BRISTOL CITY

F red Ford was an old World War 2 warrior, Londoner, cockney, and much admired. He had been in the game a long time. He was honest, direct, and loved his players like they were his own children. He had a wonderful smile, and was almost never seen to be angry.

Fred was appointed manager at Bristol City in July, 1960. I was one of Fred's first signings for the club!!

Prior to joining Bristol City, Fred had coached/managed the England Under 23 and the England B teams, as they were then known. In later years, he would have brief spells at two other local clubs, Swindon Town and the bitter cross-city rivals, Bristol Rovers.

One needs to be careful how you define 'manager', then and now. I suspect that, now, managers taking coaching sessions on a daily basis are a thing of the past.

In my day, the manager took every session that the first team participated in. It was almost unheard of for a manager to take a session with the reserves.

There were a few part-timers back then but of the group of professionals available on a daily basis, Fred would take the first team squad of, say, 16 players and Bill Harvey would take the rest. The 'rest' could be spread out between the reserves and the colts, and the opportunities of collective team comprehension was limited.

Fred was the first manager to effectively make me think about team cohesion.

"Football is all about sympathy of thought," he said in his cockney accent and 'thought' came out like 'fought.' He was blunt. One of his favourite sayings was, "It's wet tonight, you'll need long studs and stamina."

I saw him angry but once. It was when first team goalkeeper Tony Cook couldn't find his shoe! He searched the dressing room and had to go home without it.

One of the lads sees Cookie walking across the centre with one shoe, a 'dap' on the other foot, and limping!

The next day, Tommy Casey, a happy-go-lucky genial Irish international, walks through the door as Tony Cook is getting lots of banter from the other lads. The shoe turns up in Tommy's case and in five seconds they're grappling each other and it isn't friendly. They are both pulled apart, mouthing threats of some kind. Les Bardsley, whose physio room runs off the first team dressing room, is in the middle of it pulling people apart and pleading for calm. We were standing there taking it all in.

Training is barely finished that morning when Fred directs everyone to the top dressing room. It's crowded. We were all there, the players, staff and ground staff. It's a bollocking the like of which I have never seen. Fred was so angry. Nobody, but nobody, was going to own up to nicking Cookie's shoe, after that. All these years later I still do not know for sure who took it, but I have my suspicions.

"Your contracts are in my office," says Fred, "if I find out who it was, drop by, pick it up and piss off! Don't let this happen again!" It didn't.

That incident shattered morale. It's what happens when things get out of hand. Tommy knows he's innocent. Cookie isn't sure and whoever did it is on a big guilt trip.

The 1960/61 season was drawing to a close. Lou Peters and Tony Ford had been flirting with the reserve side and played a few games. I was still knocking in goals at Western League and youth team level.

The reserves were due to play the last, or close to last, game of the season at Ashton Gate against Nottingham Forest, then a First

Division team. It was my chance at the higher level.

I was 16 and struggled at the higher level. One could argue that, at that age, you would need half a dozen games to pick up the pace of the game. I had a few touches, flashed a header over the bar, and a couple of shots, but generally, I was not up for it.

I was close to the touchline, five or so minutes from the end of the game, when one of the seasoned campaigners playing for the Forest, Jeff Whitefoot, thumped me in the back and sent me sprawling onto the red gravel running track that surrounded the pitch. The crowd was baying for blood.

Straight from the concrete jungle, what did I do? I am sure you have probably guessed. I picked myself up and bellowed a few profanities and raised my fist at him. I didn't hit him. It was a non-event really, from my point of view. The ref didn't agree and sent us both off!

I looked at Jeff. He looked at me. We both said, "Ref, I never touched him," or words to that effect. This didn't help Jeff's case.

"Why are you sending me off? All I did was raise my fist? I never hit him..."

"That's enough," he said, as he raised the dreaded red card and pointed the way. I had to go. If I went because of the raised fist, then Jeff had to go too. Was that the end of the violence? No. A sweet little old lady from Pasadena, leaning over from the terraces to get to the 'tunnel' where you entered and left the pitch, hammered Jeff with an umbrella and shouted as she did so, 'You leave our Steve alone, you bully!" Sent off on your Football Combination debut. It was not the ideal start.

Terry Burt, our right back, was the first into the dressing room and couldn't stop laughing.

The general agreement was that I had a raw deal and that Jeff should have had a solo walk of shame.

On Monday, Fred had me write a report to the Football Association relating the incident. He was sure that, by doing this, I would get away without a suspension. I didn't.

I received a week's suspension and, what is more, the club was forbidden to pay my salary and I was banned from entering the ground!!

"Don't worry," says Fred, "come to training; nobody is going to bother about that." Fred misread this one.

A Bristol Evening Post reporter and cameraman come to the ground and take pictures of this young kid sent off in his first Football Combination match. I'm not even supposed to be there! Fred was furious.

At the end of the week, Fred slips me a fiver, tax-free. I got more in that week than I'd had the whole of my time at the club. No tax, no National Health stamp paid.

Truly, it is a funny game we play.

I would have to wait a few more years, in fact until 1965, before I would play another Football Combination game.

My first team appearances at the Robins during Fred's era were limited to the Welsh Cup match against Merthyr Tydfil and a couple of friendlies on a pre-season tour to the Irish Republic.

From time to time, I would be appointed as 12th man. In those days of no substitutes, being 12th man meant helping whoever travelled with the team, usually Les Bardsley with the kit bag, sometimes two wicker baskets. They were quite large.

These were enlightening times for a young boy. First up, you got first team money. This didn't mean you got £25. If your contract said ten pounds and five pounds appearance money, that's what you got. No matter that the more senior first team players were paid £25 or £30, plus appearance money, and in addition two pounds for a draw and four pounds for a win.

Worst-case scenario, I got an extra five quid, a serious amount of money in those days. If the troops won, my wages could be almost doubled. I liked the overnight trips.

The motorways were altogether not well developed in those days, so a trip to Rotherham, where I once went, meant we left on Friday, checked into a hotel nearby, say Sheffield, played the game and then had a long drive home. Once back home, Ray, the driver, would drop those that had cars, which was almost everybody, at Ashton Gate. The likes of me, if I couldn't cadge a lift, he would drop me off at home.

Before 1965, teams were forced to continue playing without a substitute if an injured player was unable to continue. Soon, a single substitute was named on the team sheet, to replace an injured player, which quickly became a single player could be replaced according to the manager's judgment, so for tactical reason, not just for injuries.

The travel, the card games, the story telling, the steaks, the waiters hovering, the pressure of the game, the crowd, the autographs, it was all a fantastic experience to me.

What can we have from the menu? Anything you like. Anything? I gloried in it. I loved being made to feel important.

Fred would hang the team sheets on the board on Fridays before training ended. There would be a hopeful rush from us kids to see if we made 12th man. This man was seen as a kind of reward for the ground staff, it was a sort of performance bonus.

I liked and admired Fred, God bless him. I don't know what he did for anyone else, but he created a football family and a certainty for Dot and I that got us through some tough late-teen and early 20's. There is nothing in the rulebook that says that you have to like the manager. He's there to do a job, and some would say that the relationship is irrelevant, but I more than liked Fred. I looked up to him as someone to trust.

My fondest memory is of him and I digging and flattening the divots on the pitch prior to the afternoon's game, him handing out marriage and baby counselling. Would you get any manager now pulling a young kid off the reserve team bus about to depart to offer advice and to dig divots? I think not.

Tuesday, January 23, 1962, was my date with destiny. It is a date I will never forget. The night a dream was realised. The night I made my first team debut.

All the hopes, aspirations, hard work, the miles of sprinting and long distance road runs, the early morning starts in the shooting box, the envy of watching the giants stride onto the field with the blood red shirt, that carried the bold emblazoned badge of the club, the rain, the warm rain or cold, you never noticed the difference on the green turf of battle, the sun, the huge yellow orb that, at season's start, leads you to breathless exhaustion, the thick clinging mud like some last grasp of a dying opponent around your feet, as your legs ached and your boots became blocks of clay; it was all worth it.

The dreams, the gaslight, they were all in the past. Not forgotten, but stored up and locked away. The imagination that fuelled my dreams would tonight be awakened and lived out in one pitiless and unforgiving 90 minutes. All of my life's dreams, since I first kicked a ball, crammed into such a brief span of time that the rest of the universe would hardly notice it had come and gone.

I had come a long way. It had been an interesting journey, with many bumps, side roads, and diversions. There could be no more hiding in my dreams. For now, they were about to become reality. Today would determine who I really was. I would be exposed. A different panel of judges would judge me. No longer would I be a good youth team player, 'the best', said the papers for a while, No longer did it matter that I was a prolific scorer in the reserve team, the star, the young bright light waiting off stage to burst upon the hallowed ground in a blaze of glory. There would be no more ifs or maybes. Tonight we would all find out the truth. You are before the most critical of judges that you will ever face. They are merciless. You can be a hero one minute, and a donkey a minute later. Many of these judges remember that they have paid to judge you, and will hold you accountable for an eternity.

You have 90 minutes to show your worth. It seems a lifetime. Yet when you break it down, it is only one 16th of a day. It will be 5,400 seconds.

You are the new boy and all eyes will be upon you. Your peers, your friends, your family, your colleagues, your manager, the staff of the club, will all judge you mercilessly, as will the Board and the Chairman, but most of all you will be judged by the paying customers, those who pay your wages. They will judge whether you are worthy to wear the shirt they hold so dear. They will compare you to those who have gone before. They will judge you against the man whose position you have taken. You understand that, because you were one of them. It's their team, their club; everything that you do from now on must be done for them. You must perform to reward them for their loyalty, and their commitment to the club, turning up on wet, soaking windy nights, when they could be at home watching the TV in front of a warm fire.

A whole new vista of imagination and possibilities will open up after tonight. Today might not be Highbury or Stamford Bridge or even Old Trafford, but tomorrow? Would any scouts be here tonight? Would one game transform you from a fringe Third Division player, in a game that, at best, three young players would remember for the rest of their life, to a superstar?

If I had never played another game of football, ever, I would have had my chance. When asked, "Did you play for the first team then?" I would now be able to proudly answer, "Yes, yes I did."

Would I say, "But it was only a Welsh Cup game against Merthyr Tydfil?" I think not.

This was the City's first appearance in the Welsh Cup since the 1930s. The reappearance was based on the premise that the Welsh Cup winners would be admitted to the new fangled European Cup Winners Cup, (which has since been absorbed into UEFA's Europa League), and hence the doorway to exotic places and, no doubt, the exotic monies that would come with such football, would open. Quite how Bristol, which is the gateway to Wales, was allowed to compete in that nation's Cup competition is problematical. The dream of playing overseas must have been immense to many of those playing and working in Wales. Our first game in the Welsh Cup, against a Welsh side, wasn't even against one of the big guns, Newport County, Swansea, Wrexham or Cardiff City. No, it was against the non league club Merthyr Tydfil.

Anyone who denies being nervous, having butterflies, or is a little apprehensive about their debut game, has to be lying. On Monday, Fred called myself, Tony Ford and Terry Bush over to train with the first team squad. Terry was a little older than Tony and myself, and had become ineligible for the youth team a year earlier than us. Steve or Tony or Terry making their debut would not have been unusual, perhaps any combination of two, but no one expected all three of us.

Terry had played his entire career at centre forward. There wasn't anything delicate about him. He was a big lad. Bull in a china shop was a good description. He couldn't play anywhere else except centre forward, although in a youth match at Swindon I had started at outside right with Terry in the middle, but Fred had changed this and swapped our positions halfway through the match with great success.

Fred knew I could play, but in the first team he had John Atyeo,

Alex Tait, Barry Meyer and, at a shove, Terry Bush. These were all centre forward options, although Alex could and did play at outside right sometimes, with devastating effect.

Terry went on to get 46 goals from 185 appearances, 17 of those as a sub. Tragically, Terry's career was cut short with knee troubles, but in my book he was a genuine lad and I liked him. He spent ten years at Ashton Gate, which says a lot about Fred's loyalty to players.

In the weeks leading up to my debut, Fred and I had a discussion about playing wide or in the middle. I told him I wasn't comfortable stuck out on the wing. I was quick but didn't have the required 'tricks'. When he announced the team for the Welsh Cup, it was, "Tony, you're playing right back tomorrow, Bushy in the centre, and Flash, you're at outside right."

Three debuts on the same night! Maybe not a first perhaps but very, very unusual.

Fred may have been influenced by a couple of issues. Jimmy Rogers was playing outside right at the time and this was to be his last season. A veteran stalwart, Jim was into a double figure career at the club. Age was against him; he was pushing into his mid-30s.

Secondly, I was on a roll in both the reserves and the youth team. Goals were flowing thick and fast, although it must be remembered that the reserves were playing in the Western League, not the Football Combination.

Fred sat me down and cleared up my dilemma about being played out wide. "We have Atyeo and Bush in the centre, and your best chance of playing in the first team is out wide. Simple!" I was not going to argue.

He'd omitted Alec Briggs, 'Von Briggs' or 'the German', as he was known, a much liked and very handsome right back, very popular with the ladies. He was tall, over six foot, blond and with blue eyes. Briggs spent 13 years at Ashton Gate. From a debut season in 1957/58, he played a sparse 13 games, through to the start of the 61/62 season, but from then on was the first choice full back; another demonstration of Fred's loyalty to players. Alec went on to become a virtual ever present in the side for almost a decade, comfortable one might add playing on either the right or left flank.

Alec got one league goal, and one other in 401 first team appearances.

I wonder if the grand kids are tired of hearing the story!

Jimmy Rogers was left out for me. Jim was a long-serving, extremely experienced player.

Alex Tait was an interesting character. He was educated. He was a trained teacher and, in those days, unlike now, football players with an education were a rarity. I liked Alex.

He always had a kind word and sound advice. He was the player from whom I learned a great lesson; that you can be educated and play professional football too. Affectionately known as 'the headmaster', he got 38 goals from 117 league appearances. He was a busy player, always doing something.

These were the trio left out for the Welsh Cup game. It was an impressive array of talent and the three kids had big boots to fill.

As I left the dressing room on the Monday to catch the bus home, the rain started. It kept coming and coming and coming. Come debut day Tuesday, the usual drill was to get to the dressing room an hour before the 7.30pm kick off. I got there at six. I wanted the team sheet for my scrapbook. I was the first, and I was alone.

When I got in the dressing room, I saw that Fred's team sheet was pinned on the board, with the Bristol City letterhead on the A5 paper he used. Yep, Stacey was there all right. All the doubts vanished in that moment.

I must remember to pick up the team sheet after the game for the scrapbook. Look, it started here, I have the original team sheet. "Is that you, Dad?"

"Yep, that's me."

I sat on the bench in front of the number seven shirt. The door opened and in came the club captain John Atyeo. John was a part-timer. Some consider John possibly the greatest player ever to play for Bristol City. I never ever saw John at training during the week. He either trained at home with the locals or came in the evenings with the amateurs. He was a schoolteacher and taught mathematics and sport. He won six England caps and scored five goals as a part-timer! He had made 700 appearances and scored 395 goals for the City before he retired in 1966.

"What are you doing here?" he asked.

"Uhhh, well, ummm, I'm playing, Mr. Atyeo," I stammered in response.

His only response was an incredulous look. He then turned and went to the team sheet on the wall.

"Ford... Bush... Stacey; how the frig are we going to win games?" He then took the team sheet from the board, looked at it again, then tore it in half and then in quarters, screwed it up, said something I didn't hear, and threw my precious memento in the bin and walked out, clearly unimpressed with Fred's team selection for this game.

I bet he went straight to Fred's office.

The rain continued non-stop. The dressing room filled with people and the pre-match buzz began. Nerves were clearly showing from the three youngsters.

The referee's whistle sounded. "Let's go lads. Remember, you need long studs and stamina tonight." Fred uttered his favourite saying as we passed him and went out of the dressing room door.

Some 3,134 spectators braved the weather to sit in the stands or huddle up on the terracing on the dressing room side of the ground. These really were the faithful. Not quite the yelling thronged masses

I had expected, but still they would all be critical judges. Be sure that they would judge you to the very highest standards. Those that turn up on nights like this are hard-core.

I'm on the grandstand side. Normally I can take the full back anytime, anywhere, but this mud acts as an equaliser. The conditions negate skill and speed.

My first touch was far from memorable. Bushy had the ball in the middle, turned, looked at me and then, with his right foot, hammered it at me from 20 yards. It bounced just in front of me, hit a relatively harder patch of ground, and in the wet skipped over my shoulder and into the terrace.

It got worse. The second bullet, hit with equal ferocity, came nicely onto the boot, but the speed of the pass was badly misjudged and went under my foot into touch. It was time for a deep breath.

Then came the most delicious moment. The ball came in from the left, John Atyeo nips between two defenders and all he has to do is to ease it past the keeper. He knees it, but the wet ball skids off his thigh and travels through the six-yard box to me. As the ball made its way to me, a grin may well have been crossing my lips as I thought, "There is a God and thank you lord." From six yards, I smacked it.

A goal on debut! Pick it out, keeper!

I will never forget the cheers of the crowd, no matter how meagre it was, or the smiles on the faces of my teammates in contrast to the dejection of our opponents.

As I jumped and screamed, I raised my arms before accepting the handshakes from my team mates, and turned to all parts of the ground. I turned and looked straight at John. I knew what he was thinking. "You lucky little buggar!"

John had his hands on his hips, his eyes to the sky, and a look of utter disbelief, or maybe it was it disdain, on his face, before he turned away and trudged back to the half way line. His reaction mattered little to me, however. This was my moment.

My mind started to race. "What will the press say tomorrow?" 'Took a difficult chance, opportunistic, superb finish, cool finish great anticipation.' Then I pulled myself up, "Come on, Steve, it's only a goal."

In the end, we won 4-2. 'Big John', 'the German, Von Briggs' and 'Shadow' Williams completed the scoring. The goal was undoubtedly the highlight for me. I struggled in the heavy conditions. I went past the full back a couple of times, but the longer the game went on, the bigger the ground became. Taking corners became a Herculean task as I tired in the heavy conditions.

There was joy in the dressing room. Given the conditions, everybody was pleased. We were far from clinical, but were effective. Most importantly we were into the next round.

We drew Cardiff at home in the next round. They were a First Division side at the time. Terry and Tony retained their places, but I was axed. I wasn't surprised. My performance hadn't justified my retention.

The only other sniff of first team football that I managed was on a tour of the Irish Republic in the pre-season of 63/64. We flew from Bristol to Cork, playing games against a Cork Hibernian team (5-2) and then on to Limerick (5-0) to play the locals.

We won both games easily and I only played a part of the first game. The day before the Cork game, we had visited Blarney Castle where the famous Blarney Stone is located. Kissing the Blarney Stone is supposed to bequeath eloquence on the person fortunate enough to have the opportunity. Well, I was held by my legs and hung out over the castle wall while I embraced the stone! The next day, an Irish lad stood on my hand and dislocated the thumb; so much for the luck of the Irish, although the team won comfortably 5-2.

In the game I played, I had only been on the pitch for 30 minutes or so. There were no on-line reports back then and only when we returned to Bristol did I read the report filed by the travelling reporter. It went along the lines of, '18-year-old Stacey is never going to replace Atyeo.' There were more similar remarks. Fred read it as inflammatory or less than honest. Fred, as I was later informed, gave the reporter a right rollocking and told him that his tour days as part of the team travelling group were over.

Fred was loyal but I was struggling to break through and pay back his faith in me. Time was moving on fast. I was 21 in the 1965/66 season. Atyeo, Tait, Bush, Meyer, Alan Williams (Rhino), and Nobby Clark were all a part of the nemesis group. I was never going to get another first team game at Bristol City, and certainly not playing at centre forward.

During one reserve match at Ashton Gate, the centre half got injured and left the field. I took his place. Harry Dolman, the chairman, always at his beloved City come rain, hail, or shine, following the first team, reserves, colts and youth team, saw the performance and was impressed.

Come Monday, Fred calls me into the office, and tells me the chairman thinks I will make a great defender, and from now on I will be playing at centre half in the reserves in the Football Combination!! For five years, I've been playing up front in the youth team in the Western League and Football Combination. Now, after less than half a game, I was now a central defender, based on a recommendation from the chairman!

Football is a game that raises some questions that will never be answered. The nuances are like the shades of light within a prism.

As for me, I was happy when the contract arrived in the post each year (yes they used to post them then!!) and although I was ambitious, I just loved playing. I never had a meeting with the manager and asked about my future, when would I get a game, or the ultimate, I want a transfer.

I realise now I was getting cosy. Perhaps the ambition was slowly but surely drifting away. I was testing the boundaries of what I could do and still play the game I loved.

Robin Perry, one of the local Bristol newspaper sports writers, was waiting outside after the game and as I left he approached me.

It was all very casual. Small talk about the game and then suddenly, "Do you fancy a move to Rovers, perhaps? I think that they may be interested in signing you."

The conversation about the Rovers was over before it began. Still, for a moment, maybe it was nothing, I wondered if there was the slightest possibility.

Whether the Pirates ever enquired, I don't know. I suspect that an enquiry was made at some point and rejected. I was never advised by the City.

That was the way it was back then.

Perhaps, no more than perhaps, Robin was sounding me out. Fred would have rejected any offer. He would have known that the Pirates weren't going to offer any huge amount to buy an untried kid. I was pretty much untested by the City and Fred would have large amounts of egg on his face if I walked into the Rovers first team and started banging in goals.

There was still an impressive array of players to dispose of, even changing to the offensive instead of the defensive role. Until I got a game, the likes of Big Jack Connor, Gordon Low, Dickie Rooks, and Gordon Parr, all of whom were taller than me – and I came in at just an inch or so short of six feet.

The dilemma was this. Fred had a guy here who could bang goals in anywhere. He was reluctant to try me in the first team, principally because he wasn't sure I could make it work or that he had too many senior players in front of me, and he would suffer if he threw in a young kid.

This was so in a defensive or offensive role.

Above all, I made great friends at Bristol City, including Ron Nicholls, an exceptional sportsman who played both football and cricket at professional level. He was signed from Cardiff in 1961 and made 39 appearances for the Robins before moving on to non-league Cheltenham in 1964.

Ron would often pick me up in the morning at our leaky flat in Clifton and drive me to work.

Often we would go to the shooting box and Ron, who was the opening bat for Gloucestershire Cricket Club at the time, would practice his leg breaks.

Gran's place at Horfield was only a short walk to the Gloucestershire cricket ground at Nevil Road. Some of the lads at the GCC knew me as a cricket buff and that I played both cricket and football for Bristol Boys in a series of matches.

I got to know quite a few of the GCC team and had a hit or two at the indoor nets.

I often wondered about what I would do during the summer football break; playing cricket and getting paid wasn't a bad idea.

SLIPPERY SLOPE

I could go on playing at Bristol City forever. But there is this thing called ambition. I badly wanted to play first team football. I wanted the glory. I wanted to walk into the supermarket and receive the nods of approval or recognition. I was surrounded by all this day after day, team sheet after team sheet, dressing room conversation after conversation, every Saturday afternoon. Something had to give.

I'm not quite sure where or when I met Gordon Butler, but he lived in East Street, Bedminster, just a short walk from the City ground, with his wife, Judy, and family. He was a few years older than me. Dot and I had moved to Maple Road, Horfield, with Michele, and Dot was expecting Nat, who was due in a few months.

I had got into the habit of visiting the bars down at the centre on a Saturday night during the season. My childhood friend, Clive Barker, had moved on. Now, Gordon had taken his place and copious amounts of of alcohol were being sunk.

Everybody has a childhood friend that they will never forget. No matter how the years flow, how long you've been apart, or not seen each other. Someone you will never forget, who will always be around the next bend. Clive Baker fits that bill in my life.

Clive stole me away from Dot and led me down the dark path of booze and sundry drinking partners! Our favourite haunt was the city centre, and we religiously did the round of bars every Friday during the off-season in search of fun, booze, and adventure. It must have been the summer of 1962; Dot and I had a serious parting at this time, and went our separate ways for a while.

Clive and I would go to the Rummer Bar and all the nearby watering holes.

Then there were curries at a restaurant in Denmark Street, just off the centre, and at that time well known as a haunt of the 'ladies of the night'.

We met auntie Beryl and her friend occasionally in one of the bars, shared a drink or two and then went our separate ways. Always Beryl, older and wiser, issued the caution. "Steve, don't drink too much and get home safe." We always got home safe.

I had met a young lady, Janice, whose family owned a pub called The Wheatsheaf on the centre. Clive and I would call in there on our travels, get shown to a private room and soon a couple of beers would be sent in!! One night, we had agreed to meet Janice in a dance club. We arrived late. The dance floor was crowded and it looked like Janice was dancing with another fellow. "Can't allow that," says my friend, so I dive in, get hold of Janice and pull her to safety after delivering a threat to the poor lad that she was dancing with. Unfortunately, the lady looked like Janice, danced like Janice, dressed like Janice but was not Janice! "Lets go, Clive …"

One night we couldn't get a taxi, massive queues. We decided to walk.

We rested in a 24-hour Laundromat just past Bedminster Bridge. Here we contemplated whether, if we dived into the River Avon, could we swim to the other side? Still drinking from a couple of bottles of Georges Brown Ale, we got to the London Inn and decided to heave the bottles at each other from across the road. Deafening sounds of glass breaking in the early hours of Sunday morning. We were out of control.

I got back with Dot. Clive and I continued on our merry way until I got the ultimatum, Clive or Dot. Clive was almost in tears when he found out that I wouldn't be picking him up on Friday or Saturday nights any more. Such is life, and such is friendship. It was fun while it lasted. He named his daughter, Stephanie, after me. No greater love has anyone, old friend! However, at that time Dot was right. I was on a downward slope. Gordon soon took over from Clive.

I was going to be 22 on my next birthday. I had ridden my luck, the club had been good to us, but the urge to play somewhere in the first team was what it was all about. It was gnawing at me.

It was a while since Fred and I, or anyone else on the staff, had had a chat about the future. I was on the margin. Fred knew I had something, but what and where to play me? I was beginning to resign myself to playing out my career in the reserves; not a happy prospect but I wasn't about to initiate a transfer request. However, things were about to change.

Gordon and I were drinking down town in search of a new watering hole, well into the evening, and were walking down towards Bristol Bridge. A young lad was walking up the slope with his lady. He was dark coloured and his lady was white.

As we are about to pass, I say something along the lines of "how are you, you old bugger?" in friendship, one like-soul to another.

He took offence and Gordon and I were quite startled. He wanted to take both of us on. Gordon was a big lad. He was taller, and thicker set, than me, robust. He picked this guy up by his lapels, then turned to me and said, "Grab him." So grab him I did, and the next thing I know we are propelling him backwards. The target was a large brick pillar separating two large shopping windows, that ran from the top to the bottom of the shopfront.

We miss our target and put this guy through the window. He went right through the glass, which shattered into a thousand pieces. He's in the window like one of the clothes-shop dummies. His girl is screaming and there are various responses from the crowd. Gordon and I are dumbstruck. We have two options. Stay and explain, or run. We run; across the road into the walkways of the buildings and watch the police cars arrive and take statements from the young guy and the crowd who had gathered to watch.

We felt safe. It was over in a flash, no names, and no addresses. Right? Alcohol, patience and common sense don't match. On Sunday at breakfast, Dot, who was not all that happy about my Saturday nights out, enquired about the grazes on my knuckles. I explained it away with some airy-fairy story, but she was not convinced.

Friday teatime and there is a knock on the door. A young police constable is standing there. "Mr. Stacey?"

"Yes."

"Mr. Steve Stacey, who plays for Bristol City?" There was an awakening here and I didn't particularly like where it was headed.

"May I ask where you were last Saturday night at about 10pm?"

I invited the young man into the living room. It is never good to be seen talking to the police on the doorstep, although there would have been many eyes behind the curtains.

"I was home here, wasn't I Dot?"

Dot was as straight as a die, no good at telling untruths, lying. The constable spotted it straight away.

"You have been identified as one of the persons who assaulted a young man at…" The rest of his words faded into the background as I witnessed tears welling in Dot's eyes.

"So, where were you at 10pm last Saturday?" He asked me again.

Looking straight at Dot, I came clean. The young constable took the details and, standing, said, "We will be in touch."

Dot was furious. She gave me both barrels as soon as he had left. "So, this is why you were home early. Saturday nights are over! I knew this would happen. Gordon Butler's no good! You have a family now…" She gave me the full shotgun. I deserved it.

The date for the court appearance was set. The young man had apparently recognised me. Being coloured himself, he knew that I was the only coloured footballer in town and the face came to him instantly.

I didn't tell Fred. That proved a bad mistake.

Gordon and I went to court and were fined five pounds each.

I am genuinely sorry and explain this to the magistrate, who believes me. The dawn has given me the realisation that my career may be at stake. It was. The newspaper people are all over the courtroom. One attempts to interview me after my appearance but I have nothing to say. I am simply too ashamed.

I ask Gran to ring the papers to ask them not to print anything. How naïve was I? It was news. It was all over the front page.

Dot was understandably furious. Gran and the girls were alarmed and felt that I was spiralling out of control. The troops at training understand and want the gory details. Then the call came. Fred wanted to see me.

Fred told me that the board had discussed the incident and weren't pleased that the club had been front page news like this. However, life must go on. He counselled me with an "I understand what you're going through" talk, and then "but in the end, Steve, it's up to you."

I was lucky the club didn't tear up my contract. I lived to play another day. More importantly, I knew I had to repair the damage with my best friend, Dot. Saturday nights out with the boys became a thing of the past.

I didn't know it yet, but the seeds for my leaving the Robins had been sewn.

TRANSFER

We were due to play Queens Park Rangers in a reserve game. On the train up to London, Gordon Parr and a couple of the other players alluded to the fact that I was being watched that day. I put any thinking on the subject aside. No one had mentioned anything to me.

It was a dismal day, grey and wet. There was not much grass on the ground that afternoon. I was playing at centre half and was marking Billy McAdams, a Northern Irish international centre forward, and, at 32, coming to the end of his career.

I can honestly say, in a long drawn out career in the great game, I can only recall a few lonely incidences that may, and I emphasise the word may, have been racially motivated.

Billy had once scored a hat trick for his country against Germany in a World Cup qualifier, only for the Irish to lose 3-4. He was a bit of a traveller, had played for eight or nine clubs, but had been a regular scorer. This was a London Combination match, so Billy was out of the first team. We all know what it's like being out of the first team. Billy must have been upset. He and I had a couple of tussles and I was on top of the big bloke. I could tell he was getting rattled, as he was all arms legs and elbows.

We had a goal kick. Our keeper played the ball out to me on the edge of the penalty area and I played it back to him. Then suddenly, I was on my face laying down and sliding in the mud at Loftus Road.

I'm up on my feet. Billy is looking at me and the ref is running toward us, reaching for that top pocket where his cards are kept. There's no doubt about it; Billy has to go. He doesn't get a lot of sympathy from anyone as he takes the slow walk of shame.

After the game, the boys tell me, "Stace, he must have run 20 yards to get to you and Pete (the keeper) was about to pick up the return ball when he clobbered you."

Talk about a late challenge. Was it frustration? He probably had more on his mind, you always do when your career is in the twilight zone. As an international, I can understand that he didn't take too kindly to being wrapped up and packaged by a young wannabe.

Whatever was going on in Billy's mind? I don't recall him knocking on the dressing room door after the game to apologise that he had 'lost it'. It's extremely hard in a professional football match to establish whether an incident, unless it is blatantly obvious, is the product of a deliberate plan. It could be a mis-timed tackle, loose elbows at a corner or free kick, or a series of other matters, niggling in the course of the game often without penalty, but enough to upset your opponent. In all of these cases, frankly, anything can happen.

You have to ask in this instance why would Billy run at someone from 20 yards, with his back to him, and climb all over him? This was not an ill-timed tackle. Frustration is my explanation. A kid was tying up a proud international player. Would Billy have done this if I was white is the question? Maybe, who knows?

It was too late for Billy. His career was over. Mine was just starting. After six years at Bristol City, without a single league game, on the following Tuesday I'm transferred to Wrexham. On the Saturday following the Billy incident, I'm in England's North West playing my first league game against Southport.

Jack Howsley, the soon-to-be scout that would handle my transfer, was at the QPR game, and was impressed by 'the young kid's handling of a seasoned international player.'

In the early days, players contracts and transfers were relatively straightforward.

The terms and conditions were clearly laid out. Generally you got a basic pay level during the playing season, say £20, plus four quid for a win, and two quid for a draw. Sometimes, at the higher levels, you got paid for the team having a position in the top four or six of the league. Perhaps ten quid for being in top spot, with graduated reductions down to fourth or sixth. In addition, there might also be a bonus based on crowd attendance. Ten quid for 20,000 and again graduated, down to whatever levels the club deemed appropriate.

Usually at the lower level of competition, in the Third or Fourth Division, the composition of the contract was even more straightforward. You received your basic pay, win or draw bonus and then had to endure a savage pay cut during the off season. If you were in line for promotion, the chairman usually made an appearance in the dressing room and put up £50 or £100 apiece if you made it.

You were entitled to receive ten percent of any transfer fee when you changed clubs. Five percent of this went to the Professional Footballers Association (PFA), and you were entitled to receive this, if my memory hasn't failed me, at the age of 35. The remaining five percent had to be spread over the term of the contract.

For instance, the club could offer you a contract for a number of years, usually one or two. They also had to offer you an option on this contract. The option could not be more, but could be less than the contract term. So you could have a one-year contract and a one-year option, or a two-year contract with a one or two year option, but not a one-year contract with a two-year option.

So, a transfer fee of £20,000 meant you got £2,000, which would be spread over four years on a two-year and two year option contract. Half of the £2,000 went to the Professional Footballers Association.

Moreover, you couldn't get the money up front, but had to wait to receive whatever was due at the end of the first year. In this case, £500. Some clubs elected to pay the money on a weekly, or other periodical basis directly into your wages, in which case it was taxed weekly.

The club could negotiate a new contract with you during the term of any initial contract. However, this contract had to be a completely new contract with new terms. These terms could not be less than initially negotiated in your original deal.

At the end of the contract term, the club could put you on the transfer list. If you and any buying club could not agree terms then your club had to offer you the option available to you. Conversely, if you were at the end of your option term and the club could not agree terms with you and put you on the transfer list, if there was no other club able to agree the transfer fee with the selling club, then when the contracts ran out, June 30 of any year, you were available to any interested club on free transfer.

This, basically, was the framework at which you were engaged as a professional footballer. The transfer circumstances were very different from today. No lawyers, business managers or accountants.

To put this into perspective, and let's say that during a 15-year career, a young player averaged £30 per week. In the 50s and early 60s, and maybe at some levels into the 70s, this was a reasonable assumption at the top end, a little less down in the lower leagues. This equates to £1,500 per year.

For an individual, that's an average £22,500 for 15 years graft.

With a 20-player list, £30,000 is a fair estimate of the annual labour costs. Over a 15-year period that's £450,000.

A far cry from what the princes at Manchester United, or their rivals over at the City, earn today, many taking home well over £450,000 per week!

Indeed, newspapers and other media outlets have hinted (2019) at colossal amounts of money into a staggering sum of multi millions of pounds on a weekly basis earned by a single player! So a general comparison might be that an EPL player today earns more in a week than the whole squad at, say, Wrexham earned in their whole careers in the past.

Think about it.

Dot and I could not afford to buy a car or a house outright, with mortgage and HP accounts, never mind furniture and the costs of raising a family.

During the close season, which began in late April up until mid-June, when pre-season training commenced, or even up to the week prior to the first league game, your salary would be reduced to almost half of what you got during the playing season.

Agents, as such, were not readily noticeable in those days. You couldn't call on anyone to assist you in contract negotiations. If I had sought advice from Bill Harvey, our trainer/coach, or Les Bardsley, our physio, for example, I would have placed either of them in an invidious position vis-a-vis their own position with the club.

You could ask a couple of older players, but basically when they had moved to Bristol, it was from a club where they had established themselves, and were in a position to negotiate.

I had no knowledge of the undercurrents present in the transfer system. My main concern was that I had to start playing first team football. The motivation to move somewhere else was mine. Although I was happy at Bristol, I was becoming restless, anxious to taste the sweet smell of the Football League. I needed the big time.

Jack Howson was a smooth, articulate player agent. He looked good, wore expensive clothes and drove an expensive car. I saw Jack after the QPR game. He didn't speak to me, but I would recognise him later. Fred called me into his office on the following Monday morning prior to a light training session.

"There's a scout here been having a look at you. I've told him he can talk to you, but you don't have to go anywhere. I need to make this clear, Steve, your contract will be renewed here. See what he has to say, listen closely and then make a decision."

I must have impressed Jack Howson. He was at training dead on the dot, 10am the day after.

"Steve, I'm a friend (scout, agent, Mr 10%) of Jack Rowley. You know Jack, former England and Manchester United player, now manager of, (wait for it) Wrexham."

Where's Wrexham, and how much? was all I was thinking.

"Wrexham are in the Fourth Division, (the lowest division of the Football League at that time) and he's looking for quality players to move the club on."

He continued, "He's asked me to talk to you about the move and I have the OK, from Fred Ford, to talk terms."

At that time, I would have been on about £14 a week at Bristol City, plus any first team appearance money, maybe ten quid, or, as usual in the reserves, two quid for a win and a quid for a draw.

"Jack's offering you £22 in the season, and £14 in the off season, usual win, draw bonus, and straight into the first team this week."

"Who are they playing?"

"Southport away. Club house is yours too, ready to move in rent a pound a week."

"What about…"

"Fred's agreed to pay you £250 benefit money."

The deal was done, simple as that. Although I played it cool.

"I'll talk to my wife."

It wasn't really a hard decision to make. I was just drifting along at City. Keeping a young player for five years without substantial first team appearances was a little out of the ordinary, although Fred had run the same course with Alec Briggs.

I explained the situation to Dot. She wasn't much surprised. Our conversations about moving from Bristol when the time was right had been fairly frequent. Now we had the opportunity. We also had more money, I had first team football and we had a house of our own.

I signed the next day. Bill Harvey, City's coach, made arrangements to drive me to Wrexham on Friday, February 25. We would stay in Wrexham that night and drive on to Southport to meet the team at the Southport ground on Saturday. I was included in the team at right back.

I had a great debut. Bill and I talked to a scout from Sheffield Wednesday after the game that Bill knew. Wednesday were then in the First Division. He made it plain he would be keeping tabs on me for the rest of the season.

How do you go from a reserve player in the Second Division, to a Fourth Division full back, who had never played in that position before, to a player who might be First Division material in one week?

My career at Wrexham blossomed as a full back from the start, and later at left back, a position I had never played in at Bristol City, or anywhere else. Truly, the world moves in mysterious ways!

My first experience of transfer dealing came some months after I had left Bristol City. I was talking to Jack Rowley. I mentioned that I hadn't received my promised benefit and could Jack include it in my pay packet next week. Was it best to have it all at once or bit by bit for tax purposes?

Jack blew his stack. As far as he was concerned, the monies should have been paid by Bristol City immediately on my signing for Wrexham. I was to receive them the pay date after the transfer. In those days, you got paid in a brown envelope in cash on a weekly basis.

He rang Bert Bush, Bristol City's secretary.

I was outside Jack's office when he rang Bert. The conversation started cordially. It ended in language I wouldn't use in front of my mother.

The good news was I got my long-awaited benefit the next payday.

Jack was kind of a father to the players. He rarely took training; neither did his sidekick, Ken Roberts. Non-interventionist might be the word to describe him.

Ken was seen more as an administrative person of sorts, who failed to convince the playing group that he had any more grasp of leadership training or tactics than Jack Jones, the older ex-player and confidant, did. But still, Ken was the youngest player ever to play for Wrexham at the tender age of 15.

The training regime was left to 'Old Jack', Jack Jones, who had been with the club forever and a day. At a guess, Jack would have been in his 60s even then. To be fair to Jack, he didn't have a lot to work with. It was a grave mistake.

Coaching, as we now know it, never happened. There was little tactical awareness, or organising of the back four, closing down in midfield and the like. JJ warmed us up, did a few sprints, some shooting practice sometimes and then it was a small sided game. Come match day on a Saturday, we just went out and played!

Jack Rowley had a wonderful record as a player and had the respect of everyone for his tour of duty with Manchester United and England, but he never pushed it.

He relied, I suspect, on his reputation and his ability to talk it up to players on the day.

We finished bottom of the league in my first season 1965/66, 92nd out of 92. It doesn't get any worse. In fairness to Jack Rowley, he arrived late in the season, January 1966, and couldn't do enough to halt the downward spiral. I arrived in February of that year, when the season only had about ten weeks to run.

In retrospect, it's easy to analyse, but with a little more subtlety, coaching and organisation, we wouldn't have finished bottom in

1966 and therefore would have avoided the embarrassment of having to apply for re-election to the then Fourth Division. Secondly, we would have clinched promotion in 1966-67.

Jack didn't lead. He left the important issues of fitness and tactics to Jack Jones who, bless him, didn't have a clue about the modern game. Jack Rowley came from a world where skill, in a general sense, came second to brawn. Jack got me a pair of the new-fangled boots when I arrived. Like now, the industry was in a constant state of flux with different designs and colours; mine were brown.

Jack asked me if I liked the new-fangled 'cloggers'.

Coaches today would be dumbstruck by the lack of information, training scenarios and tactics on the training ground then. It was almost as though you were expected to play by remote control. No one knew quite what to expect on Saturdays. Anything could happen and usually did.

When I got to Wrexham, the club was struggling to shake off a series of losses that had placed them while not quite at the bottom of the table, but in a precarious position. They had won five games, drawn three and lost the remaining 14. They had scored 29 goals and conceded 53. No wonder Jack was looking to strengthen his team.

I must have done some homework on the precarious position the club found themselves in, but if I did, it vanished off the radar. I don't recall being concerned about the position or whether, in fact, I might well be playing non-league football next season.

The Red Dragons' New Year was a buzz. Four consecutive victories, two at home (Barnsley, 6-3, and Barrow, 3-1), and on the road (Lincoln, 2-0, and Stockport, 4-2).

Two losses followed, at Hartlepool 2-4 and promotion hopefuls Torquay 1-3.

The New Year had brought seven games, five wins and two losses, but the signs were still there for all to see. The ten points for the wins had cost them 16 goals against for 22 scored. We were leaking at least two goals every game.

The rest of the season, 17 games, saw only three wins including the local derby, at home to Chester, six draws and eight losses. We conceded 35 goals and scored 21. We had only managed to secure one clean sheet in all this.

We suffered five consecutive losses in April, three of these at home, to Notts County, Newport and Crewe. The 17 games since I had joined the Red Dragons at Southport were less than commendable.

There was some minor consolation. On May 7, during the home game against Halifax in a 2-2 draw, I got my first league goal. Jack Rowley, in his wisdom, had decided to play me at centre forward. On a dry, dusty, bumpy pitch one of the lads, Peter Jones, chased a lost cause at the 'covered' end and miraculously pulled it back from close in on the left goal line. The Halifax defence had just about given up the chase for the ball and, almost unchallenged, I got a header from close in. I did enough celebrating for the whole team who must have wondered what it was all about.

My first league goal that's what! After numerous finishes in the reserves and the youth teams, here it was, never to be forgotten!

Then came the first ever episode that had me wondering about whether there were problems with players about my being black.

It was April 25, a home game against Newport County, and an evening kick off. I'm at centre half, marking a big lad at the back, and as the high ball is on us, a back hander catches me across the nose and down I go. It's a deliberate back hander, so the boys tell me. A few of my teammates are around the offender making their views plain. Full consciousness did not return until I was back in the dressing room. I had been stretchered off and taken to hospital with a broken nose. The game is lost 0-1.

It was quite a smack. I had bruises around my eyes and admit I was fairly shaken up. The club bought me a pair of sunglasses to hide the bruising. When I got home to Bristol, Michele starts to cry. So bad is the bruising, she doesn't recognise her dad. Dark on dark!!

I had a couple of days to get over it, and missed the next two games, one home and one away.

The last game of the season is at Newport and my 'friend' is on the pitch as we line up. Early in the game, there was a fifty-fifty ball and as we close in, he comes over the top of the ball. Now, any pro will tell you about a purpose-built, over the top challenge. It is impossible to disguise, it's a leg breaker.

He catches me full on my protective shin pads and down we both go. I'm ashamed to say that, for the first and only time on a football pitch, I lost my rag.

I stood and as he was still lying on the floor, I kicked him twice. One left and one right.

Now he's up in a flash, the boys rally and the site of the engagement becomes a mass of players. I'm sure that he will get sent off and there is a very strong possibility that I'm going, too.

The referee eventually moves everyone out of the way and it's the three of us.

"This is where it begins and ends," he says. "Any more, and you're both gone."

I'm not sure that he even booked us! We don't shake hands and he's moved to another part of the pitch, where we won't clash. I'm outraged! I had now come to the conclusion that this was personal. The two incidents together made me think this guy had a problem. I managed to get over the rage boiling inside of me. The game ended in a 2-2 draw. All the talk was why the ref hadn't sent us both off.

Jack thinks we both should have gone, and so does everyone else.

The referee's thoughts may well have gone along the following lines: if I hadn't retaliated, the ref would have sent him off, but because I did, he thinks I would have kicked him too, if he had done that to me. He knew he couldn't send him off and leave me on. It was both on or both off.

Looking back, did I read this right? Did our friend have a problem? I like to think not but some doubt remains.

In early April, we played Notts County home and away within four days, a strange fixture arrangement which did us no favours; we lost both games 3-1. This put us into the bottom four and hence re-election territory for the first time in several months. One can only guess that the nerves in the Boardroom began to jangle a bit.

Around this time, the chairman, Mr. Bill 'Porky' Evans, came into the dressing room and offered us £50, two weeks wages each, if we avoided having to apply for re-election.

We finished bottom by a mere two points, but no matter the margin, we were bottom, rock bottom!

20. Chesterfield	46	8	9	6	37	35	5	4	14	25	43	39
21. Rochdale	46	12	1	10	46	27	4	4	15	25	60	37
22. Lincoln City	46	9	7	7	37	29	4	4	15	20	53	37
23. Bradford City	46	10	5	8	37	34	2	8	13	26	60	37
24. Wrexham	46	10	4	9	43	43	3	5	15	29	61	35

There were few positives to salvage from the wreckage. Even another win would not have saved us from the bottom spot. We had the worst defensive record in the league.

However, there are some interesting comparisons though. We scored the same number of goals (72) as Darlington and Torquay, who finished in second and third place respectively, and were both promoted. Only eight teams in the whole of the 24 scored more goals (72) than we did!!

Yet it was fair to say my first season in the real league had not been as satisfying as I would have liked.

In the beginning, I stayed with Keith Webber and his wife. Keith had been signed from Everton, but this was to be his last season at Wrexham. Sammy Mac (McMillan) and his wife, Norma, had a bit more room so I shared their place whenever the need to stay overnight came. Sam was a genial Irishman, with a wicked sense of humour, who could play up front or at wing half. Generally, he was always among the goals.

After a game, travel was a bit of a rush. Most teams kicked off at 3pm on Saturday, but for some reason Wrexham kicked off at 3.15pm. My connecting train was Wrexham, change at Shrewsbury, then direct to Bristol Temple Meads. I had an hour or so to get off the park, change, shower, have the obligatory beer, and get to the station. From the last stop at Temple Meads, I would often take the short walk to downtown Bristol, the Rummer Bar or other old haunts I used to visit with Clive. I needed to unwind!

Whereas 1965-66 was a disappointment for the club, I thought that I had done OK, and the local newspaper, The Wrexham Leader, thought so too. Ron Challoner, the sports writer, gave me a great compliment or two, although the consensus was that Wrexham needed half a dozen players before they would be any real threat and become promotion challengers.

Lincoln (43 votes), Bradford City (43), Rochdale (40) and Wrexham (40), were duly elected back into the Football League Division Four as expected. It was a bit like an old boys club, vote the boys back in, it might be your turn next year!

As a family, we were about to move - lock, stock and barrel - to North Wales. We finally settled into a clubhouse on Windermere Road, Wrexham, in June, 1966. It was a nice little two-bedroom bungalow and Dot, myself and the kids were very pleased with it all. The feeling of 'I made it' was upon us. It felt like Steve had finally arrived.

Kath, Dot's sister, and her husband, Fred, came up with us and helped us move in. The girls sewed all the curtains by hand. Indeed, Windermere was to become a haven for the family, from Eve to Kath and Barbara, and my sister Vanessa. The 'Boss' lived just round the corner, in Richmond Road. School for Michele was five minutes away and a drive to the Racecourse took no more than ten.

WREXHAM DAYS

J ack had savaged the playing staff at the end of the season. Small town Wrexham had 30 professionals on their books when I got there. Next season, there would be only 24.

New faces came arrived, including Dave Carrick, Mickey Evans, Tony 'Plonky' McLoughlin, Terry Oldfield, George Showell, Johnny Schofield and Don Weston.

This is a massive challenge for anyone, considering that all these new players would be considered first team material.

Don Weston was probably the quickest thing on two legs over a short distance that I had ever seen. He was quick and deceptive with it.

A new era had arrived at the Racecourse Ground, a venue that is now recognised by Guinness World Records as the world's oldest international football stadium that still hosts international matches, having hosted Wales' first ever home international in 1877.

The squad was a blend of youth and experience. Terry Oldfield (27yrs, 132apps) from Bristol Rovers, George Showell (32yrs, 211apps) from Wolves, Don Weston (30yrs, 228apps) from Huddersfield Town, and Johnny Scofield (35yrs, 212apps) from Birmingham City, were no mugs, and brought a wealth of experience from the First Division, FA Cup Finals and European competition. These were seasoned veterans. The dressing room was alive again!

Albert Kinsey, Dave Carrick, Mickey Evans and Tony McLoughlin were a new breed of youngsters about to break into league football, very much like myself.

Dave Grant was among them, but Dave never played as much first team football as the rest. I knew Terry Oldfield, from his time with Bristol Rovers. His career was to end very shortly, following a nasty incident at Cardiff.

Plonky, Dave Carrick, Albert Kinsey and Davy Grant would. from time to time, stay overnight with Dot and I after a game before driving back to Liverpool and home. They all fussed over Dot and the kids like mother hens.

It was looking good in pre-season and expectations were high. This was more like a true band of brothers. We had all moved in and we all wanted success. The atmosphere at the club had changed. People had been jogging along with the wind. Now a new horizon was about to be born, or so we thought.

Don Weston, who had a previous spell at Wrexham from 1958/1960, moved back in 1966 and became a friend. We went shooting and fishing.

Dot marvelled at the salmon we caught in the River Dee.

Don was still capable of going past just about anybody over the first ten yards. I think sometimes he surprised himself. As with all these types of players, Don would flatter one minute only to deceive the next. But he still knew where the net was. I'll remember Don for all of this and how he used to make his roll-up cigarettes and puff away. He had once gone AWOL from the army to play a game for Wrexham; now, that's my kind of player!!

Arfon (Griff), Sammy Mac, who I had 'lodged' with for a while, and Alec Lucas, Nat's Godfather, and myself were regulars in the Pant Yr Ochain pub out at Gresford, usually on a Wednesday or Thursday night, perhaps the White Hart at Llangollen or the Bridge Inn at Chester. These were our regular gathering places, and it's fair to say that, on most Thursdays, we would be out there somewhere.

We were recognisable of course and everyone was keen to get the gossip on last week, or next week, or what was going on at the club. Mind you, you had to be careful; one wrong word and there could be trouble for this reason; the in town establishments were usually off limits. Go west, young man, or at least somewhere out in the country where you wouldn't be subjected to unwanted conversations or a cryptic analysis as to why half the Wrexham team was out on the town. We would usually keep a low profile and hide away in some corner.

Maybe it was because we all got on that there was a strong feeling that this was going to be a special season. In fact, as it turned out, 1966-67 was to be a good year for me. Along with John Schofield, I played in every first team league game, thereby earning the coveted title 'ever present' for all 46 fixtures. In addition, there were two FA Cup, one League Cup and five Welsh Cup appearances. A total of 54 first team games. The only game I missed was an early round of the Welsh Cup against Rhyl, which we won 5-0.

A game against Liverpool in a pre-season friendly was one of our early games at the famous Anfield Stadium. Sadly it was a game played behind closed doors, but I am not sure we would have attracted a full house. It was still special to play against that formidable, intimidating side, one of the greatest English League teams ever. Liverpool had won the League Championship the season before and had been beaten by Borussia Dortmund in the European Cup Winners Cup Final. They were at the height of their glorious best.

Jack picked me to play at wing half that day. I had never ever played at wing half before Bill Shankly stood on the left hand touch line, shouting all kinds of messages of support to me, "Well done son, oh good touch", etc. Was I on the road to Anfield, I thought?

I had a good game, if you can believe that. Good first touch, didn't give much away, flashed a header over the bar and got in a couple of shots.

I also crunched a few tackles, and showed I wasn't intimidated.

I even got a "well played" from a couple of players and Bill Shankly after the game ended. I got the impression that all eyes were on Steve. This was in spite of Liverpool beating us 9-0!

Fred Ford and Bill Shankly were good mates. They had met in the services during the war, although Shankly was in the air force and Fred in the infantry. They may have met during the numerous wartime matches played all over the UK with teams that were conveniently close to the local military bases.

Maybe that is where the "well done, son" comments all came from. I did all right but we didn't have much of the ball and the superiority of his fine team was overwhelming.

In October, 1966, just as the transfer talk began to hit a crescendo, Peter Wall and Stuart Mason, who played as full backs in that game, got transferred to Liverpool for a combined fee of £26,000 pounds. I was gobsmacked. There is no disrespect here for either Peter or Stuart, but I thought that, then, I was a better player than either of them.

I felt that I had been stitched up. I asked for a meeting with Jack Rowley and we sat in his office. I fronted Jack. He launched into some verbal crap about how the club needed me, and that neither Stuart nor Peter would be appearing in the Liverpool first team yet. I asked him why, given the circumstances, I hadn't been on the Liverpool shopping list. "More valuable to the club", "you have a bright future here, not at Anfield", "You must be joking, the club needs you" and the like is what I was told. I percieved it as nonsense.

I never forgave him, but I promised myself that I wouldn't let it affect my performances.

Years later, the truth emerged relating to my transfer from Bristol City to Wrexham.

Fred had been reluctant to sell me. He wasn't sure. He had no way of knowing, without giving me an extended run in the first team, how good I was or wasn't. I fouled up at Bristol with the downtown incident. Without that I may have been there plodding comfortably along for another five years.

Perhaps he was after monies for the new Ashton Gate facilities that would soon transform the ground.

Fred hedged his bets.

Sure, he sold me for £5,000, but added that, if Wrexham sold me for any more, Bristol City would get half of everything over that sum.

It suddenly all became very clear.

Pete and Stuart go for £26,000, Wrexham pick up £26,000 clear.

Steve goes to Liverpool, or anywhere else, for £26,000, then Bristol City get half of £21,000 – that's £10,500, plus the original 5K, £15,500 in total.

Wrexham were struggling to attract sponsors, having finished last in the league. If they sold me, they would have collected LESS than the club that sold me to them.

It gets even more convoluted if I go with either Peter or Stuart.

How much is Steve worth in the deal, half, 5K, 10K, 20K? Ten pounds!!!!!!!

This was the deal that was concocted without my permission and without my knowledge. If this had been discussed with the most important person in all of this, me, things would have been different. I probably would still be at Bristol City.

Whichever way you look at it, Wrexham would have been the big loser if they had decided to transfer me instead of Stuart or Peter. There's no business in it for them at all.

Did I see, know, and have knowledge of any of the financial details or any of the other transfer details? No.

It would have taken hundreds of issues akin to this that the PFA took up on behalf of players to bring some equality into the game and in particular to the messy issues of player transfers.

Let's linger here a moment. Where's my agent?

It was always going to be difficult for anyone to break into that Liverpool side which leads to the obvious conclusion that anyone that Shankly signed at that time would be as an insurance policy for cover for those two fine Liverpool full backs Gerry Byrne and Chris Lawler. Stuart never made a first team appearance and Peter had to wait until the March 16, 1968, before getting his debut.

To me it was all a little less than honest. Disingenuous would be a good word to use. In the context of the convoluted contract deals now being struck between players, agents, accountants, solicitors, business managers and Uncle Tom Cobley and all, this was small change.

I have often wondered how the contract negotiations would have gone between Bristol City, Wrexham, Ipswich and myself with a little outside professional scrutiny. Or the difference it may have made had I been able to have in my corner someone who knew their way around the shadowy world of player transfers. Was I taken advantage of? Yes, definitely, as were hundreds of others. Was I naïve? Yes, that too.

I was furious with Fred and Wrexham for agreeing to the deal, and I lost respect for Jack.

This is what the Professional Footballers Association (PFA) would fight for over the years; the right for a player to be included in, and to have knowledge of, all the details of a transfer deal.

To be allowed to earn more than £20 a week, for clubs to stop treating players like some dumb-assed idiots just off the street, to be used and manipulated as a commodity rather than a person.

Ditto, ditto and ditto again.

What hurt me the most was that nobody had asked me if I would agree to all of this. Nobody.

TRANSFER SHOCK

W e should have won promotion to the Third Division in 1966/67. It was a lack of foresight and discipline that cost us the prize. Of those that appeared on my debut game at Southport a few short months ago, only Arfon Griffiths, Dave Powell and Sammy McMillan made the cut the following season.

We opened the season with a 0-0 draw at home to Exeter City on what was, for us, a blistering hot day, in the 70's F. The week after, away at Hartlepool, and I mean no offence, but at the time it wasn't what one would call one of the most impressive places in the UK in my opinion, we lost 1-2. The week after, we trounced Halifax Town at home 4-0 on September 3, and then incredibly went unbeaten for the next 15 games until we lost in a top-of-the-table clash at Stockport 0-1 on December 2. In all, we went unbeaten in 16 games, winning seven and drawing nine.

Our inability to finish teams off, to administer the 'coup de gras' would be our Achilles heel. But in that short length of time, although beaten only once, we used 18 players. This seemed an extraordinary amount considering we had lost only one game.

On the other hand, it could mean that Wrexham were taking a close look at opponents before they had got to play us, and changed the team and tactics appropriately to support this.

I don't recall any team briefings on this theory, neither do I recall being taken aside with the "… Steve, this is the plan and your role in the plan is this…"

During this unbeaten period we scored 34 goals and conceded 15. In successive games during October and November, we drew by the same score, 1-1, at home to Crewe and York and away to Barrow,

Southend and Lincoln.

During this spell only myself, Micky Evans, Arfon Griffiths, Sammy Mac, 'Plonky' McLoughlin and Johnny Schofield were ever present. That's half a team.

I don't recall the injuries during that period so I may be being a little unfair here, but you would expect a mostly unchanged team during such a time. Albert Kinsey, Graham Turner and Terry Oldfield missed a handful of games between them so, early on anyway, it was a fairly settled environment. Saying that I played in eight different positions during the season confirmed my versatility!

In all, during 1966/67 we used 24 different players in the search for glory, which in itself tells another story. This clearly is not a settled team, or perhaps it's someone searching for an answer.

Sammy McMillan got 18 goals from 45 games (a goal every 2.5 games) and was our top scorer.

If we had been able to defend, we would have won the league, but that would have required a change in the way we played. Even I scored two that year. But I had to play in eight different positions to do it. These weren't the days when you had numbers for ID and players wore them all the time. Every shirt denoted a position on the field. Eight was inside right, six was left half and nine was centre forward, and so on. I wore the following jersey numbers that year: 2,3,4,5,6,7,9 and 10. When Johnny 'Schoie' Schofield, our keeper, signed from Birmingham, he hurt his hand in a game at York City and could no longer play in goal. Remember this was the pre-substitute era; who went in goal? Yep, you guessed right, I did, the utility player.

Jack left for Bradford in April, 1967. We had only lost six matches all season, but drawn 17! We must have been the favourite on everyone's Littlewoods Pools coupon.

Having had a season in which a team only lost six games, you would expect the manager to stay, but maybe there was no money available to strengthen the team.

The problem was we just went out and played. We had some luck, but we grafted a lot. We would sit in the pub on Thursdays and organise the formations. Terry Oldfield was particularly outspoken on this issue. Everyone liked Jack but he was absent from the battlefield over the important issues, as was his sidekick Ken Roberts. There was still potential glory ahead the Welsh Cup final and prospects of playing against the giants of Europe.

Then Jack shocked everyone, or no one, by resigning. The 1-1 home draw with Barrow was his last game. This was two weeks before the first home leg of the Welsh Cup final. He took Ken Roberts with him, so it probably was Cliff Lloyd and old JJ in charge, or a self-managed effort by the senior players. I just don't recall.

We'd beaten Bradford Park Avenue twice that season, a 6-0 thrashing at home in October and a 3-1 win at their place in March the following year. When Jack took over, they were 22nd in the league, with 26pts and had only won nine games all season. We were seventh on the table and with a bit more finesse could have been well and truly in the promotion race.

You have to ask yourself why anyone would leave a club two weeks before a cup final that could take you into Europe, for a club in the same division that offered no more prospects, probably fewer than the club that you were already at. I am still unable to comprehend why Jack chose to leave before the first home leg of the Welsh Cup final.

I don't recall the details, but at the time, rumor had it there was some big money floating around at Bradford PA. When Jack left, he asked me to go with him. I said no.

Alvan Williams, from Southend United, was appointed as the new manager. Alvan had played for the Red Dragons in the 1950s.

He was a vicar's son, although to imagine Alvan anywhere close to the priesthood was stretching things.

He had been Assistant Manager at Bangor City and managed Hartlepool United for just over a year before handing over the reins to a certain Brian Clough and moving to Southend-on-Sea in June, 1965. His main claim to fame was he had 'led' Bangor City to the first round of the European Cup Winners Cup. In fairness, little Bangor beat the Italian Cup winners Napoli 2-0 at home, only losing the second leg 3-1. The subsequent decider, played at Arsenal's Highbury, saw Bangor dismissed from the competition 2-1. It must be said that Alvan was not the manager of Bangor City at the time, but Assistant Manager. The 'Manager' mantle went to a Thomas George Jones. How much credit Alvan should take from the success of Bangor in European competition is open to conjecture.

On the other hand, the success would have made the marketing of the Welsh Cup a lot more viable going on into Europe. Maybe that was why he got the job.

For us as a club, the Welsh Cup was where our success lay that season. It wasn't unusual for teams from England to play in this competition, and from time to time Tranmere and Chester had entered. And don't forget, I had made my debut with Bristol City in this competition several years before, against Merthyr Tydfil.

At Wrexham, we steamrolled Rhyl (5-0) and Merthyr Tydfil (7-1) before we found ourselves in the two-legged semi- final against local rivals Chester. In five days in March, we slogged out a goalless draw away and then demolished the pretenders 4-2 at the Racecourse. This set up a two-legged final against Second Division side Cardiff City.

The stage was set. This season, the winners would gain automatic entry to the European Cup Winners Cup.

This was no small matter. AC Milan, Standard Liege, Valencia,

Bayern Munich and Hamburg SV were all in the pot.

But it was too early to dream of those teams. First we had to win the final.

The first leg was played on a Monday evening, April 17, 1967, at the Racecourse Ground. It was a cold, damp night and 11,473 fans turned up to cheer us on. This was a disappointing crowd and one that we had surpassed in league games on five occasions this season.

When we lined up, my opponent was Barry Jones, a renowned Welsh international, capped 15 times and definitely no mug. Mr. Gow, a first class International referee, was the man with the whistle. I was determined that Barry would not get the better of me.

Barry was probably at his best at this time, a virtual cornerstone of the Cardiff team, which he had rejoined in March 1967 from Plymouth Argyle, just a few weeks before the cup final. Sadly, his career at this level was to be ended prematurely a year or so later with a broken leg.

The first ball out to him was best described as hopeful. Both the ball and I got to Barry at the same time. I cleaned him up. We all went down in a heap. Barry was hollering, Mr. Gow was whistling, and the crowd was roaring.

The Cardiff bench are on their feet.

What did you say you would do to me after the game?

All I could hear from the crowd, the players and the Wrexham bench was: "What a great tackle, Stace!" Maybe the tackle was a little unrestrained for what was, after all, cup final night!

I looked up at Mr. Gow. He was wagging his finger at me. "Last time, son," was all he said. Barry was giving me the look. Barry took revenge on me the best way he knew how, he vented any anger he had by having a ripper and tore me to pieces.

It was not a game to remember. Definitely not the dream I thought or hoped it would be. It was a big disappointment for me.

Luckily, with a team not at full strength, we managed to hold Cardiff to a 2-2 draw, and on the balance of things we were quite happy.

All the goals came in the first half-hour. My mate Barry put Cardiff in front after less than a minute. One of our replacements for the walking wounded, Dave Campbell, made it all square on 11 minutes and the reliable Albert Kinsey put us ahead after 21 minutes.

We laid siege to their goal but to no avail. King equalised for Cardiff after 27 minutes and although the game seesawed from end to end, that's how it ended, 2-2.

Two divisions separated the clubs, but on the night you wouldn't have known it. We were happy with a draw, and on this showing we had a chance at Ninian Park. We also knew that a few of our regulars would come back in for that game.

Cardiff would have been happy, too. We had battered them for a good 40 minutes or so, and in some respects they were a little lucky. However, after earning a draw away from home, they would have been confident that they could finish the job at their place.

The manner in which they would achieve this task is still a bone of contention in Welsh football.

To sum up our confusing season, Tony 'Plonky' McLoughlin and Don Weston would be back for the second leg, but only three players, Sammy Mac (10) 'Big Ray 'Mielczarek (5) and our keeper, Johnny Schofield, retained the same jersey for the game! I do admit that it was 16 days and three games later, but that was still eight positional changes. Not the ideal preparation for the second leg of a cup final. Was it panic, or confusion? Quite possibly both.

The second leg loomed. Eve had not travelled to Wrexham to see her son's first cup final appearance. Kenny, my brother, had a car. The deal was done. With no motorways, the journey would take you up north through Gloucester, a pleasant enough drive through the Cotswolds, across the Severn at the aptly named Over, and down through the western side of the river, past Newport and Chepstow and on into Cardiff. That would have been the trip, almost as tortuous as the four-hour haul to Wrexham to watch the first leg.

We lunched at a hotel on the way down. Most of the team would, as usual, have a steak. Ninian Park was rather empty, just over 8,000; I suspect half of them from Wrexham.

Arfon Griffiths put us ahead after eight minutes, Don, on his return to the first team, smacked the post and for the next 25 minutes we had them on toast. Plonky was inches away with a 20-yarder and, as usually happens, instead of closing it up and taking ten minutes to frustrate them, we said: "We can do this, another couple and it's over." Dean equalised after 25 minutes and they were right back in it, with their tails up.

Ten minutes after the break, George Showell gets in the way of a dubious cross and the ball rebounds into the net to put them in front. Now they close it up and the going gets tough.

Gareth Williams, a Welsh international who should know better, challenges Terry Oldfield for the ball. Is this a deliberately malicious challenge? Well, for me, for anyone to challenge for the ball and to dislocate someone's knee, is reckless, careless and has no place on the football field. Tackles are meant to be at ground level.

It was a very large dislocation. It was horrendous. Terry's knee was out and he was screaming with pain. Albert Kinsey vomited his steak on Ninian Park and there are more than a few yellow faces around. It was the worst football injury I've ever seen.

In an amazing turn of events, referee Gow allows Williams to stay on the pitch. He gives him only a yellow card. We are furious, the crowd is furious and Gareth is looking distinctly nervous. He's surrounded by most of the Wrexham team who are outlining what his fate is likely to be over the next half an hour. To my shame, I'm one of them. 'Get Gareth' becomes the catch cry, and the game degenerates into who can kick Gareth as hard as possible first. He hides as much as he can.

'So, Gareth you can break a leg/dislocate a knee and get away with it, well, boyo, wait until we can do you, and God help the referee if he sends us off.' So bad did it get that the BBC (Wales), on showing the game that night, refused to show the last 20/30 minutes. Who could blame them because 'it wasn't football.'

Cardiff had most of the ball for the last 20 minutes or so, as we forgot the issues concerned with defence or attack, simply seeking retribution from the Cardiff captain. Cardiff could well have shoved another five past us, as we were past caring.

The rough part came at the end, as the final whistle blew and Cardiff are 2-1 winners on the night and 4-3 on aggregate. To add insult to injury, the Welsh FA (FAW) chairman presents the cup to the Cardiff captain, Gareth Williams.

By this time, we are about to riot. We sulk and fester over this dastardly deed. Terry has played his last game. He never played again. He wore a caliper on that leg for as long as I continued to know him.

The medals were presented to Cardiff. Then, Alvan refused to let us go and collect ours. They were later delivered to the dressing room and Alvan throws them out into the corridor and tells everyone who will listen what he thinks of Gareth! He tells anyone who approaches to 'go away', in no uncertain terms, and that they can 'stick the medals up their backside'. No one was going to cross Alvan at that point in time and collect their own medal.

Alvan had a lot riding on this game. Previously, he has had small town Bangor City in the European Cup Winners cup. Now, Wrexham should have become the second team he coached to make it to the European competition.

Two Welsh Cup final appearances with two clubs are definitely a big plus on any CV.

Understandably, he is mad.

I don't know about any of the other players but I'm still waiting for my Welsh Cup Final runners-up medal. Several request to the Welsh FA have been rejected. I know not why.

Incredibly, Cardiff went through to the semi final of the European Cup Winners Cup the following season. SV Hamburg were the opponents, and a 1-1 draw in Germany only flattered to deceive as they lost the return leg at home 2-3, aggregate score (3-4). Heartbreak for Cardiff; 2-1 up with 12 minutes to go, they conceded two goals in five minutes to lose in a most devastating manner.

Eve was disappointed. She felt for her son, poor little love. It's only a game, Mum!! She was proud though. She sat in the stand in the best seats and thumped her chest when her lad had the ball. She was remembering years ago, when she managed my signing-on fee for Bristol City. This match whetted her appetite for more negotiations. Ted was there, too. My stepfather never said much and tonight was the same. A word or two, that was all... thought we should have won and mentioned Gareth. My stepbrother Ken is shy and spent the whole game in the car park!!

TRAINING ON A MOUNTAIN

Alvan's appointment was a strange one. After what could only be described as an ordinary performance at Southend, including a club record 9-1 loss against Brighton, he became the first manager in the club's history to suffer relegation. It is still a mystery to me why Wrexham would hire a manager that, a season ago, had just seen his side relegated. Perhaps he was very persuasive in his interview. Perhaps he had said that it was far more important that the club remain solvent rather than the welfare of the players, and the performances of the team.

I have a feeling that he told the Board not to worry about the transfer fees, promised to take a lower salary and, instead, a percentage of any transfer fees for players he sold. This way he would help guide the club out of debt. The cherry on top, was probably the promise of a youth policy that would make the club a fortune. Looking in from outside in later years, I'm convinced that this was the scenario.

He was a man inclined to speak his mind, regardless of circumstances. A reputation as a more than vocal persona proceeded him.

He talked and shouted a lot. He never demonstrated to me that he had an understanding of tactics, or about what made players tick. He failed to motivate me, and I always felt that he was a short-term solution.

He would later manage public houses in Wales, Blackpool and London. In later life, he would be charged with the murder of a man outside the public house he ran in North London. He went on trial at the Old Bailey. There was insufficent evidence to convict him of murder, but he was jailed for 12 months for affray.

When Alvan left Wrexham, in difficult circumstances, under the drama of a drink driving conviction, and took up the license at the Ship Inn at Bala, it was his last involvement in football, or so I thought. But just prior to his passing, in December, 2003, he received a special merit award from the FA of Wales for his services to the game. I'm unsure what these services were related to, Alvan created chaos at Wrexham. He may well have set up a youth programme, but this was not anything unusual. Rather, it was par for the course for what was happening at the time. If anyone deserved credit for the youth development policies, it surely would be John Neal. Maybe I'm being picky. One thing I do know is Alvan was a different kettle of fish to Jack Rowley. I liked Jack. I never warmed to Alvan.

If, as I surmise, Alvan promised to buy players cheap and sell at a profit, as well as develop and sell established players, the tricky part is working out who you sell and who you buy. It appeared that the Board trusted him. There was 'an understanding'.

In the end, Alvan took it upon himself to sell half the Wrexham team and he paid the ultimate price.

Alvan's plan was out in the open for all to see. It's clear now that the Board had no idea that he intended to transfer me. I believe that they were as shocked as anyone when the news hit the boardroom. Why else would they react so vehemently when the news broke? In my opinion, Alvan had clearly breached the trust between them and the 'agreement' on buying/selling.

Dave Powell has been sold to Sheffield United just days before. Had Alvan given the Board an assurance then that this was the last throw of the dice, or had he been seduced by the agreement and the assumed percentage of transfers?

We can only ponder.

The events were described in the Wrexham Football Club Annual like this:

'Racecourse fortunes suffered a severe setback with the resignation of Mr. Alvan Williams on 17th September. He arrived at The Racecourse on a wave of enthusiasm and appeared to be on the threshold of success until he announced the sale of Ray Mielczarek (to Huddersfield Town) and the subsequent transfers of Dave Powell (Sheffield Utd) and Steve Stacey (Ipswich Town) brought matters to the point at which the Directors clashed with the manager on various aspects of policy and his resignation was accepted.'

Question?

Didn't Alvan discuss with the Board that he was initiating these transfers?

Disappointment among the general body of followers was reflected in the decision of the Supporter's Association to write a letter of protest to the Club following the transfers of Powell and myself. They wanted the board to reconsider the policy of parting with players who, in the Association's view, were needed to gain promotion.

After the previous season, the feeling had been that this was surely to be *the* season. The messiah had arrived; Alvan Williams. But right from the start there was something that said we had a wheeler-dealer. Something said, be careful. Time would tell. He arrived smoking cigars and driving an XJ Jaguar, if my memory serves me correctly, a bit flash for Wrexham.

Alvan wasted no time in recruiting and brought with him from Southend Ray Smith, Tony Beanland and Steve Ingle, as well as Eddie May. Terry Bradbury came from Leyton Orient and the best signing of all, John Neal, whom Alvan had worked with at Southend, came on board as first team 'trainer', as the coaches were known then. Alvan wasn't in the same class as John, either in his knowledge of the game, or man management.

Straight away, half the team had Alvan's own mark on it. Sadly, Sammy McMillan, who was a crowd favorite at Wrexham, was soon to travel in the opposite direction and sign for Southend.

It's fair to say that the locals at Wrexham viewed the players coming into the squad with a certain level of suspicion. They were labelled brash, loudmouths, frigging city boys, and these are only the printable versions. He immediately created a 'them and us' situation that manifested itself into various little scenarios.

When you have a manager who has just got a side relegated and then brings half of that team with him, how would you react?

At least with Alvan I settled more or less into a regular position. It was left back, with a new number. Traditionally, the left back wore the number three.

With the introduction of the 'new' four-four-two style of play, the numbers changed. Why, I don't know. Maybe some managers believed that they could confuse opposing teams as to their line-up So, the keeper stayed one, right back two, first centre back three, second centre back was four, and the left back was five.

Generally, both Alvan and John Neal were on the training pitch.

Pre-season training was a revelation. We were going to run to the top of Mount Snowdon.

Snowdon is in Snowdonia, a magnificent part of Wales. It's really and truly a mountain, standing some 1,085 metres (3,560 feet) above sea level.

Off we trooped in the bus. Snowdon boasts a magic little railway that takes tourists almost to the top of the mountain. As a railway enthusiast I was naturally intrigued. The total railway distance from top to bottom is about four-and-three-quarter miles, or seven-and-a-half kilometres.

It was a warm summer day. We ran, walked and jogged our way

to the top. Facing numerous challenges along the way, such as scrub, tourist avoidance, rocks and ankle-breaking countryside. There was no road that led to the top.

Tourists gaped and pointed fingers at us. Little kids jumped up and down in excitement. Why are they running? Why don't they catch the train?

Alvan finally stopped us on the way up. He got us all together, found a quiet little spot, uphill 20 yards, almost vertical, and had us all doing doggies!

Hughie and Ralph paid a visit to a couple of the lads. I don't know how long it took. We all made it eventually, and the view from the summit was stunning.

On clear days both the Isle of Man and the Wicklow Mountains in Eire, just across the Irish Sea, are visible. But we had no time to enjoy the view, as it was time to retrace our steps. One thing I will say is it was easier going down, but there were some inevitable falls.

I was concerned about my knees. The downward momentum meant that you were continually putting the brakes on to slow up. I let Alvan know how I felt, and I wasn't alone.

At the bottom, my chest was heaving. I, along with all of the squad, even the young ground staff boys, were rooted. Sweating profusely, we all had scratches or marks of some kind, dry mouths, aching limbs and tight chests. The man's mad, was the general consensus.

He was happy. The press were out in force and the pictures were splashed all over the local papers, along with Alvan, crouched, fist clenched, giving it the 'come on, marines, let's do it.' There was no compromise on fitness, none whatsoever. This was a case of run 'til you drop.

Later in the week, there was another cross-country run through scrub and woods.

This was not as demanding as the 'mountain walk', as the

Snowdon episode had been dubbed, but was a trial in itself.

I was behind Albert Kinsey. Albert had slowed almost to a walk. "Get a move on Albert." The track was single file and it was dark. The sun barely shone through. All of a sudden, "what the frig!" Albert is moving like greased lightning, but backwards.

Albert started hollering about a snake and he's off, like an Olympic sprinter, all dappled in the sunlight. All you can see are Albert's heels. No one else saw the snake, leaving Albert defending the quality of his eyesight for quite some time.

Ally McGowan was a real genial ex-Wrexham player. I have to say he was the most liked and affable man you could ever wish to meet. We had many a long conversation about the ins and outs of full backs. Ally had played over 400 games for Wrexham in the full back position, so we had quite a bit to talk about. A broken leg finished his career early, although he was in his 30s, he reckoned he had another ten to go. I used to chide him about his goal scoring record. "Ally, 400 appearances and only two goals, what's going on? I've done you in my first season." When I was first at the Racecourse, he had a dual role of looking after the kids and working as the groundsman.

Wrexham was a cosy little place, of all the clubs I played for I count the Dragons as the best loved time of my career.

One morning, we had gathered at the ground during pre-season. We all enjoyed a chat with Ally. There we were in the stand, chatting and watching Ally seed the pitch. He was having trouble, though. We could hear him up in the stand muttering "frigging pigeons." The birds were eating the seed. Ally can't prepare the ground and shoo the birds at the same time.

Alvan appears, and he wants to know what the problem is.

"Birds," was the answer and some ribald comments followed.

"Pigeons."

We're laughing at the situation as Ally gets louder and louder and more agitated. He can hear us. "Get off your backsides and sort it!" he yelled at us.

Alvan has the answer to everything. He disappears, and reappears with a .22 calibre rifle. Why would a manager just happen to have a rifle and ammo in his office?

Imagine, half the Wrexham team in the main stand, armed with a rifle and plenty of ammo, taking it in turns to pop the pigeons. The sound of the recoils was quite loud. People would have heard it outside the ground as it echoed around the empty stadium.

Wrexham was unusual in those days, as at the top end of the ground, and from memory actually inside the ground, was a public house, yes a pub. It soon became obvious that the publican had called the police.

The siren was heard long before the car was seen. Clearly, the constabulary wanted to let us know they were coming. Dead pigeons are littering the field.

"Get the shovels you two, the rest pick up the pigeons", was the order.

The ground staff kids shoot off for the shovels, we the players quickly disperse all over the pitch, picking up dead, half dead and dying pigeons.

Where to now? The back of the stand was the answer. This was the covered stand, standing only, on the opposite side of the Mold Road sitting area.

By the time we get around to the pigeon burial area, there are two or three holes already dug. Little Ken and his mate on the ground staff are sweating, digging, sweating and more digging. In went the pigeons, the holes were filled up and the freshly turned earth stamped on.

The police arrive and there we were, this band of brothers, a dozen or so all up, standing in the middle of nowhere, waiting.

The conversation went something like this.

"Who's doing the shooting then, Alvan?"

"What shooting's that, then?"

"We had a report that there has been some endangerment to wildlife. Shooting from the stands."

"Just practicing."

"Pigeons, is it then?"

"What pigeons is that, then?"

"The pigeons that's eating your seed on the pitch."

The policeman who is talking, in that lovely lilting Welsh accent, has elbowed one of our group out the way, and is now standing on pigeon cemetery, patting his feet up and down on the newly-turned earth.

"It's illegal you see, the discharge of firearms in a public place, and if I found any guns here, I'd have to confiscate them, wouldn't I? Particularly if there was no gun license to go with it."

By now we are all about to fold up laughing; even the policeman is finding it hard.

Alvan's all red in the face.

The policeman turns to go, stops, looks at the grave and says, "Starting a veggie patch are we, Alvan?"

The troops find it hard to contain their laughter.

Question.

Why would the manager of a football club have a .22 rifle in his office?

There had been an indifferent start to the season. Of the first nine games, we had won three, drawn three and lost three. We had quite a good record at the Racecourse though. We had won three and drawn two and only conceded a single goal on the opening day of the season against Luton.

Even so, questions remained to be answered. Only Tony

Beanland, Terry Bradbury, Arfon Griffiths Johnny Schofield and myself were 'ever present'.

A few weeks later, Alvan wanted to see the players in the dressing room after training. The season was not going as planned. We had slipped to 14th in the table, five points behind the early leaders, Alvan's old club, Southend United.

On Saturday, we had been beaten 2-0 in the 'local derby' at Swansea.

Promotion hung in the air. The sweet smell of success lingered like an expensive perfume. If we were not careful, that sweet smell would soon disappear.

What was Alvan telling the Board?

He's brought half a team from Southend. Why?

These are the players that will propel us into the promotion race? If it didn't work at Southend why would it work at Wrexham?

Alvan must have been considering the fact .

Next Saturday's game was at home to another fellow mid-table team, Hartlepools United, another of Alvan's old teams.

We're going to have a mid season break to Anglesey, Alvan's birthplace. Two days away from it all would refresh the group, install new vigour and get us back on the road.

A boat trip was planned for the afternoon. Just an hour or so up and down the straits, the manager said.

Now, I don't swim. I would rather have not gone, but when in a team one does as the team does.

The Menai Strait is a narrow strip of water separating the Isle of Anglesey from the Welsh mainland. It's a dangerous piece of water, a wide opening with strong tides pushing water up through a gradually narrowing estuary. As you can imagine, this creates some interesting tidal configurations.

The team was in a boat in the middle of the Straits. We had been out for a while, cruising around.

Then someone asked, "Isn't this boat down a little at the back?"

The thing was sinking. A quick look at the well deck at the back shows us taking on water in the stern.

We're going down at the back end.

"Don't panic, lads!"

Don't frigging panic! We're sinking in the middle of one of the most dangerous stretches of water in Wales! I, and I suspect I'm not alone, am not a swimmer. Even if we were, the stretch of water isn't particularly friendly, and this fool is telling us not to panic!

"Get the life jackets."

Problem: there aren't enough life jackets.

"What do you mean, there aren't enough lifejackets?"

Ray Smith suddenly admits that he can't swim. Join the club, Ray!

We find a jacket from the heap. It's doubtful who got there first but Ray is doing a good job of putting it on.

"Ray, I got to it first."

"No you didn't, I did. And anyway I've got it half-on." he argued, possession being nine-tenths of the law.

Ray and I are in the middle of this boat, both standing, both with two hands on the life jacket, arguing like kids. "It's mine!", "No, it's mine!", "No, it isn't!" All rather undignified, but when you can't swim, and the water's going to be over your head, if you go overboard....well pull harder!!

I cast a forlorn look around the boat. All the jackets are taken.

Three or four of us are standing around, ready to walk ashore.

"Don't worry, it's only a precaution."

"Well, if it's only a precaution, give me your frigging life jacket."

The boat is turned gently. What are the boys in the jackets thinking?

"Glad it's not me. Don't worry, Steve, I'll save you," and "Do we really need you after the way you played last week!"

The boat limped back to port. It's a long 20 minutes or so and I was willing it home all the way.

There was no sign of any rescue boats. We disembark quickly.

Those without jackets are friends for life; we are a different breed to the rest. We braved the Straits and won. I remember as soon as we were ashore feeling quite ill.

The favoured drug of professional footballers? Alcohol.

Alvan lost his job at arguably both Southend and Wrexham due in part to the consumption of alcohol. He was the leading figure in having a bar installed at the Racecourse.

Most players, along with tobacco during my career, were frequent users.

It would not be unusual to enter a dressing room to see players with a cigarette and a bottle of beer directly after the game.

Lemmo Southway, years before, would pass round the quart of White Horse in the Robins' dressing rooms before the game had started.

At Wrexham the after game party was a ritual. Practically after every home game, the question was where's the party tonight? Bacardi and Coke and Wrexham Lager were the drinks of choice. We would often have to go to the Miner's Welfare Club late at night and get Mr. Evans to fill the empty bottles with lager.

On October 2, 1967, we played Brentford. It was a Monday night game in front of 8,670 fans.

Johnny 'Schoie' Schofield had been signed by Jack in the summer of 1966 as a replacement for our front line keeper, Graheme Beighton, and had become the regular keeper. Along with myself, he had been an 'ever present' in the 1966/67 season.

'Schoie' has played the first four games, in which we conceded six goals. Young Gordon Livsey plays the next four, presumably for

Alvan to have a closer look at him, and we concede just two goals. 'Schoie' returned for the Newport game and we get beat 3-2.

'Schoie' is in his mid-30s and has a string of stories to tell about his time at Birmingham. He rarely travels to Wrexham, only for the odd training session and on match days. It must have been part of the agreement when he signed. We get on quite well and I tended to lap up the stories about the 'big time'.

Come half-time and, the game is goal-less. After 57 minutes I get the ball in the left back position and start to cut inside. I cruise past a tackle, squeeze past another defender and, as two more close in, somehow give it the one-two shuffle and I get to see the goalmouth.

What now? I didn't hesitate, and smacked it from 20-odd yards into the corner. It was some goal, even if I say so myself. It was a cracker. The crowd certainly seemed to love it.

We were bubbling now and put them on the rack, and for 15 minutes we are in no danger and have got this game in hand!

However, 15 minutes later, though 'Schoie' makes a mess of collecting a cross, stumbles over one of our defenders and eventually palms the ball against Ray Smith for an own goal. The crowd, the players and the bench are stunned. We had this well under control.

Five minutes later it gets worse for 'Schoie'. He dropped a tame effort and the resulting tap in gives Brentford a win they never deserved. In the cold light of day, 'Schoie' has cost us the game. The whistle goes and Brentford are naturally delighted. We players are stunned and so is the crowd.

In an ominous sign, the manager's bench quickly empties. Little was said leaving the park. We all know 'Schoie' has had a real bad one, but that comes to us all once or twice in a career. The problem is, of course, that when you are a keeper, these bad ones can easily cost the game, and tonight it has.

The last man enters the dressing room, and Alvan slams the door.

"Great goal Stace", was his first comment and then it starts. The finger pointing, the shouting, the swearing, raised voices, accusations, points about ability and things that simply can't be repeated.

The unkind word is better left unsaid.

I have never ever seen anything like this in any dressing room that I've been in. Alvan is all worked up, red-faced. Along with others, I'm stunned at what is happening, it's clear there will be no coming back from this.

'Schoie' has done his "sorry, lads" bit, which is all you can accept. Next week it may be you under the grill. But clearly this tirade has affected John; it's almost a big man in tears. There's a quick shower, a brief farewell and 'Schoie' is off.

I understand that his contract was either paid up or he was simply told don't bother to come back. It was a terribly sad end to a great career and a personal friendship.

Alvan's actions in front of the team made him few friends. This should have been done behind closed doors, but Alvan wasn't that kind of man.

As for John, 'Schoie', I never saw him again.

Saturday, October 28, 1967, was Michele's fourth birthday. The event is etched in my mind. We were at home to Workington and we had so far recorded five wins and five draws to complement our five losses. That meant that we had accumulated 15 points. A point a game is not promotion material. The Board knew it, the fans, knew it, the players knew it and Alvan knew it.

Many in the dressing room think Alvan has promised promotion. Workington were anchored with the bottom group near the foot of the table. A win was expected, which we did comfortably 5-0 in front of almost 6,000 of the faithful.

It was prior to the game that that was of concern. There was myself and players 1, 2, and 3, who shall not be named for obvious reasons. Alvan walked into the bath/shower area.

I thought the discussion was going to be along the lines of a tactical issue, or a gee-up to several senior players. Instead, Alvan reached into his pocket and brought out a small glass medical pill bottle. He goes on to say, "They're good for injury prevention or assisting recovery from injury. You don't need to tell anyone else about these."

A short silence fell over the group. I'm unsure which of us held out our hand first. We all took the pills on offer. Walking off after the game, I had a certain bounce in my step. Player 1 mentioned that he felt he was skipping over the ground and players 2 and 3 thought that the medicine had given them a lift; one used the phrase 'I couldn't stop running'.

The handouts continued for four or five weeks and then vanished, never to be seen or mentioned again. We lost just one of the next seven games.

Was it a placebo? I'll never know. Alvan was a high-risk taker. Players including myself were foolish, and should have said get lost, certainly. Had I, or did I, ever indulge in anything of the sort over the years? No.

What was I thinking? If "one of England's top teams", as Alvan had indicated, are or were taking these pills, and they were one of the best in the land, it must be OK.

How naïve can you get?

Concerns about medicinal aids then were limited to concerns about the Chinese 'bulking up' for the Olympics. Drugs in sport were virtually unheard of.

It wasn't a happy end to the season when, with some luck, we could have reeled in a promotion spot. It was so close yet still so far.

After Christmas, we had a shocking time that cost us promotion. The 2-1 home win over Swansea promised so much yet, like the winds of fate, only deceived.

We lost four on the trot, at Hartlepool (0-3) and York (1-3) and at home to Newport County (0-1) and Bradford City (0-2). The fans knew it, too, and gates dropped to around 3,000.

Consistency is the key in any season. We had a terrible spell with those four consecutive losses, but from the next 16 games, only Chesterfield were able to beat us. From March 2, away to Darlington, to the final game of the season, at home to York, we: P16, W9, D6, L1, F26, A13, points 24. This impressive record boasted seven clean sheets, six of them on the trot!

It was, however, too little, too late and we finished the season in 9th place, five points off a promotion spot. When you look back, 'Schoie' had cost us two against Brentford.

We were not far off, so close.

I was not a fan of Alvan Williams for many reasons but, in fairness to the man, the quality of training and fitness improved substantially in the 1967/68 season. I thought John Neal had had a great deal of input, too. In fact, from my point of view, I always discussed technical matters with John and asked him how I could improve my game.

But the question needs to be asked.

How does a team, any team, embark on a run of double digit games without a loss, without a goal against them for many matches... and then collapse in a heap? It needs another book, but the here and now of club psychology may hold the key.

HAMSTRING

Injuries were part and parcel of the game in those days and players were frequently expected to play through minor injuries, knocks and bruises and so forth.

My injury of 'choice' was my hamstring. It plagued my football life. The injury had a massive cause and effect on my career, and understanding it today allows me to contemplate what went on during the treatment periods and at those critical times while I was on and off the field.

Warm up in the early days consisted of a couple of laps around the track and maybe a few ten-yard sprints at half-pace. Generally, this was done on an individual basis; in other words, unsupervised. There was no collective 'stretch the muscle' philosophy.

From the beginning at Bristol City, I was plagued by minor hamstring issues, spending considerable time in the treatment room. I was given the inevitable ultra sound and told 'no sprinting until Wednesday.' I would play three, maybe four, games and then the inevitable strain would return.

This infernal injury, which had plagued me since the Bristol City youth team days, and was destined to end my career, would not go away.

At Wrexham, in October, 1967, against Darlington and then, in November at Bradford, I'd had to leave the pitch for treatment and was substituted. Luckily, despite having to leave the field, I didn't miss any games at that time, but the warning signs were beginning to show.

Against Rochdale over Christmas, I collected a fairly serious knee injury, my right ligament being damaged. This was the home match on Boxing Day, which we won 2-0. But in the return match, four days later, we lost 3-0. I missed the next three games, spread over quite a period of time; this included the 'local derby' against Swansea. That Swansea match, according to the records, is the only game we played in the month of January. I returned to the side for the home game against Newport on February 10, having enjoyed six weeks of rest.

Sadly though, my hamstring problem was well and truly coming back to haunt me. Inadequate treatment was part of the problem. Returning to action too early certainly did not help; neither did the lack of a good warm up with specific stretching.

On March 9 at Chesterfield, again I couldn't finish the game. I had stretched the 'hammy'. That meant I was consigned to the bench for the home game against Aldershot the week after. I entered the game close to the whistle.

I remember I collected a Ray Smith header at the far post and snuck home the winner with just a few minutes left on the clock.

However, in doing so I smacked my knee up again. It wasn't looking good. That put me out for four more weeks. Training on a gammy knee, and at risk of a hamstring pull, made it difficult to get anywhere near fit. I missed the next eight games, either because I was injured and unable to play or because I was sitting on the bench, more in hope than anything else. I played the last four games of the season; we won three and drew one. That season my hamstring had led to me missing a quarter of the scheduled games.

As a team, we blew it again. Eight players had played 30-plus games: Tony Beanland (42), Alan Bermingham (32), Terry Bradbury (38), Arfon Griffiths (44), Albert Kinsey (37), George Showell (32), Ray Smith (44), and myself (34).

After playing the first 24 games of the season, the injuries allowed me only another 10 full games,

Packed house at Perry Lakes Stadium as the locals take on Manchester United.

Brian Green (L) Australian Director of Coaching, Alan Vest Western Australian Director of Coaching (R) and myself. Football was beginning to boom in Australia and the 1970s laid the foundation of future international success.

I was one of the lucky few to undergo the training to become a fully qualified Australian registered coach. Here with Brian Green, Director of Coaching.

Steve Pateman collects a cross at Perry Lakes versus Middlesborough. We drew the game but it was, in my opinion, Western Australia's finest hour.

Sometimes it gets crowded in and around the goal area! Here
I get trampled on by the Middlesborough centre forward.

Where's the ball? A close call at Perry Lakes against Middlesborough.

Legia Warsaw were one of the giants of Europe at this time. In the 1970s, Denya was one of the world's top players. They proved too much for us at Perry Lakes.

Floreat Athena versus Tricolore in a top four play off game at Perry Lakes. In a strange twist at that time, you could finish at the top of the league, which qualified you for a series of play offs with the other top three clubs. Hence you could finish top of the league, but if the fourth team beat you in the top four play off, it was, as a Bristol Rovers supporter would say, 'Goodnight Irene.'

I was captain of an Australian Representative team that won the Marah Halim tournament in Medan Indonesia in 1975. We beat Japan in the semi final.

I should have done better with this header in front of goal in one of the group matches. Dave Brooks, a stalwart player, is to my right.

Ken Morton, ex-Manchester United, puts this one into the side netting. After all these years Ken and I are still firm friends.

After-tournament victory celebrations. Coach Alan Vest, standing front row at right, Alan was the most successful coach in Western Australia's history and remains a firm friend.

Come to W ere e Fie

Every picture tells a story. I was, and still am, deeply honoured.

I broke a thumb during one of the play off finals. Ken (pictured) put it back in place and sent me back on.

One guess!! Vava (Edvaldo Izidio Netto), the great Brazilian player who won world cup winners medals in 1958 and 1962, and me in Geelong Victoria. I'm proudly wearing my Bristol City blazer. At the time, Vava was manager/coach of the Brazilian youth team playing in an international tournament. This picture is at Geelong where I was working at the time. Vava kindly brought the team to town to play a couple of 'warm up' games against the locals.

Dot, myself and the children, Michele and Natalie, at Yanchep National Park. A not-to-be-missed spot if you are visiting. credit Stacey family collection]

A family shot just after arrival in Australia. L to R: Dot, Michele, Natalie and myself. credit Stacey family collection]

Dad, Clarence and I downtown New York in the 1980s. We had taken a while to track him down but find him we did. (Stacey family collection)

My two sisters, Joyce (L) and Valerie. Meeting the whole family was a revelation, and an amazing experience, one that Dot and I will never forget. (Stacey family collection)

With my 'new' family in NY/NY. At front Clarence Jnr (L) with Valerie(R) and at back Michael (L) and Joyce(R). (Stacey family collection)

Downtown NY/NY. Dot and I with Clarence and Joyce. From memory, that's an old WW2 aircraft carrier behind us. (Stacey family collection)

Sister Joyce. Joyce is the one that pushed and pushed me to visit the 'family history' in Mississippi. (Stacey family collection)

Miss Daisy is not driving anymore. Clarence's wife, the mother of Joyce, Valerie, Clarence jnr and Michael. A loving and caring woman and it's my privilege to have met her.
(Stacey family collection)

In the front, my father Clarence Sims in the Bronx with his mates. (Stacey family collection)

Daisy, Dot and Junior (my nephew) in front of Clarence's former house in the Bronx. (Stacey family collection)

I have this thing about Vietnam. It's the American part of me. Here at this war cemetery in the north, I shed a tear or two. (Stacey family collection)

Clarence, far left, showed me the house of an old friend in Mississippi while taking me to visit Aunt Currie and Aunt Julia Mason, and to explore my ancestral roots. (Stacey family collection)

An old slave shack in downtown Mississippi. (Stacey family collection)

AFRICAN ANCESTRY

August 24, 2010

Dear Mr. Stacey,

It is with pleasure that I report that our PatriClan™ analysis succesfully identified your paternal genetic ancestry. The Y chromosome DNA that we determined from your sample shares ancestry with the **Balanta** and **Fula** peoples in **Guinea-Bissau** today.

We studied polymorphisms (different forms of DNA) on the non-recombining portion of your Y chromosome (NRY). This segment of DNA is transmitted identically from father to son. A panel of nine genetic markers (also called polymorphisms) on the NRY was analyzed using standard Polymerase Chain Reaction (PCR) methodology. The polymorphisms we examined consisted of the slowly evolving ALU insertion/deletion polymorphism; and 8 highly mutable microsatellites or short tandem repeats (STRs). Differences in chromosome markers correlate highly with the ethnic and geographic origin of the individual. When compared to Y chromosome markers in large databases such as our African Lineage Database (ALD), Y chromosomes collected from individuals like you could be interpreted as genealogies reflecting the paternal lineage history of the human species. Although the informative stretches of genetic information along the Y chromosome represents less than one percent of your entire genetic make-up, it has proven to be a powerful tool for indentifying and defining paternal lineages.

This result means that you have inherited through your father a segment of DNA that was passed on consistently from your father to son to you. This segment of DNA is presently found in Africa in Guinea-Bissau. We have enclosed several materials that reflect the results of your analysis and that may help you to research your historical and cultural ancestry. There is a copy of your Y chromosome polymorphisms. We have also included a Certificate of Ancestry authenticating that your polymorphisms matched with the Balanta and Fula in Guinea-Bissau. You can display it with pride among other important family documents. In addition, we have included a full colour map that geographically depicts your ancestral region. Finally, we have included the *African Ancestry Guide to West and Central Africa* to help you learn more about the peoples and cultures in Guinea-Bissau.

Thank you for your support and interest in African Ancestry.

Sincerely,

Gina Paige
President

AFRICAN ANCESTRY

Steve Stacey

Y Chromosome Polymorphisms

MARKER	DYS388	DYS389I	DYS389II	DYS390	DYS391	DYS392	DYS393	DYS394	YAP
ALLELE SIZE	12	13	30	21	10	11	15	15	+

Sequence Similarity Measure: 100%

This means that your sequence is 100% the same as sequences from the Balanta and Fula people in Guinea-Bissau today.

CERTIFICATE OF ANCESTRY

African Ancestry hereby certifies that

Steve Stacey

Shares Paternal Genetic Ancestry with

the Balanta and Fula peoples in Guinea-Bissau

Based on a PatriClan™
analysis performed on

August 24, 2010

Rick Kittles, Ph.D.
Scientific Director

Guinea Bisau

Guinea Bissau is an old slave trading country. My gene testing tells me that this is where my ancestors, of the Balanta and Fula, lived and died. Many were shipped across the Atlantic to the American slave ports in Mississippi and Florida.

At least the core of the team was in place, or so we thought, but as everyone knows, consistency is the key. The mid-season loss of form was our downfall.

Our inability to handle away fixtures clearly hampered us. We came home well but it was a case of too little, too late.

The 1967/68 campaign was clearly a disappointing one. We had been out of it for most of the season and flattered to deceive in the run in. We had been hammered 7-1 away at Bradford City in the FA Cup First Round. I had a game to forget that day. We beat Bethesda in the first round of the Welsh Cup, only to have Cardiff stick it up us 1-3 at home. The League Cup was no different. We lost in the first round at Tranmere 2-1, so we had no cup runs to fall back on. It didn't happen for us this season.

In the shape of things to come, Alvan had sold big Ray Melczarek to Huddersfield for £20k and the likeable Sammy MacMillan to Southend for £1.5k. This was a transfer I never understood as Sammy and Albert (Kinsey) were, in my opinion, the most lethal up-front combination that we had. What had we done on the pitch under his stewardship?

A close inspection reveals that the team conceded more than four goals on nine occasions, and let in three goals on six occasions. As a result, our season went up in smoke.

So, a new season dawned, 1968/69, and Dave Carrick, 'Plonky' McLoughlin, Johnny Schofield, Sammy Mac, Ray Melczarek, George Showell, Don Weston and a few lesser lights had all gone, either transferred or, in George's case, retired to the backroom staff. Stuart Mason returned from Liverpool, without playing a single game for the Merseysiders. Peter Wall was soon to leave Anfield for Crystal Palace, leaving me to ponder what my own fate may have been.

Eddie May had arrived in the close season, as did Ray Charnley from Blackpool, and Ian Moir, half-way through the previous campaign. The ground staff started to appear, youngsters in the form of Booth, Macreath, Purdie, Jones and others.

I was in a dilemma. I had signed for Wrexham in February, 1966, and my contract ran until the end of June that year, with a new one-year contract and a year's option. My deal with Wrexham ran out on June 30, 1968.

Wrexham either had to re-sign me on a new contract or, if we were unable to agree terms, put me on the transfer list. The danger was if no one made an offer within a set period of time, I think it was a month, it may have been longer, and I refused the terms Wrexham offered, then I was free to sign for whomever I liked.

Information is the most valuable resource. Only Alvan knows which clubs made offers for me during the past two years. Wrexham still had to give Bristol City half of any agreed transfer fee. This clearly delayed my departure from Wrexham by some 12 to 15 months.

Alvan had a problem. He had sold half the team, but had kept me on the back burner, basically out of greed. He could sell everyone else and get the full value price and his commission. In his, and the club's terms, I was the least valuable because of the deal with Bristol City, which at the time, I had no knowledge of.

Now he had to negotiate a new contract with a player who was clearly upset that he wasn't getting the kind of money he should have been getting at a First Division club.

In those days, home telephones were a luxury. I'm sure that today, my phone would have been running hot. However, the nearest phone to our house was in a phone box at the top of Box Lane, half a mile away!

Only Alvan knew who had contacted the club, and he wasn't telling me. I took Dot and the kids to the meeting in the Wrexham Board Room. Only Alvan was present. He poured me a scotch and Dot a Bacardi and coke. The kids were told to sit still and the negotiations began.

He tabled a deal of a two-year contract on £24 a week, and £18 in the summer. Two wins a week, and the bonus put me into the £30 a week or more bracket

Dot looked quite impressed, but cool as you like, and without prompting, said "We've got two children now, Alvan..." She must have been talking to Agent Eve, I thought.

"OK, £25," was his immediate response.

I'd seen a wage packet in the pay office, so I knew that one of the Wrexham stalwarts was getting more than what Alvan was offering here. I felt like telling Alvan where to stick the contract, and sit it out.

Dot, what's that agent's number again?

I looked at Dot and the kids. I didn't want to put anything at risk, even though I knew that, in the end, I had all the cards. I should have demanding £30 or more a week, all year round, plus a signing on fee, free housing rental, appearance money, top four money, blah, blah, blah, turned around and walked out with the family. I didn't.

I forgave Jack and his ilk, and pondered the fact that player's agents were invaluable.

I lacked information. He knew more than me. He knew what I was worth at a First Division club. He'd seen the contracts.

In truth, I was happy at Wrexham. I was a big fish in a small pond. I liked the club, the friends, and the environment. I was being paid more, to do what I enjoyed doing most. It was a win for me, but we both knew it was temporary.

I knew the First Division awaited, Alvan had kept me and he would get his cut in the end.

Blackburn Rovers, Manchester City, Sunderland, West Bromwich Albion and Liverpool were just some of the First Division clubs that were mentioned as being interested in signing me during my time at Wrexham.

In pre-season, we played a game at home against Blackburn Rovers. I faced Bryan Douglas from left back, and England international. He saw out some 15 seasons with Blackburn, making 438 appearances and scoring the magic 100 goals. A goal every four games, not bad for a winger. Every manager alive would settle for that from the main striker, never mind a winger. He played 38 games for the national team, scoring 11 goals, and appeared in two World Cup tournaments, in1958 and 1962.

He wasn't quick enough to do me on the outside, so he kept cutting inside.

I missed a couple of tackles that would have sent him into the main stand, had I connected. I don't think my performance in that game did enough to alleviate any doubts that I was better than anyone else who might have been under consideration.

The back four at that time was myself, at left back, the twin centre halves were David Powell and Eddie May, while Steve Ingle was at right back. Eddie May had been signed from Southend in the close season, arguably one of Alvan's best decisions, and a young Gareth Davies was about to establish himself in the Wrexham side. It was getting lonely. Few of the players who had been at the club when I joined were still there. I was beginning to think that there was something about me that didn't gel!

I kept telling myself it was only a matter of time before I moved. The newspapers were full of transfer talk, so it had to happen. One Saturday paper reported that I had signed for Sunderland for £20,000-odd during the close season.

"Don't know anything about it," said Alvan as I flew down to the Racecourse Ground to find out what was going on.

Hmmm. I know he's lying.

Bring in the Agents.

The season started with a 1-2 loss at Aldershot. Then we had an unbeaten run of five games, including a League Cup win at home to Port Vale (2-0).

During this run, we did not concede a single goal, beating Bradford (3-0) and Grimsby (2-0), and playing draws against Workington (0-0) and Swansea (0-0).

On September 4, we were due to play Blackpool in the League Cup at home, and then it was on to Alvan's old stomping ground at Southend. If a replay were necessary with Blackpool, it would happen on September 9, a short five days after the original fixture. Unusual, but, in hindsight, it proved lucky for me.

Little did I know, but my last three games had been closely watched and they were all rippers. A draw at home to Second Division leaders Blackpool in the League Cup, a single goal loss at Southend, and a three goal defeat in the replay at Blackpool. It was never a game that warranted a three-goal margin, and I thought that we were hard done by on the night. The seeds of my going had been sown.

For the time being, the hamstring had been put to bed. It would soon be wakey, wakey time.

MATCH DAY TICKETS

T he home league game against Grimsby that year would end up being my last at the Racecourse as a Wrexham player.

Grimsby's Manager was Bill Harvey, the very same Bill who, two and a half years earlier, as coach at Bristol City, had driven me to my debut game for Wrexham against Southport.

Wrexham was a small town. Everyone knew the members of the local football team. If you did something, anything, somebody knew somebody who knew the inside story.

Dot would go to the butchers, Glyn, and would buy half a pound of mince, a pound of sausages and a couple of chops. When she went to pay, it would be, "OK, love, don't worry about that, ask Steve to leave a couple of tickets for the game on Saturday." She had no choice; Glyn would not take her money.

Two hundred weight of coal was delivered and it was the same thing; "Can Steve leave a couple at the gate and get my Billy's autograph book signed?"

Then there was the bloke at the fish and chip shop on a Friday night. A long queue watched me come in. Our favourite was cod and chips with curry sauce. The queue would shorten and he would say, in that Welsh lilt, "OK, boyo, good game on Saturday, how will we go?" Now everybody knew I was in the shop. I guess it was a form of advertising. We would have a little banter. Then I would order the usual cod, chips and curry. I would go to hand over the cash. "Tickets at the gates, OK Steve?" and he would push the money back. I'm not going to argue with him in a chippy, so off I go.

Les, the veg and fruit man from Liverpool; how he ever made any money, I don't know. He would come all the way from the 'Pool in his van to flog fruit and veggies around Wrexham and Chester.

Les was an older guy, and we became quite friendly. He seemed lonely and rarely talked about his family. He'd often stop and have a cup of tea with Dot and myself.

"Yep, two tickets Les, sure we'll have a beer after the game."

Players usually got two tickets each. On Saturday morning, when Dot said, 'Don't forget the tickets for Les.' I realised that I had failed to keep tabs on my commitments. I needed 13 tickets!

Picture this: all the tickets were left at the main entry door. You put your name on the envelope and the name of the person it was meant for. Your guest would turn up: "Steve Stacey has left me a couple of tickets."

"Name, please? Sorry, nothing here from Steve. Next please."

I canvassed the players. Sometimes you could swap dates if, for some reason, the boys didn't need the tickets. Dot had one spare; I managed to get another four from the lads. These were repayable, and would take four weeks to clear. If you were lucky, you could cash what you owed at an away game, if you had nobody travelling. Dot very rarely went to away games, because taking the kids with her on a bus trip half way across the country was, well, a little bit too much of an ask.

Sometimes, people didn't turn up at the gate and collect the tickets. This was no good to me. You didn't know the result of this until the game started and even then they may turn up late. Sometimes you could get a ticket from the office, but this would be for the less desirable area of the stand.

I needed another eight tickets. I had some promises, but I wasn't counting on any more from the team.

All the lads were assembled at 2pm. My only option was to heavy the ground staff kids, if I could find them. They had one ticket apiece.

There was one last resort, Bill Harvey, Manager of Grimsby Town

Football Club.

I hung around outside the dressing room waiting for the Grimsby coach. There were two problems with this plan. If the supporters' bus came with them, the odds were fifty/fifty I would get any tickets. It all depended on how well the people who travelled knew the players. If relations didn't travel, then you had a good chance. You could then let it be known that I would return the ticket favour when we played at Grimsby.

Secondly, I had to get to them before the home team supporters. Lots of punters would hang around the visitors asking for tickets on the free before they actually bought their own on the day. Pre-match sales were almost unheard of in those days.

Would Bill be a manager who got off first or last, I thought, hopping from one foot to another. If he got off last, the players may have already dolled out the tickets to supporters or hangers on. Luckily, Bill got off first.

Bill had been Fred Ford's managerial assistant while I was at Bristol City in the early days.

"Flash!" he said. "How are Dot and the family?"

"OK, She's looking forward to seeing you after."

"Aye we'll be on our way to the dinner stop after the game. Not having dinner in Wrexham." He said. Most teams made it out of the town they played in to have dinner after a game.

"How's Sue?" Bill's daughter and Dot had gone to the same school in Bristol and knew each other.

There was no supporter's bus as yet. Grimsby to Wrexham is about 150 miles. My guess was the bus was fairly close behind.

No good messing about, let's get to the point, "Bill, I need some tickets."

"How many? Four?"

Well, it's a start. Grab as many as I can get. I didn't stay to explain the nitty gritty.

Bill went into the dressing room and said something along the lines of "Give us your tickets, lads, if you got nobody travelling, it's urgent or I wouldn't ask." Another strategic planning arrangement for when we played at Blundell Park for me to put in the diary. Bill gave me the tickets.

We didn't do Bill any favours on the park, we blew them away 2-0.

SIGNING ON THE WING OF A PLANE

In between league fixtures, we took part in a charity game at Ellesmere Port, up near Manchester. Joe Mercer, the ex-Manchester City and England manager, was introduced to the teams. He got to me, smiled, took my hand and said to me, "Know anybody who wants a full back?" I was on a roll.

At the reception after the charity game, John Neal came to me and said, "We've agreed terms with a First Division club for your transfer."

He said he couldn't tell me who, but to be ready to be picked up at 8am the next day by him and Alvan.

Can you now imagine a player being called into the manager's office, or indeed the players agent being told a deal was lined up, but not being told who with?

Where's my agent?

Eight o'clock the next morning, the two amigos arrived. The only comment I could get out of either in the car in relation to where we were headed was when we were half way to Blackpool, and they revealed that was where we were going.

Blackpool, that made sense. I had just had two great games against a class Second Division team, who were likely to soon be a First Division team, those performances had obviously sealed it.

Then my mind suddenly registered that Blackpool was the home of the Football Association, then headquartered at Lytham St Annes. In order to have your transfer cleared, the papers needed to be lodged at Football HQ 48 hours before the kick off time of the game in which they intended to play you.

I had made an erroneous assumption.

Finally, Alvan revealed the truth. "Bill McGarry is flying in from Ipswich to talk to you."

"Flying? Bill who? Ipswich? Where the frig is Ipswich?"

Alvan knew, and so did John, that, after all the talk about Sunderland, Liverpool and Manchester City, Ipswich, last season's Second Division champions, who were about to play in the top league for the first time since early in the 60s, were unlikely to be my most popular choice.

They were right. My first reaction was, "Stop the car I want to get off. Let's go home!"

My thoughts raced. Think about it, Steve, it's still the First Division. No, wait it out. You're bound to get a more fashionable club come in for you, now that they know you're on the market again.

I wanted to call Dot, but there were no phones. There was no way of contacting her. I knew an immediate decision would be required, if these guys are flying up from East Anglia. Would Dot trust my judgment? If I say no, it's likely they will turn to their second choice. That's why they have a plane, Steve. No rushing down motorways, waiting for trains or buses, or hiring a car; just hop in the plane and fly off to the next target at Bury or Swindon. They've got you by the balls!

We drove to Blackpool Airport, and walked into the smallish terminal, but it had a lounge room and we went in there, where Alvan introduced me to Bill McGarry, the Ipswich manager, and Wally Gray, the club secretary.

"We'll go out here, Steve, on the tarmac," McGarry said.

"OK."

"Has Alvan told you anything about the move?"

I opted for a polite, "No, Mr. McGarry."

"Wally, give me the contract." Wally handed him the contract.

"No, the other one." Bill was exasperated.

I was right! Wally had given him another contract with another name. They were off to other hot spots if I wasn't agreeable. Difficult for Wally to mistake me for most of the other chaps currently playing professional football! Flying must have made him nervous.

Bill unfolded the contract on the starboard wing of a small aircraft nearby I looked back at the terminal as I walked to join him. Alvan and John were looking distinctly nervous, heads down, walking around and puffing on their interminable tobacco, John a cigarette, and Alvan the usual cigar.

I still hadn't made up my mind. Everything was up for grabs.

Remember, I was on £20 odd, a week, £4 for a win, and £2 for a draw, then £14 and Parkers bakery or Schweppes in the summer.

Bill lays the contract out on the wing of the plane and turns to me while he smooths out the paper with one hand.

"Steve, the contracts for two years, a one year option; £40 a week."

First team appearance money, £20. Usual win and draw bonus, £4, if we're in the top six in the league we pay, and he reeled it off, if the crowd exceeds…" off he went again.

Bottom line, in the top six and pulling in 20,000-plus crowds, I was on £100 a week. £100 a week! I had never seen £100 in one place at the same time in my life.

"You'll get your ten percent over the contract term. What do you say?" He concluded.

My response should have been: "Can I speak to the clubs taxation agent please, Mr McGarry?"

Again I point out, why, why, why wouldn't clubs pay out what you were due the day you signed?

Remember, some clubs would put you and the family up in a club house… and charge you rent!!!

What would Bill have said if I had responded: 'OK, Bill, I'll talk to my 'wealth agent, accountant, financial advisor, wife,' where am I going to live, in a barn?", or "OK, Bill, I'll take 40% on signing and the rest over the next 6 months!", or "Sorry, Bill, my tax agent says I need it all at once in order to buy a house and build my wealth," or, perhaps, "OK, Bill, I'll take all the money now and talk to the taxation people about paying anything due through the contract period."

Remember, he's got another contract in Wally's briefcase.

I was still in shock. Eventually I asked, "The £40 during the season, Mr. McGarry, how much during the close season?"

He gave me a quizzical look before answering, "£40. £40 every week, even during the close season."

"£40 every week even during the close season." I repeated, incredulously. McGarry must have thought he was dealing with an imbecile.

"Yes, £40 a week, every week of the year."

I had been cocooned at Wrexham for two years. From the club's point of view, why would they offer one of their best players more money if they could get him for peanuts year after year. This was where the fatherly advice I so much needed went AWOL.

I very much relished playing at Wrexham. Dot and I enjoyed the great social atmosphere, I would have gone on playing there for the rest of my career. It's not correct to say that I did not consider the future, over the possible progress or the advancement, I was comfortable, perhaps more comfortable than ambitious.

When I wanted a better contract, more money, someone to negotiate the club selling me the clubhouse, I had nobody to light the fuse. I let people lead me when I should have been the driver.

How easily the doubts are cast aside, for greed! No, it was not greed. It was practicality. I had a wife and two kids. I had the chance to double my salary overnight. Bill spread the contract on the wing of the plane again. He gave me the pen.

Then he indicated where I must sign. He signed the document, and asked the now returned Wally to witness both our signatures. Bill knew all about Dot, the two kids and me. He knew Fred very well. There were smiles all around, followed by handshakes and congratulations. The local photographer appeared and I redid the signing on the wing of the aircraft.

"I'll need you in Ipswich on Friday night," Bill said. "You can train at Wrexham for the rest of the week, then drive or catch a train. Train I think would be better." He then gave me the name of the hotel to register in on Friday. "You'll be in the first team, centre half."

Here was another twist of fate; what was going on in my life? I made my debut at Wrexham in a position I had never played before and now I was going to be making my First Division debut in a position I had hardly played at all, except in a few Western League games at a club where I was well and truly recognised as a full back.

I never asked who we were playing or where the game would be. We could be travelling somewhere on Saturday morning. I didn't ask!

Alvan and John were all smiles. We all said our farewells. I just hoped that Dot and the kids would like East Anglia. We travelled in silence for a while.

"Travelling on Friday, Stace?" said Alvan, breaking the silence.

"Yeh. Who we playing, John?" I asked.

John pulled out the fixture book.

"Holy Moses… Liverpool at home!"

I went over the contract terms again and again. Dot would be pleased, I thought. Then it hit me. Friends, good friends, we would miss them. Mrs. D, Mr. Evans, The Miners Club, Glyn the butcher, Les the travelling grocer, Bill and Ben's baby sitters, the boys, cards in the back of the bus.

When you have to go, you have to go. You can't stay for the good times. This is yours and your family's future.

The local paper, the Wrexham Leader, led with the story on Friday. It was a bad week for stalwart Wrexham fans, who had been in the wilderness for years without any success.

Dave Powell had gone to Sheffield United on Wednesday, for a fee reported to be £18,000, but the inside story put it at more, quite a bit more; big Ray Mielczarek had gone to Huddersfield previously and now I had been sold. The paper had a few things to say.

The paper asked all the right questions:

How can you win promotion if you sell half a team?

Has the club got any interest in promotion?

Were the Directors only interested in protecting their own interest (financial) in the club?

Do we have to watch Fourth Division football all our lives?

The sale of three star players that clearly represented the backbone of the defensive set up was not something that could be hidden away. It's a lot to ask patient fans to handle. The Leader's sports writer, Ron Challoner, predicted that fans would desert the club in droves.

Only 48 hours earlier, Alvan had denied that a bid had been made for Dave and reiterated that the club would be 'reluctant' to sell any more players. Not very savvy for a manager to pursue that line, when clearly it was untrue. This was Alvan's problem; he wasn't believable.

The question remains. Was Alvan on a percentage of player transfer fees in place of a higher salary?

Had the Board given him the ultimatum?

Alvan you promised promotion… where is it?

This is what I think.

Alvan's on the brink; he promised promotion and a thriving youth development policy.

He's got a forward plan… remember, after leaving Wrexham he goes into the pub business, and now he realises he can't deliver on his club issues. He needs collateral.

I've postulated that he's been given the results-or-else quandary.

So he sells Dave and I, along with big Ray's previous departure.

The club sack him, but he has his percentage on the players sold, Dave, Big Ray and me.

After Dave and I left, Wrexham lose four games on the trot without scoring a goal, the residue of selling half a team.

Alvan was sacked as manager soon after my departure, and the man who everyone respected as a more effective leader, John Neal, was appointed in his place. My biggest regret on leaving Wrexham was that I wasn't about when John Neal had the job, and shared in the subsequent unqualified success that the team enjoyed over the next few years.

We were sad to leave Wrexham, Dot and I. We had many friends and had not only enjoyed the football but the social life that made it a club then. The kids were just making friends of a sort. Michele was at school and Nat not far away. Wrexham had made me feel good about my family and myself. I'm not sure that this kind of environment is generated any more. It was something special.

TOP FLIGHT FOOTBALL

I pswich had gained promotion to the First Division, as it was called then, during the 1967/68 season by a single point (59) in front of QPR and Blackpool (58). QPR pipped Blackpool by the smallest of margins, goal average.

What should have been the highlight of my career turned into a 'Welcome to my bad dream… nightmare, even.'

Every player's ambition is to play First Division football. Any boy with any aspirations to play professional sport wants to play at the highest level possible. They want to test themselves alongside and against the best. I was no different, and the move to Ipswich looked like I was going to have the opportunity to realise that dream.

Sadly, I can only say that my time at Ipswich was not as memorable as I would have liked. The nagging hamstring that I had dealt with for most of my career was about to become the most important issue in my career to date, for my whole career even.

I was due to travel to Ipswich by train on Friday after the training session at Wrexham. We were doing some sprints on the Friday morning at the Racecourse and I felt a tightening in my left hamstring area. It was definitely a twinge. I eased up and just jogged around the track a couple of times and followed that with some stretches. All seemed fine.

I bade my former teammates farewell and they generously gave me some advice on how to handle the Liverpool team the next day. I was on my way to the big time.

I was leaving behind a smoking time bomb. Alvan was under pressure from all sides; the chairman, the board, newspapers, fans and players. I was sad to leave but excited about what lay ahead.

Reg Tyrell, one of the youth team scouts, and support staff, met me at the station and took me straight to the local hotel.

A photographer popped in to take a few photographs, but other than that I was left on my own. I must say I thought it strange that there was not a more formal greeting, but still, I had an evening to myself. I went to the cinema and saw Anzio, with Robert Mitchum, which was about the allied landings in Italy during WW2.

On my first day, the only other person I met associated with Ipswich Town was a young Laurie Sivell, the reserve team keeper who was sat in front of me in the cinema with his girlfriend.

The next day, Reg picked me up in the morning and duly delivered me to the ground. I was nervous. Most of my football career had been spent in the backyard of the Fourth Division, and now I was being asked to test my mettle against arguably one of the best teams in Europe, playing at centre half, where I hadn't played on a regular basis since my last days at Bristol City. Today, I would be marking Roger Hunt, a Liverpool and England favourite. The thought of that was enough to make anyone nervous.

I was conscious in the dressing rooms of the inquisitive looks, which seemed to all say, "Can this guy play? From the Forth Division, this is a tough ask…" Never did I think, for one minute, that any of the looks had anything to do with the colour of my skin, even though I was the only non-white in the dressing room. I had become used to that loneliness.

It wasn't a good start. All I wanted was to get a first touch, whether it was some delicate little flick or a hump to the stand. I admit I was overawed by it all.

There is the old saying that a game is just a game, but this statement eliminates the notion of anxiety, inner confidence and self-doubt about whether you are going to measure up. I had never suffered nerves as I did that day. Making this huge leap of three divisions and slotting straight into the first team had always been the dream, but in reality it was a gigantic step.

Was I good enough? McGarry thinks so. I told myself, 20-odd grand, that is a lot of money. With that price tag comes expectation from the Ipswich faithful and hierarchy. Here I was, for the first time, doubting my own ability. I felt even more isolated as the dark stranger on the biggest stage in English league football.

To some, although it was never spoken of at the time, I was this flag bearer for coloured footballers, but when I should have been standing proud, I felt isolated and doubtful. I felt so alone I may as well have been on a desert island.

I finally got my first meaningful touch and won a free kick on the right hand side of the park, which led to a great cheer from the crowd. Not long after, I froze at a corner and gave big Roger a free header. Luckily for me, it whistled over the bar.

As my confidence started to grow, I began to get forward, and took on Emlyn Hughes on the edge of the box. He bowled me over and I looked to the referee, pleading for a penalty. The referee waved play on, and as he does so, smiles at me as if to say 'you are kidding, son, aren't you?'

I felt as if I was just settling into the pace of the game. It was very different from Wrexham, there was more control and patience shown by all the players. Liverpool played a long ball down through the middle of the park and Ian Callaghan and myself were in a race, which I was winning, when I have this sharp pain behind the left thigh. It's the hamstring.

I fell over immediately. The sensation was just like being kicked in the back of the leg and, in desperation, I claim that Ian has kicked me. He hasn't, of course! It was simply how a severe hamstring strain felt like. I tried to stand but couldn't without help. Jimmy Forsyth, the trainer, came on and helped me up and then led me off, to much sympathy from the crowd. What a start! Just 30 minutes into my debut and it was all over. The pain was excruciating.

In the dressing room, the club doctor comes in and gently feels my leg. He nods and says that it is, as he suspected, a hamstring. He knew as soon as I went down what the problem was. It's bad and he tells me I will be out for a while. I was devastated.

At half-time, and at the end of the game, which Liverpool won 2-0, there are condolences all round. The manager, Bill McGarry, has a few words with me, but what can one say?

I have to thank this man for giving me the chance at the big time. I wish I could do something about it, but I can't. He gambled and lost. What I would call the biggest day of my fledgling career has ended in disaster. I sat there in the home dressing room, head in my hands, thinking, what have I done to deserve this?

I get the train to London, along with the Liverpool team, and onward to our northerly destinations. Bill Shankly bought me dinner and invited me to join the 'lads'. I was too disappointed and spent most of the journey in miserable isolation. I could read it on the faces of the troops. There but for the grace of God go I.

We had a conversation, Shanks and I. It was a fatherly chat. He encouraged me, and told me to forget what happened today and get on with it. He told me I was a decent player and had a future in the game. He didn't mention Fred or the fact, as I believed, that he might have been interested in signing me at an earlier stage of my career. He was a likeable man and I regret not having been able to play for him. His taking the time to encourage me after such a shattering day showed what a leader he was. I have never forgotten that time spent with a true football legend.

I got home and Dot wasn't up to date with the news, having heard nothing, and she was devastated when I told her.

I duly reported to Portman Road on Tuesday. At that time, the venue had a reputation for an almost perfect lush playing surface, and I thought that perhaps this might have contributed to my injury. I had mentioned this to a reporter after the match and the groundsman Fred - whose surname name escapes me - wasn't happy!

I tried to explain myself by telling him it was a tribute to his skill as a groundsman that the playing surface was so good. I am glad to say we parted as friends.

In November, Bill McGarry departed to become the Wolves manager and was soon to take Danny Hegan with him. Cyril Lea, the genial Welsh international, and first team coach, took on the managerial duties. Cyril remained in charge until early January, 1969, when Bobby Robson was appointed. During this period, I spent a great deal of time on the treatment table, and seeing doctors as well as the inside of hospitals.

Jimmy Forsyth was an old gnarled Scottish ex-player, and in his time had been manager, coach and physio at the club. In my view, he was a lovable and compassionate veteran of the game. He and I had some long discussions. I was on the table twice a day for a long period of time, so we had time for conversation. I think I discussed with Jimmy, more than anyone else at the club, the problems and challenges that I was facing. He, like Fred Ford, understood the deeper issues and I was thankful for his advice and support.

I want to put into perspective how serious this injury issue had become. The Liverpool game had taken place on September 14, 1968. The original diagnosis of two weeks was sadly wide of the mark. As soon as I returned to Portman Road, it was confirmed that the injury was as serious as the club doctor had anticipated. It wasn't until 28 days later that I made my comeback, in a reserve game at Bournemouth. But I never made it through the 90 minutes.

At the first sign of the twinge, I signalled to the bench and off I went. It was a hamstring strain on the original injury. This is what happens when you try to return too early.

The next two months were probably the worst of my career. I honestly thought that it was all over. I finally walked onto the pitch at Birmingham. I have never been more apprehensive. I don't remember much about the game. The longer it went on, the more I expected to feel pain at the back of my leg. It never came. When the referee blew the final whistle, I was ecstatic. It had been 63 days since I walked off the field at Bournemouth!

I joined Ipswich in September, 1968, and left finally for Bristol City in October, 1970. There were 42 games in the league season at that time. Ipswich had played just eight games when I joined them, so there were 34 games left.

In 1969/70, a whole season, there were another 42 league games. In 1970/71, I finally signed for Bristol City, after a two month loan period.

There was a total of 84 possible league games I could have played for Ipswich, but the record shows that, between joining and leaving, I played just three first team games and made 33 appearances in the London Combination or reserve team.

The rest of my time at the club was spent overcoming my infernal hamstring injury. That was 36 games in total, out of a possible 84.

I spent loan periods at Charlton (two games), Chester (one game) and Northampton. I don't recall playing a single game at Northampton. This may have been due to a return of the injury during training.

The bottom line is this: in 1968/69, I played 17 reserve team games at Ipswich. In 69/70, I played 12 and in 70/71, before I left, just four. I think this gives some insight as to the nature and severity of the injury. It was unbearable; all I wanted to do was play football. To spend so much time out of the game makes it very hard to maintain your effectiveness as a professional football player.

In order to reinforce my newfound status, as a First Division player, I had upgraded my car!! A glitzy dark blue V4 Ford Corsair replaced the Ford Anglia. Once in Ipswich we moved into a clubhouse in Belstead.

Opposite lived Danny Hegan. Peter 'Diesel' Morris was at the bottom of the road, and John O'Rourke just a short distance away. Next door to us lived Bob and Sheila Coombs and their sons, Tom and Bill.

Bob was an American Vietnam veteran attached to the Woodbridge/Bentwaters USAF base. The young lads were extremely polite and friendly. I took them down to the ground a couple of times and they lapped it up. I think youngsters everywhere look on in awe of the facilities and people that they meet at professional sporting venues.

As for Bob's wife, Sheila, she was English and came from the very same place that Dot was born, Plymouth, in Devon!! I think it fair to say that the families bonded. Through that family, and an airbase sergeant, I spent some happy hours with the Americans at the airbase.

There were times when I thought of Clarence up on the base. I imagined him driving his lorry to deliver or collect goods from or to the airbase during WW2.

There were no footprints here. Just a little of America that allowed me to dream on for a while. Would I ever see my father?

Bobby Robson was appointed manager of Ipswich on January 13, 1969.

Most people know of the great man's career so I won't repeat it here, except to say that, prior to Ipswich, Bob had coached, in conjunction with the Hungarian star Ferenc Puskas, the Vancouver Whitecaps, and then at Fulham, where he was dismissed after they were relegated from the First Division.

Ipswich had, at this time, a group of older professionals who, as some would say, 'thought that they owned the club'. The stage was set for a showdown. The new manager was keen to impose his will and style on the club.

The first time I met Bobby was just after he was appointed. I was walking through the stand area where the offices were located. I was in the corridor, and there was no one else around. We couldn't miss each other. I was walking one way and he the other.

I looked at him, and he looked at me, and we both kept walking on and past each other without a word being said. He must have been deep in thought. Maybe he had no idea who I was.

Players pick up vibes about managers. I liked Fred and Jack Rowley. I disliked Alvan Williams and, for some reason, felt that I couldn't warm to Bobby Robson as a person, a different issue to whether someone is a competent or successful manager.

It was soon clear that there were other players around the place whose feelings went deeper than that, who publicly vented their anger at the new manager. Perhaps they thought that he was not fashionable enough for them and their perceived 'positions' in the club as elder statesmen, but let me say this; Bobby Robson was the first manager that I knew who explained exactly what he meant and what he wished from his team.

He represented change in the way he did things; in how he explained tactics, and how he wanted his team to play. He stressed the importance of possession above all else. He communicated with his players about his goals and what he wanted from them. It was all business with Bob.

Our training would differ. There was much more emphasis on fitness. He valued elegance rather than crunch. His mantra was; 'When we have the ball, we attack, all of us attack, and when they have the ball, we defend, all of us defend.'

We would do so many thousand yards of sprints. The so called 'doggies' were in abundance; pre-season training meant no excuses, be careful what you eat and drink because if you didn't, everyone might be privy to what you had for breakfast the next session.

I smoked my last ever cigarette at Ipswich, a Benson and Hedges filter tip. I recall one of the sessions around the practice area adjacent to the ground. I was struggling a little, and stopped to clear my throat. I then proceeded to bring up a dark thick mess that scared the life out of me, and from that day to this, I have never smoked a cigarette. Thanks Bob!!

My gut feeling about him was that he was detached, a rather cold personality.

I realised early on that I wasn't going to go far with Bob at the helm, and was sadly resigned to that fact. Foolishly, I allowed the feelings to get personal.

It wasn't about me or whether I fitted into the plan, it became 'its all Robson's fault,' and I put my failure to progress in the manager's court. Of course, it was nothing of the sort; what you do in training and on the pitch is exclusively in the realm of the player. I thought that I was being treated unfairly. I regressed into childhood.

I was nowhere near to getting a recall to the first team. Mick McNeil, a former England player, got the nod over me when I may have expected a game, but in the end it was all about certainty. Mick was a touch player and I wasn't. Even then, I thought my days were numbered.

Towards the end of the season, in April, 1969, I finally made it back into the team.

In hindsight it looked as though I may have conquered the hamstring. I'd put together a few games in the reserves and now I had my chance.

What I wanted was for someone to say to me, "Look, Steve,

understand the problem; you've got half a dozen games to justify your next contract with a First Division club."

Southampton at home, and I took another wallop. I thought, "this really hurts." I clenched my teeth and carried on. For a moment, it looked as though I was going off, and the silence around Portman Road was deafening.

I thought that I did all right. We drew 0-0 and I retained my place for the next game: Liverpool, at Anfield.

Thursday before the Saturday game at Liverpool, Robson made it clear. "Have a beer or two tonight if you wish, but we have a big game Saturday." We also had a hit on the local golf course.

At Anfield, Bill Shankly, Liverpool's much admired manager, is in the corridor leading to the changing rooms and, as we pass, he's talking to no one in particular, "...look at 'em, can't play, we're going to do it today," and other such comments to put us off our game.

As it happens, he was right.

We were comprehensively outplayed, and lost 4-0. Mick Mills, later to play for England under Robson, had a bad day. Peter Thompson took him to pieces and scored the first goal. I thought that, given the circumstances, I did OK at left back. I was marking Bobby Graham at outside right. Bobby's claim to fame was that, on his debut, he scored a hat trick against Aston Villa! I contained him on the day, but the nerves got to me with my ball distribution. I was prone to the longer pass, rather than keeping possession.

I was dropped for the next game against WBA and that, as they say, was that. It was my last game for the Ipswich first team and my last game in the First Division.

I had a conversation with Cyril Lea as the next team sheet went up. These weren't the days when managers told you that you were dropped, or what the reason was, if any. It would have been be nice to know. The team sheet got pinned on the board and my name wasn't on it.

Cyril was honest, although reluctant, as most assistants would be, to contradict the manager. Cyril gave me a nod when I asked if he would have kept me in the side.

One of the other issues that failed to lift my relationship with Robson was a more personal one. The team went to Canada to play a friendly with the manager's former club, the Vancouver Whitecaps. The decision on who was to go was made and he never spoke to me. Whether I was going or not was immaterial. What I was seeking was some polite kind of talk or discussion that I wasn't going and being given the reason why. I was quite hurt by this. I took it extremely personally.

I took Dot and Bill and Ben to Spain for a holiday, instead of Vancouver. One of the first bars we went into had a team picture of Ipswich on the wall. After a bit of a discussion with the owners and a passing policeman we all decided it was, indeed, me in the picture.

At the beginning of the 1969/70 season, I was on a downer.

During pre-season training, I had left my beloved Ford Corsair in the car park, and the firm that was painting the floodlights failed to take the proper precautions and my treasured vehicle ended up covered in gray spots. After wasting time dealing with the insurance company, who didn't want to pay, but eventually coughed up, I eventually had the car repaired and re-sprayed into a more favoured gray with a black roof.

I managed 12 reserve games this year and still couldn't shake off the injury problem. I got Dot to ring John Neal at Wrexham. She told him I was keen to return. John promised to do what he could, but it was too hard. Ipswich wanted their money back and neither John nor Wrexham had £20k-plus. I was going to have to wait it out.

The 'McGarry Crew' was very much against the new manager and his new ways. Billy Baxter and Tommy Carroll were two Ipswich veterans. Shortly after Bobby's arrival, we were undertaking one of the new training sessions. It was along the lines of three-on-three, and if your opponent receives the ball, and you are more than two yards away from him, you had to do press-ups.

Bill and Tom were having none of this. They sulk and refuse to take part. They told Robson, "You're treating us like wee bairns." Well, that was the start of it. At some point it led to punches being thrown and then players, including myself, pulling the antagonists apart. It was a pitiful scene.

Then, at the beginning of the season, several players had failed to report for pre-season training. I am sad to say that I was one of them, along with Baxter, Carroll and one or two more. I don't know why I chose this course of action. I guess sometimes, the innocent are easily led. In my own mind, I felt I was being treated unfairly. The club had paid £20k-plus for me, why am I not being given a game? This, and other convoluted thoughts, addled my brain.

After a few days I, along with the others, turned up for training. Nothing was said. Then I found out that Bobby had fined me a week's wages, £40, a fortune then. I had no other means of support, no savings, so this was going to be difficult. I had not thought through the consequences of my actions.

I rang the chairman, John Cobbold. He and his driver, Roger, used to roam Ipswich in a red Rover 2000, fitted with a television. He would front up at the local downtown pub on a Wednesday (he owned Cobbold Brewery) and, as all the players knew, he would always buy a meal and the drinks were on the house.

I explained to him what had happened and that it was going to be difficult to feed the family this week. "Don't worry," he said, "I'll fix it." About an hour later, Roger turned up on the doorstep with an envelope with £40 in it. As he handed it to me, he said, "Mr. John says… trust this will be enough and, in the future, and I quote Mr.

John, 'f…..g behave yourself.'" I asked him to thank the chairman, and tell him I would take note of his advice. He was a gentleman who will never be forgotten.

I was not in a good place in my head, and the inevitable happened, I had my first real confrontation with the manager. I had been selected as 12th man for a reserve game. I decided, in my wisdom, that this was beneath me and told Bob so.

In the warm up for the training session on Friday, which was usually a very light session, I felt the hammy playing up. I told Cyril Lea, who sent me off to see Jimmy Forsyth. I was on the table when Bobby burst in and, in no uncertain terms, asked Jimmy if I'd be fit for Saturday. Jimmy asked me, and I told Bobby that it was very sore and that I would rather not play. Heated words were soon exchanged.

I think that, with the 'McGarry Crew' making life hard for him, he felt that this was another part of the playing group undermining the manager. This was not true.

I didn't play, but on Monday I asked to see Bobby after training. I asked for a transfer.

The meeting was cordial and he tells me, "Stace, where could I get a player of your calibre for £25k?" Of course, I know he is just trying to make me feel good. I had no answer. In fairness to the man, he never again condemned me to the reserve bench without a game. Time was running out for me, I knew that. Clearly, I was not included in the manager's plans, so it was time to wait until an opportunity arose.

My sojourn at Ipswich was almost over.

I had loan games at Chester, Northampton and Charlton.

I had had a conversation with Wrexham's John Neal, but Bobby wanted Ipswich to get their money back.

Wrexham didn't have therequired £20k-plus.

Dave Bowen, the Welsh international team manager, was at

Northampton, and the well-respected Eddie Firmani was manager at Charlton. Bobby had chosen the potential loan clubs well.

Bobby had made up his mind. I think, in the end, he was actively looking to offload me. He may have rung Bristol City to see if they would be interested. I received a phone call asking if I would be interested in a loan arrangement.

I always believe that going back to an old club is not a good idea. Wrexham was a different kettle of fish, Dot and I both wanted to go back there. So Dot and I formulated a plan. We would go back to Bristol, check it out, and if we didn't both favour the move, then we would go back to Ipswich, and seek a transfer. Then they would have the problem of either negotiating a new contract or getting rid of me on the cheap.

At the back of my mind was this old dilemma. The epitome of professional football was to get to the top, play in the First Division, alongside and against the best in the country. Why leave unless you had to, or had no control over the situation? Getting to that level is the hardest part; only the best make to the top. Therefore, you need to hold on as long as you can, hold on until you can chose the moment to leave, and when it is a move that will suit you.

I get it.

Taking the family back home to Bristol was a gamble. I knew in reality that asking Dot and my family to go back to Bristol and then to leave again was not going to work, so we moved, lock, stock and barrel, back to Bristol. We moved into a hotel first and then a flat. Alan Dicks, the manager, asked why I couldn't stay with my parents. This was never an option, there were four and there simply wasn't enough room.

As we left for Bristol, I knew in my heart that we were leaving Ipswich for good.

BACK TO BRISTOL CITY

I rejoined Bristol City for a loan period. As usual, the contract details were furthermost in my mind. City added a fiver to my basic pay, making it £45 a week and the usual bonuses.

My first game back for the Robins was a game on a Saturday at Sheffield United's Bramall Lane on September 5. The lads were staying overnight in Derby and I caught up with them there, having safely deposited Dot and the kids in Bristol.

I roomed with Trevor Jacobs. Trev was a full back who was having a bad time at the club, and I was going to replace him. It was an interesting decision to pair us up.

I started the game at right back and, before you could blink, we were soon three up and cruising. It was just as well we scored a few early in the game as, by the end, we were hanging on at 3-3. In the end, we were lucky to escape with a draw.

My habit of collecting injuries continued, but not the hamstring this time. I got a four-stitch cut after a tussle with the superbly talented Tony Currie. I returned to the fray in a desperate attempt to help the lads hang on to the point. I met Currie in the treatment room after the game and had a little 'discussion'.

Despite the wound, it was good to be back. Being back at your old club put a different perspective on things. At least there was a reference point for discussions regarding players and managers. The manager at the time was Alan Dicks, who led the Robins for 13 years from 1967. He was another one of the new breed of managers, much like Robson, in many ways. But it was clear at this time that there were some serious changes afoot in the way that clubs and players were to be managed in the future. It was a long way from the 60s, and the game was to profit greatly from this change.

Alan, like Robson, was a little aloof, not necessarily wanting to be your friend. He was all business, and talked the modern language of football development.

He had had me watched at Ipswich and mentioned that the report had contained a few issues, but in the main he welcomed me back for the trial.

At this point it's worth considering the kind of season that City were eventually in for. In Alan's first season, (1967/68), City finished 19th with 36 points and, for a couple of seasons after that, it didn't get much better. In 68/69, they were 16th with 38 points and the following year, 69/70, 14th with 39 points.

In my first season, the team finished 19th with 31 points.

The club was going nowhere fast, and some may have considered him a very lucky manager to survive at such an ambitious club. Nevertheless, the defensive flaws were being exposed as we also drew the next game, at home to Hull City, 3-3. We were 2-0 up close on half-time, when goalkeeper Mike Gibson, rolled me a ball on the edge of the box, which I completely stuffed up, and Chris Chilton put Hull back into the game.

It wasn't until after the away defeat at QPR, and the home draw with Blackburn Rovers, that we managed a win at home to Birmingham City, a game watched very carefully by Bobby Robson. Bobby said that I did alright, but clearly it wasn't enough for him as I was about to sign a final permanent deal with Bristol City.

Bristol City are drawn away to Blackpool in the League Cup. Blackpool are with home ground advantage and are clear favourites.

I was at right back on the night and my direct opponent was Tony Coleman.

At Blackpool, I had him in my pocket. He couldn't get past me at all and he was becoming increasingly frustrated as the game enters its climax and Blackpool are eliminated at home 1-0.

There had been one or two scuffles, close encounters with elbows and legs flying, during the game, but at the final whistle, as we march off down the tunnel, the home crowd are venting their disappointment at their players. Tony eyed me down the tunnel, having refused the post match handshake. I could not have cared less, I had done my job and we had won. As I brushed past him, he took offence, pushed me and had a kick as well.

A fight breaks out. It was a scuffle and a half. We had to be separated and I was wondering what the problem was with this idiot. I know he had a reputation, but trying to sort it out in the tunnel was unusual.

Was this frustration, racism or just a player asking where has the stardom gone?

It's a difficult call and one I can't answer. There was no verbal assault, no name-calling. Maybe that is because, on the field, we are all brothers. What goes on in one's mind, however, is a far different issue. It may have been racial but most likely it was simply a case of it was not happening for him that night, and this guy on the opposing side happens to be black.

It proved to be a defining season for Bristol City. The next seven games on the trot were lost; only two of them were at home. In the end, the Robins were four points clear of relegation. It was a very close call.

The club must have considered themselves very lucky indeed. Alan must have considered himself even luckier. His four-year stint as manager had seen the Robins average 36 points per season and an average table position of 17th. Most managers would surely have been asked to leave with such a dismal record. Maybe the Directors saw something that others couldn't.

Dot and I, along with the children, were staying at a hotel in

Clifton, paid for by the City, and we later moved into a flat in the same area. Alan gave me reminders every couple of days as to how much it was costing the club, and why couldn't I move in with my parents. I got a bit fed up with all this and I told him one day to 'give it a rest.'

In the meantime, the City had pointed me in the direction of what was then a small village, some 15 miles or so south of Bristol, called Nailsea. The club was, in truth, terrific. They paid the deposit on the house, £500, which then was a lot of money for a house that cost £3,500. Stephen Kew, a board member and a solicitor, did the legal work for free. We were proud of our Nailsea home, Dot and I. It was our first home that we owned and I was, to the best of my knowledge, the first in my family to own a house.

On October 20 I played what was to become my final game with the Robins. We had played at Sunderland on the Saturday and moved on to Middlesbrough for the game on Tuesday evening. We had lost at Sunderland 0-1, and the same fate befell us at Ayresome Park. I did my hamstring in the first half and had to leave the pitch. I was devastated again. 'How long can this go on?' I asked myself.

I would have been shattered if anyone had told me then that I had played my last game for the City.

I had a couple of run-ins soon after with Alan, or AD as he liked to call himself, that contributed to my demise. However, let me point this out first up; in my rush to get back home, I had neglected to check the contract details, didn't listen properly or both. I signed the papers in front of me, but I didn't check the detail. So I was at fault.

What the City had done was, in essence, take on my redundant Ipswich contract. This expired at the end of the current season, June, 1970. Careless of me yes; foolish, yes; my own fault, yes. I could not blame anyone else. So, a couple of run-ins with the manager certainly didn't help my cause.

Near the end of the season, I received a message to go and see the manager after training. He told me I was leaving and showed me the contract. I was gobsmacked. Why didn't I read the contract earlier? He clearly had me by the short and curlies.

I could not understand why the City went to all that trouble to settle us in Nailsea, if my playing career with them was to end when the season did. I was pretty depressed. I'd come from one dark place at Ipswich and walked into another.

I had seriously been contemplating on my decision to return to Ashton Gate but now it was too late. The decisions had been made for me. For the first time, while still in my mid-20s, I considered putting football second and getting a 'real job.'

I was blaming everyone except myself; Fred, for selling me to Wrexham without telling me about the 'on sale' clause; Alvan, for manipulating the transfer to Ipswich when other clubs had been in the hunt; Bobby Robson, for the perceived snub on keeping a £25k player in the reserves; and AD, moving me on from the City after just a few months.

I reflected on the fact that I had no one to talk to about these issues. I'm not making excuses, but I just wish I had had another male figure around to bounce ideas off. My depression worsened when I realised that it was me, and me alone, who had made these weak and ineffective decisions. Dot was amazing, she would have moved anywhere with me. I am not sure that I realised that at the time, as I was so wrapped in my own career and living the dream.

Now I had to contemplate where the next contract was coming from.

We were well settled in Nailsea. Dot was a section manager at the local supermarket, and the kids loved school. We had lots of friends, some of whom we still see from time to time. All I needed was a club.

One day, I received a telephone call from one of the all time football greats, John Charles. He was a giant of a man and a truly great player. Despite playing for Leeds United from 1948/49 to 55/56 in the Second Division, which is quite remarkable given his status, he was best known for his time at Italian giants Juventus. He won 38 Welsh caps to back that up and played in the 1958 World Cup finals. He was a giant of a man, both on the pitch and literally.

One would have expected that one of the major clubs at the time would have snapped him up as their manager, but instead, he became player manager of Merthyr Tydfil in Wales.

The previous season, 1970/71, he had been managing and playing (34 appearances and 12 goals) for Hereford United, who played in the Southern League at the time.

"Steve, I'm taking the lads on a trip to France, four days, and a game at Brest. I've checked it out with the City and they say it's OK for you to come."

It wasn't a good start!! I caught the train to Bath and met the boys there. It wasn't until I met the coach at Bath that I realised I had forgotten my passport. We had to get moving as we had a boat to catch at Southampton. The police, thank goodness, retrieved my passport from Nailsea and ensured that somewhere along the way I had the precious document in my hand. It made back page news in the Evening Post!

We finally arrived in Brest after an interesting ride. Dot had asked me to fetch her back some French lingerie!! In my broken French, I asked the lady who owned the hotel to direct me to where I could find some lingerie and 'du brassiere.' Those schooled in French would realise that she must have thought that I was mad asking to buy some lingerie and a shop!

The confusion was alleviated when the young receptionist went upstairs and returned with a black brassiere, held it across her chest and then pointed and said in French, "Is this what you're looking for?" She then offered to take me to the shop and buy the items Dot had requested. I accepted, and so, too, did half the team who took great pride in her choice of bras and pants!

We had a grand time. We ate beautiful food, drank wine, diluted of course, at breakfast, had a visit to the dry dock, which once housed the mighty 'Tirpitz', and had numerous chances to practice our French with the locals.

Come the game, I played alongside John in a dual centre half role. He was in his 40s then, but still his huge physical presence and his dominance in the air was impressive.

It lifted me out of my doldrums. I must have made an impression, too, because after the game I was asked to stay and play for Brest FC!! Also, John said that he would be happy to have me at Merthyr.

The deal was to train twice a week with the team. The money wasn't as good as at the City, of course, but a job was promised at the local accounting office owned by one of the directors. A house would be provided, and I was assured that the club would 'look after me'. I trusted John.

John promised to call me in a few days, and he did. However, while waiting for that call, John Newman, from Exeter City, had called me and offered me a guaranteed two-year contract.

He knew about Merthyr, and knew what he was up against. He didn't have much trouble in persuading me to join Exeter, who were then in the Fourth Division. The club agreed to pay the same as I was on at Bristol City.

I rang John Charles and told him that I had been offered the chance to stay in the football league and that this was the major determining factor in my decision. He understood, and wished me well. Before he hung up, he said something akin to "Don't forget where we are." I assured him that I wouldn't.

EXETER CITY

John Newman was a well-respected player and manager, having played for Birmingham, Leicester, and Plymouth before moving on to Exeter, where he became manager in 1969, and remained in charge until 1976. He was player-manager until 1972.

On August 14, 1971, I made my first appearance for Exeter. It is strange how, the longer you hang around in life, the more that coincidences spring up. My first game for Exeter, as it had been for Wrexham, was at Southport. It was memorable for all the wrong reasons. We were beaten 4-0.

In those days, Exeter and Plymouth were arguably the most travelled teams in the league. Exeter to Bristol was 80 miles and on to Plymouth was 40 miles. This meant that, every other week, you had this long haul until you made any headway into the trip. Barrow, Workington, Hartlepool, Crewe and Carlisle were marathon coach journeys. Going there wasn't so bad; it was the long journey home, especially if you had been beaten, that was the problem.

Exeter, in fairness, was the first club at which I wasn't moved all around the park, position-wise. In all my time there, I either played at right back, or, most often, left back.

Training was interesting and thoughtful. Again, there was a strong emphasis placed on fitness.

Our first season was a bit ordinary. I was back on the old familiar hunting grounds, Lincoln, Crewe, Barrow, and Grimsby. It was like a trip 'back to the future'. Wherever we went I recalled past struggles with Wrexham, who had been promoted, so at least I was spared the revisit. At Aldershot, I remembered little Nat being born; at Grimsby, I thought of old Bill Harvey; I remembered my loan periods from

Ipswich at Northampton and Chester; and so it went on.

We won only one of the eight opening games and found ourselves 21st in the last league in the land. Here we go again, I thought. We had lost the opening game of the season at Southport 0-4. We were then trounced at home in midweek by, of all teams, the Pirates, Bristol Rovers, in a League Cup game 0-3.

We lost the first home league game of the season to Grimsby 3-4. That was 11 goals we had conceded in three games.

John Newman called us together and, quite deservedly, gave more than a rocket or two. 'Nutty' or 'Nut', as he was affectionately called, thought that he might steady the ship himself. After the first two league games, he included himself as player-manager against Northampton away. We drew 1-1. He played again at Workington away and we had another draw, this time 0-0. He kept his place for the 3-2 home win against Peterbourough, and for the trip to Doncaster where we won 2-1. The ship had been steadied.

Our problem was we were so inconsistent. We would win three on the trot only to lose the next three, and so on. We never got out of the bottom half of the table all season long. Victories came slowly.

Bob Wilson, the keeper – not of Arsenal fame- became a good friend of ours. His wife could down a pint of Newcastle Brown in no time! I soon realised that there wasn't this sense of togetherness among the players as there had been at Wrexham.

Not that it mattered. I had my own cheer gang. Exeter and the environs at that time was home to the Royal Hampshire regiment, and also a Commando Unit. For some reason, the little corner of the ground opposite the main grandstand became 'Army HQ' and the troops (literally) would cheer everything I did.

Colin, an army sergeant, and his wife, Pauline, became good friends. They lived quite close to us and we would meet them often. We sadly lost touch when I moved on and Colin was deployed back to Northern Ireland.

I became the coach of the regiment's team, who were participating in the Army Cup at the time. We were not crowned champions, but we did OK, and won a game or two. At training sessions, some of the lads were allowed to miss normal duties, which was apparently a win of sorts. There was much incentive for them to get into the squad!

I was often invited to the sergeant's mess for a beer or two, which was a privilege, and I believe that I was only allowed in, as a civilian, because I was the team coach.

Johnny Giles and Steve Morris, who had been with me in the early days at Bristol City, appeared at Exeter for a while, but both were released at the end of the 1971/72 season.

It was about this time that Dot became quite ill, which led in future months to her being hospitalised, where she eventually underwent a hysterectomy.

If I thought that my injury problems were to be solved here in beautiful Devon, I was very much mistaken.

These two issues, my injury and Dot's illness, were to have a large bearing on where life would take the kids and us over the next two years.

My hamstring injury inevitably returned, along with a bad groin injury and, worst of all, a torn Achilles tendon. The latter saw me in plaster for several months. Luckily, some of that time in plaster was spent during the off-season.

It was during the home game against Southport, on October 16, that I had to leave the field because of my hamstring. I missed the next three games, and made a return against Scunthorpe. However, in the next game, at Southend, I had to leave the field again. I missed the next game at Colchester, but made a return at Brentford. This must have been the last gasp saloon because I missed the next game at Peterborough only to return for the next two at Chester and Aldershot. I had only finished four of the last 11 games. I was frustrated and depressed.

In March, Nutty decided to try something new and I played at wing half at Barrow. I hobbled through the game, a dreary 0-0 draw, with my troublesome hamstring. While the game would not have excited many, Barrow was remarkable for other reasons.

Barrow is a very bleak town. Forgive me, but the only possible reason it exists is that, years ago, the government thought it would be a good place to build ships, and submarines in particular. The town is situated on the southern tip of Cumbria, at the northern end of Morecambe Bay.

The reason I have memories of Barrow-in-Furness is because it was here that, along with Fred Binney, I was arrested. We successfully penetrated the sub gate.

Our travels had taken us to Barrow on March 20, 1972. Barrow v Exeter City, a Fourth Division English Football League game. We would be lucky if 2,000 fans turned up. It was a small, sloping ground, with typical old-time shelters, not much in the way of a stand. To match the atmosphere, we played a boring, meaningless and uninspiring 0-0 draw. Maybe that was because all the excitement had happened before the game.

It was a long trip north from Exeter, over 300 miles. We stayed overnight ready for the game on the Monday night.

When we arrived in Barrow, there were no particular room ups in those days, it was left for us to work out between ourselves. I used to room with the club musician, the mercurial Fred Binney.

Fred was a genial country lad. He played the guitar, scored goals and thought he could sing. He was instrumental, if that is the right word, in producing the Exeter City club song. It was so bad that, when it was played as we ran onto the field, I used to plug my ears.

Really, it was bad.

Fred never stopped talking, but what I liked was that he always kept thinking about the game. He would get the cups out and they would become players. He was so enthusiastic that you forgave him the rest. He could take unbelievable slanging about his guitar and his singing, but he simply kept on playing and strumming.

Fred and I went out for a walk and found the dockyard gate. We thought it would be good to go and have a look at a submarine. We mixed in with the workers and entered beneath the austere steel gate, although we must have stuck out like sore thumbs, a little dark lad and a hippie!

There were what seemed like hundreds of workers going through the gate. No one spoke. No one looked at each other. We followed the flow and then the vista ahead of us opened up. There was a fence, the sea, gray and cold looking, stretched out before us. There were people in navy uniforms and the biggest submarine I've ever seen in my life.

We stood watching for a while as men came and went. Then Fred opened a gate and in we went, too. We walked up to the ship and had a really good look up close. We even asked if we could come aboard. That produced some strange looks. We were just about to leave, and should have left a lot earlier. We spotted a big hole. In seconds, it occurs to us that we are gazing at a nuclear submarine.

Two tall, stern-looking, men asked us for our passes. They had no uniforms on, just civilian clothes.

We attempted to explain ourselves, but our feeble efforts were met with a curt response. We were taken to an office where questions were fired at us like a machine gun.

"Empty your pockets. Names, addresses? What are you doing here? If you live in Exeter, why are you here? Football? Likely story!"

"Ring the manager, ring John Newman," we pleaded, realising

that any punishment from him would seem mild compared to what these people had planned for us.

"Don't worry, we will. Sit in there and keep your hands on the table."

Fred and I were feeling very nervous, sweating and trying to understand what our fate may be. Whenever we asked something, one of them would say, "We'll tell you when we want you to know something."

I had only ever seen a prison from the outside. The thought crossed my mind that this was going to change soon. The office was small, just a desk, a chair, a dim light, a filing cabinet, drab curtains and dull painted walls. Papers were spread on the table and there was a telephone.

Eventually, John Newman is reached on the phone and explanations given. Not long after this, we were released with a stern warning to make sure that we know where we're going next time we go for a walk.

I have never been to Barrow since!

I played only two of the remaining 12 games that season. After Barrow, I couldn't front up for the next six matches. I got through the game against Colchester but didn't make the 90 minutes against Hartlepool in the next. That, as they say, was that. My last appearance in a disappointing season, both personally and for the club.

It's easy to look back and make excuses but, at league level, you have to be the best to get there in the first place. Staying there requires a level of commitment and fitness that you can't let slip. The minute you do, your career starts to slide.

I knew that the hamstring injury wouldn't go away. There was nothing that I could do about it.

I would get in early in the mornings and do the stretches. I did every exercise they told me to do to try and keep my troublesome muscles in tune. Then, along came a groin injury that was so severe that there were times when I literally couldn't walk. I had to hobble.

I would play on Saturday, but the pain would return. As a result, my fitness deteriorated.

Towards the end of my first season at Exeter, I tore my Achilles tendon. It may have been the imbalance in the groin that actually caused this, or vice versa.

Nutty was brilliant in helping me to get over this series of injuries.

I had seen a surgeon in Exeter, who was reluctant to try surgery on the Achilles. Instead, I had the whole of my left leg put into plaster in the hope that a long rest over the close season would stabilise the injury.

We had moved down to Exeter in the meantime and, when the kids were in school, Dot and I had found a couple of nice country pubs where we would go and have lunch. Quite often we would take the kids on a drive and an afternoon out to the beaches which, in this part of the world, are so pretty and plentiful.

On one such excursion, we stopped for a drink in a pub at Dawlish Warren on the coast. Mine host was Bert Hoyle, the old Rovers goalkeeper. We had a long old chat about my days when I watched and his days when he played.

I had a two-year contract at Exeter. Dot and I, and the Flower Pot Men (Michele and Nat), had moved into a clubhouse at St Thomas. Dick Plumb and Tony Scott had joined the club, along with an understudy keeper for Bob Wilson, and a couple of local young players.

Clearly, Scott and Plumb were the key signings. Dick had been at Bristol Rovers and Charlton and had spells at Yeovil, then a non-league club, in between. The other signing was Tony Scott, who had several England youth caps, spells at Villa and West Ham, and had also played locally, at Torquay and Bournemouth. In retrospect, along with Dave Gibson, this was a serious injection of experience for a team at this level.

As with most footballers, we started the season feeling confident that this was going to be our year.

Regrettably, once again we had an indifferent start to the season. No matter how much you prepare, there's nothing like the real thing to get you going. For the second season on the trot, almost to the day, we lost the first game at Southport, 0-1. We then hammered Bradford City at home, 5-1. I got the run around at Mansfield from their left winger, and we lost, 0-3. We drew at home with Hartlepool, 1-1, but there was nothing in our performances to set any tongues wagging.

But then came a run of success that saw us climb to second in the league table on January 27.

Sadly, the final 17 games derailed our season and our hopes of promotion.

That disastrous final spell was our death knell. How do you go straight from a long run of form that has promotion written all over it to a point when you can beat hardly anyone? It's not a short little spurt of five or six games, it's about half of the entire season. How do you know that you're on the throes of a bad spell? If anyone could answer those questions they would make themselves a world beating manager.

I was approaching what might be called a nervous state. Dot was in and out of hospital, Nat had been to the specialist, and the travelling was getting to me.

I had had several discussions with John and he was very understanding.

During the periods that I was injured, Nutty would take me on trips to watch the opposition; Swansea, and several visits to our neighbouring teams, Plymouth and Torquay, come to mind.

We had moved back to Nailsea. Dot had a hysterectomy and was fronting up OK. But the relationship between Dot and I, the kids and this depressing state I was in playing football, the travel and the anxiety, all got to me. In the end I made what was, in my view, a very brave decision.

Dot and I discussed the issues, and she made it quite clear to me that any decision that I made would be mine. I had a long talk with Nutty. I didn't want to leave the club in the lurch, but I'd had enough of these injury issues. John was so accommodating that he had even suggested and I took up the offer to train by myself, or get over to the Rovers or City to do the training.

I was so fearful of something happening to Dot, and my need to be with her that, on March 24, when I hobbled off the field after a defeat by Newport County, I knew it was to be my last professional league game. I was almost in tears. I looked at Nutty and said something along the lines of, "I've had it John." He looked at me and said, "We'll talk about it Monday." So we did. We both knew it was over, but parted as friends.

In two years at Exeter, I had managed a start in just 66% of all league games. In other words, I came up fit for only two of every three games. The club agreed to pay me through to the end of my contract, which terminated on May 31, which was very good of them and much appreciated.

In a strange way, I was happy. Would I miss professional football? Yes, of course I would. Was I happy to be at home with Dot and the kids? Yes, I was happier than ever.

AUSTRALIA BECKONS

The first job I had outside of football was as an Equity Insurance salesman! It was an interesting change.

Dot, myself and the children had often talked of the 'American Story', Clarence and where was he now. What was he like, and all the issues that would relate to meeting a long lost father.

I was constantly scanning the papers for a 'proper' job and was attracted to an advertisement for a Travel Manager at Hourmont School Travel. I was interviewed and, a couple of days later, got a phone call offering me the job. This was a nine-to-five scenario and just what I wanted. It didn't pay as much as professional football but it was enough to pay the bills. For once in a long while, we were all happy.

One of the perks of the job was free travel for holidays and I thought that was just up my street. The job, as the title suggests, was to organise the travel arrangements for teachers to take their pupils on 'Educational Visits' to places of historical, musical, cultural importance and other places of interest.

It was a busy place and fun to work at. One thing I had not banked on was how fast word travels in the football industry. One day, I had a phone call at work from a guy who was looking for players to play in the States.

I was interested, more from the Clarence angle than from the pure football experience. In the end, it boiled down to the Dallas Cowboys or the Seattle Sounders. Both contracts were for six months, but they wouldn't pay for the wife or the kids' travel. The money was more than reasonable, but I kept telling myself not to get too excited.

In six months, it would be back to the same old nine-to-five job. In the end, I decided that Clarence could wait, and Dot agreed.

The phone still kept ringing. Roy Bence from Bath City, then in the Southern League, offered me two nights a week training and a few quid to back it up. I would be earning as much as I did at Exeter if I accepted this offer, and kept the Hourmont job. Dot and I thought long and hard about it and, in the end, I decided to give it a go.

John Sydenham, an ex-Southampton and England Under 23 international, signed around the same time as me, and we immediately became good friends. John reminded me that I had actually marked him as a winger when he played for Aldershot against Exeter a year or so before!

Roy soon got the dismissed talk, and Fred's old nemesis Bert Head took over. The first thing he insisted on was that we would all have a training session on Wednesday, but in the afternoon. Despite strong protests that most of us worked on Wednesday, he went ahead with the session. I managed a couple of sessions but I was stretching my luck and so were many of the other players. Some were slipping out of work without telling the boss.

One day, John took me to one side and said, "Stace, I've had this guy call me, he's over here on a scouting mission and looking for players to go to Australia. I'm off. Are you interested?"

I was. So we met the 'agent' from Australia, Gerry Corulla, acting on behalf of Floreat Athena. Two weeks later, we were on the plane via Singapore and a boat, the 'Patris' ('Homeland', in Greek), from there to Western Australia.

We were guaranteed a return ticket, the kids were paid for, and housing was provided as well as employment. The contract said I would be paid $5 per week for playing, but the final details would be concluded once we were in Perth. What is it they say? 'Beware of

Greeks bearing gifts!' Nothing of the kind happened.

We made the trip with our friends, Andy and Les, and their son, Richard; Les was pregnant with her second child, Andrew.

We arrived safe and sound. Then, rather than being shown to the accommodation that was to be provided, we were shown some places we could rent.

At least I had a job. Then came the punch line: "One of the committee has a bakery and you could become a bread vendor." Back then, bread was delivered door to door. I was not proud and was happy to accept the role, when the next sentence was spoken: "But he hasn't any vacancies at the moment!"

The good news was my contract would see me earn \$20 per game. What about in the summer, the off-season? No play, no pay was the club's answer. I have to say that they were very nice people but the move was 'challenging', to say the least.

Dot, Les, Andy, myself and our kids rented a house in the northern suburbs. Andy and I started delivering bread, not as employees but as contractors, for a firm called Tip Top. Technically you had to provide your own mode of transport, and after a while we did, but we played on the patience of the management by using the red Tip Top vans to deliver our goods door to door. We got away with it in part because the manager was the same manager who ran Parkers Bakery in Bishopsworth, Bristol! He had given me a job during the summer months in Bristol while I was playing for Wrexham. Talk about a small world!

The football wasn't that crash hot. In all honesty, I think that Sneyd Park, my first amateur club, would have won the league with points to spare. It was all a bit of a farce. The lads were, in the main, nothing more than honest amateurs, but the support that these clubs managed to attract was intense.

You were playing for the heart of Greece at Athena, or at Windmills for the Dutch, and at Azzurri it was the Italians. There were clubs representing Croatian expats, Macedonians and Portuguese, and the whole community supported the club, it was a community based around football.

Our coach was Jimmy Pearson, who had played for Australia when the country tried to qualify for a World Cup finals tournament for the first time in 1965. Scottish-born Pearson had played for Greenock Morton and Aberdeen before emigrating to Melbourne in 1962. He then moved north and played for Sydney side Pan Hellenic, and it was here that his performances on the wing earned him an international call-up. He played eight times in all for Australia in 1965.

Jim had a solid background as a player, but very little experience when it came to man management skills.

I found it difficult to grasp the lack of professionalism on the pitch - or open meadows, which is what some felt like - or with internal club issues.

The bottom line though was this. I wasn't getting what had been promised. I made it plain that I wasn't happy. I was up at four in the morning delivering bread. Dot was working in a coffee shop, and the kids were all over the place, it was a complete shambles.

A few weeks down the track, Dot and I were watching television in our flat in Doubleview when there was a knock at the door. It was a bit late for visitors. When I opened the door there were two men standing outside. They offered me money if we lost some games. I told them that it wasn't something I would do. Get lost.

They continue to plead with me, but their begging meets with the same response and eventually I usher them out of the door. I watched out with interest at the results over the next few weeks, and sure enough there was a blip.

One day a person with ties to Olympic Kingsway asked whether

I would be interested in coaching the team.

I knew that almost certainly I wouldn't be able to play, as Athena would ask astronomical money for my transfer, but coaching was a different proposition.

Athena still owed me money, housing and a job. So I accepted the offer.

I should have known that all hell would break loose. It was bedlam. "You can't do that, Stacey! We'll honour your promises." I had heard it all before.

Off I went to coach Olympic. There were no problems, everything that we had agreed happened. Then I ended up being strung up and hung out to dry. Athena appealed to the Australian Football Association, the West Australian Football Association, and every other organisation that would listen.

It was clear it was time to go home. I'd had enough of this place, except for the beach, the BBQ's and the fantastic weather.

The whole family was at the airport when, out of nowhere, the police appeared and arrested me. What for? I was arrested for breach of contract, and leaving the country while owing money. It seemed every accusation that may seem feasible was levelled at me.

Nobody wanted to know my side of the story. Even the judge, who ruled in favour of Athena and who sentenced me to a night in the slammer for breach of contract, would not listen.

I went to jail and was released in the morning. However, I copped a worldwide ban on my football activities and was then escorted back to the airport and onto the plane home.

As we soared to 30,000 feet, I thought 'screw Australia!' Never did I for one moment think that I would return. It had been a memorable time, but for all the wrong reasons.

Once back in England, I contemplated returning to the travel business. Instead, for the first time in my life, I was on the dole. We had rented out the house in Nailsea while we were away so luckily we had a few quid to keep us going. Conscious that a career in football was short-lived, and that plans needed to be made for the 'afterlife', I had, while in Perth, answered a call to take a mature age entry exam for entry to Teachers Training College (TTC) at Nedlands campus. Not long after we arrived back in the UK, I received a letter telling me that that my application was successful.

Now we faced a real dilemma. Mundane, safe Nailsea and work in the holiday industry, or exciting, exotic Perth that offered long term benefits, even though our start to life down under had far from lived up to expectations. We had a family discussion. It was decided that we would head back to Perth.

Amazingly, we were to be paid family benefits to attend Teachers Training College at the Nedlands campus, right next door to the University of Western Australia.

Since I had been accepted as a mature age student, an alternative to teaching was offered. The Federal Government had taken note of Australia's success in the Olympic Games and had introduced a programme aimed at the local level to encourage mass participation in sport and recreation. Recreation Officers were to be appointed to local authorities to facilitate these issues. I chose to take this course.

I soon found out that getting paid for a full-time education, magnificent gesture that it was, just wasn't enough to support the family. So I took 'other' jobs. These included driving a fish delivery van for Mike Kailis, the Athena president, as well as writing a football report for the Sunday Times, and acting as a Recreation Officer for the Catholic Family Welfare Bureau. I also cared for Aboriginal Wards of Court at a place called Wandering, south of Perth, and drove a delivery truck for Coca Cola. It was certainly interesting.

One day, I fell off the truck at a delivery on Wanneroo Road and unfortunately crunched my back and was on sick leave for a while.

While I was recuperating, I accepted a job offer from the City of Stirling as a Recreation Officer and thus set out on my 'career' path.

Despite the unsavory parting, on my return to Australia, I was offered the chance to coach Athena football Club. Certain committee members had left and a new regime was in place. I accepted.

In Australia, if you finish top of the league table you are not crowned champions but 'premiers'. To be the season's champions, you must win the 'finals' series, which has seen the top four teams play off. We won the Top Four, which made us the champions. One played three, and two played four. The winners played off and the winner of that game was proclaimed the season's champions.

This was a great growing period for football in Western Australia. The state team was selected to represent Australia in an overseas tournament in Medan, Indonesia, named the Marah Halim Cup, after the governor, I was privileged to be appointed captain.

We won the tournament. On our return, we played some great European teams who toured Australia, including Legia Warsaw, Manchester United, Middlesbrough and Glasgow Rangers. Astoundingly, our 'band of Brothers' from the parks and back streets of the UK and Australia became the first team from Western Australia to beat an overseas touring team, when we defeated Glasgow Rangers.

This was followed up by the defeat of the touring Canadian champions, Toronto Metro. Despite the victory over Rangers, in my view the best performance was the game against Middlesbrough. Jack Charlton, the 'Boro manager, declared that he did not understand what touring warm up games were, and that his team would be seeking to play us off the park. They came, they saw, but they failed to conquer, and we drew 1-1.

There has been some discussion over the years about the best players to have represented Western Australia. Undoubtedly, after the trauma of WW2 and the immigration from Europe, some excellent individual players came to Perth.

However, I believe that the essence of the game is to transform individuals into a team. That group of players that won an overseas tournament (Marah Halim Cup) after many previous overseas tournament visits, the defeat of arguably Scotland's premier team (Glasgow Rangers), and the dismissal of the Canadian champions, (Toronto Metro), never achieved before, and will never, given the change in Australian football, be achieved again, says it all.

This group of players was Western Australia's finest and needs to be acknowledged as such.

Like all good things that work properly, a car for example, no matter how finely designed it is, it will not function properly without a driver. Our driver was Alan Vest. I must declare that Alan has become a close friend of mine, and he was the driving force behind our success, Western Australia's success, and football's success.

Alan called the shots; I did my best to carry out his wishes on the field. He was undoubtedly the best coach I ever had the privilege of playing for in Australia. Alan was born in Barnsley but represented New Zealand's All Whites and had the distinction of scoring on his international debut. He came to us via Christchurch, in New Zealand, but in my view he was wasted in Western Australia. He deserved something a lot further up the scale.

I left Athena. I can't remember the exact circumstances; I probably had too much to say. Perhaps it was because I chose to go to Medan to represent the State rather than stay behind, and play for them. The Board at the Soccer Federation of Western Australia, despite most teams sending at least two players to represent the state, chose to continue playing the league games. This was madness and some clubs were not happy that players chose what they saw as choosing to take a career boost over playing for them.

If you thought that was bad, the best is yet to come, believe me. I was asked to coach Rockingham United in the Second Division. Rockingham is an hour south of Perth and I was working at the City of Stirling. It was a bit of a journey with the freeway not running that far in those days, but we managed.

I put together a pretty useful team, older guys in critical positions, in goal, and at the centre of defence. A young kid called Neil Allingham played at outside right, Davy Sharp in the wing half position. He had experience in the UK. Then there were the infamous McCanns, Hughie and Pat, difficult to control but players who contributed 110% week in, week out. I played a few games, but I wanted to control the play from afar, I found it hard to be the coach and play.

We worked our way to the top four very quickly and we stayed there. Soon, we were at the top and contested the top two positions. It was quite clear that we were soon going to be promoted to the First Division. In those days it was two up and two down.

Then we heard that there was to be a special meeting of the SFWA. They announced that they had changed their minds, and only one team would be relegated and promoted instead of two!

Remember, we are nearing he end of the season! In any other part of the world, revolution would be on the agenda. Maybe it had something to do with the West Australian version of the FA cup, the D'Orsogna Cup. Second Division Rockingham had knocked out First Division Athena in the quarter finals. We spanked them and sent them home, tails between their legs.

For the semi finals we got Azzurri, another First Division club. It was the same story; we spanked them and sent them home.

So, Second Division Rockingham had won promotion and, in addition was in the D'Orsogna Cup final after crushing not one, but two, First Division teams.

Ascot, another First Division side of English-based players, as were Rockingham, beat us in the final.

Davy Sharp took too much time on the edge of the box in dealing with a disposal, got robbed and that was that. We were terribly unlucky but what's the point of berating Davy. He knew more than anybody what the cost was.

It had been a great season. Sadly though, even promotion was snatched from us. I am unsure why the club never appealed to the Australian Football Federation about the change in the number of clubs that got promoted, but they didn't and we had to spend another season in Division Two.

Can you imagine?

England the First and Second Divisions.

It's three games from the end of the season.

Team A are to be promoted to the First Division and a couple of games from seasons end so are team B.

Hey, sorry, team B, this is the Football Association. We've changed our minds, only one team this year.

Sorry.

What the…?

It was all about being unable to manage the change in the country regarding immigration and population changes.

Teams represented the heart or Greece or Italy or Croatia.

Rockingham, English, you must be joking.

This was about the time that a career became more important than football. In fact, that decision was a major catalyst. The game was poorly administered, too ethnically factional, and, in my opinion, was going nowhere.

So we moved to the other side of the country, to Geelong where I would continue a career in Recreation, with the Shire of Corio, as a manager of the recreation section.

I couldn't resist it. I started to write a football review for the local paper, the Geelong Advertiser, mainly match reports covering sides such as Hamlyn Rangers, Geelong, North Geelong, and Corio

I encouraged the formation the Association of Geelong Football Clubs, and arranged for a few visiting teams, including a magnificent gesture from John Adshead who was then the manager of the New Zealand World Cup side, to come and play en route to Barcelona for the World Cup. They played our Geelong Select side.

Vodjavina, a visiting European side, came to play and Ken Morton, an old friend, also brought Woolongong Wolves who were then a National League side, to come and have a game.

The Brazilian Youth World Cup team also came to Geelong to hold a couple of training sessions, and give some advice to players and coaches. I had the pleasure of having some long discussions with former World Cup star Vava.

Maybe I couldn't play or coach, but in my time as someone in the recreation field, I did what I could, when I could, to help football along its way.

I looked back on my 'life' in football.

Football in Western Australia was sadly run by a group of people who were concerned with their own ethnic self-interest. What they wanted was continuity. Change was not on the agenda, self-interest was.

In later years, I had upset some of the games so-called 'power-brokers' by pointing out that football in WA was going nowhere the way it was structured. Nick Tana, who was then the president of Balcatta FC, and owner of a chain of fast food outlets, agreed with me. Nick was pivotal in pulling West Australia out of its quagmire and launching Perth Glory, now part of Australia's premier competition, the A-League. Nick sold the club soon after the A-League was started, after watching the team win two National

Soccer League titles – the competition prior to the A-League – and some have questioned the direction the club has gone in since. It has been caught up in repeated bad publicity, including being stripped of points and excluded from the finals for breaking the imposed salary cap.

Prior to the birth of Perth Glory in 1986, the WA Government engaged me to prepare a discussion paper: 'The Future Direction of Soccer In Western Australia.'

Soon after its release I became public enemy number one. After WW2 ended, European immigration communities needed some form of unity. Football, a European institution, fitted the bill perfectly and these ethnic clubs had given the game life in Australia, and the members of these communities sustained the clubs and the game. Yet the game's development would be stifled by the continuity of the development of football being left solely to these ethnic groups.

My comments were deemed to be anti the ethnic clubs, when in fact they were stating that, for the game to thrive, it could not survive relying on these clubs to be the sole ones developing top-level players. There had to be an organised structure that would increase the local talent pool from which these clubs could choose to raise the standard in the local competition.

At that point in time, the game's development and growth to the casual user was limited.

The proverbial then hit the fan. Alistair Norwood, then owner of the High Street store Jeans West, and one of WA's emerging multi-millionaires, wanted to build a stadium to incorporate rebranding, ethnic football teams, and play all local games at the same stadium and build a National League.

The government agreed and allocated several million dollars to implement this. They appointed me to run the committee that would handle this delicate issue. The clubs, however, saw this as an attack on their national identity.

I thought we were all Australians?

We may have come from afar but we were now all Australians, but some could not let go of their past.

One of the problems was that the clubs had their own administration. The SFWA (Soccer Federation of Western Australia) had club members, or diehard supporters, on the board. Change was virtually impossible. Time has vindicated the questions asked. The clubs, sadly, held the game as a whole back, purely to protect their own interests.

Someone like myself, who had been around a bit, and tried to effect change, was not welcome. I became the centre of the 'Get Stacey' campaign. I had won the championship with Athena, caused probably illegal change in the SFWA with the Rockingham episode, (change of the number of promoted teams half way through the season), captained the state team that had won the Marah Halim Cup, and the state to its first win over a European touring side. I had written a weekly article for the Sunday paper. I had been critical of some, and was the author of the government-sponsored 'The Future Direction of Soccer in Western Australia'.

The capacity for causing antagonism with some of these issues is obvious. Football in Australia had opened new doors for me and seen me make new friends, many who have lasted a lifetime.

MY FATHER'S VOICE

I am the first African-American to have played professional football in the UK. I'm not sure if this is an issue that means anything to anybody, but it certainly does to my family and I.

The issue never bothered me during my football career.

We were watching 'Roots' one day, when the question was asked. "Dad, who are we, where do we come from?" This led me to our search for Clarence and our American family.

It was only when my playing career was well over that I was made aware that I was the first African-American to play in the Football League. When I was playing for Wrexham and Ipswich, I am not sure that anyone was bothered about such an issue. Having had time to contemplate this news, let me say this. I am proud of this fact.

Dot and I and the children only just made it into the Land of Oz.

The White Australia policy ended around 1973, when a series of amendments preventing the enforcement of racial aspects of immigration law were implemented.

It has also only recently been pointed out to me that my move to Australia could be deemed brave by many, as Australia had only just abolished its White Australia Policy.

This policy can be traced back to the 1850s. It is said to have originated following white miners' resentment towards industrious Chinese, which came to a head and ended in violence on the Buckland River in Victoria, and at Lambing Flat (now Young) in New South Wales.

As a result of these flashpoints, governments of both of these colonies introduced restrictions on Chinese immigration.

Then, in Northern Queensland, it was the turn of labourers from the South Sea Islands of the Pacific. Paranoia spread and there was a groundswell of support to oppose all forms of immigration, which might threaten jobs, particularly immigration by non-white people whom it was thought would accept a lower standard of living and work for less pay.

Leading politicians in New South Wales and Victoria warned that there would be no place for 'Asiatics' or 'coloureds' in the Australia of the future. In 1901, the new Federal Government passed an Act ending the employment of the Pacific Islanders.

The Immigration Restriction Act 1901 received royal assent on December 23, 1901. It was described as an Act 'to place certain restrictions on immigration and to provide for the removal from the Commonwealth of prohibited immigrants'.

There were numerous restrictions placed on immigrants. There was no place for the insane, for prostitutes or for people 'of a loathsome or dangerous character.'

With these severe measures, the implementation of the 'White Australia' policy was warmly welcomed and accepted. In 1919, the Prime Minister of the day, William Morris Hughes, hailed it as 'the greatest thing we have achieved.'

It was not until 1966 that a review of the non-European policy saw the Immigration Minister, Hubert Opperman, announce that applications for migration would be accepted 'from well-qualified people on the basis of their suitability as settlers, their ability to integrate readily and their possession of qualifications positively useful to Australia.'

It was not, however, until 1973 that the Whitlam Labor government took three key steps in the process to remove race as a factor in Australia's immigration policies. One of these was to issue policy instructions to overseas posts to totally disregard race as a factor in the selection of migrants and ratify all international agreements relating to immigration and race.

Australia, however, effectively remained 'white' on the immigration front until 1975 and it was only then that the implications of the new policy were tested by the refugee crisis following the Vietnam War.

So for Dot, myself, Natalie and Michele to move to Australia in 1974 again made me a front-runner, and again I was not aware of the fact. I wasn't aware of these restrictive practices.

Even though we were now living on the other side of the world, we had not left behind our past.

Once in Australia, Clarence's name was coming up more and more. As the kids got older, they became more inquisitive and, being unable to answer some of their questions about their grandfather, the demand to find Clarence grew greater.

Dot, as always, was supportive. We had discussed moving to America to facilitate the process, which led me to apply for a position at Fordham University, without success.

We were now in Geelong, in Victoria, I was working for the Shire of Corio and Dot was working in a nursing home. The owner of the nursing home was a lovely lady called Sue. Her friend, Pauline, dropped in and the talk soon came around to the subject of missing parents. Pauline had the same issue as Dot and I and recommended a few avenues for us to explore.

Eventually, we got a call from lady in Los Gatos, California, Edith Smith. She found people and asked if we needed her help.

I was at my desk working when a call came through from the United States. It was collect. In other local authorities, collect calls from overseas were unusual, and to accept one could lead to a reprimand, maybe worse. Not so at Corio.

I mean this sincerely, almost everyone knew that I was looking for my father, and I had daily enquiries from different staff members about how it all was going, from the boss, Barry McMurrich, and even the Mayor, Gerry Smith.

When I agreed to accept the charges and the caller was put through, Edith was in tears. "Steve, I've found your father!" I will never forget those words and how they sounded. This was a moment frozen in time.

"Are you sure?"

"He gave me your full name, and that of your mother and her sisters, and your date of birth as well as that of your mother. He wants to know whether you will talk to him?"

"Next Sunday. Tell him I'll call him at home." I told her.

Edith then explained how she had managed to track down the father I had imagined all my life, but had no memory of.

When I called at the given time on Sunday, a young girl answered the phone. I learned later this was Valerie, my sister. I asked if a Mr. Clarence Sims lived there.

She told me that he did and I asked if he could come to the phone.

When he came to the phone, I heard him pick the handset up off the table. Then he uttered my name. "Steve?"

It was spoken in a way I have never heard it said before or since. It was a tone that indicated that he was dumbstruck. The tone of his voice as I heard him say my name for the first time in my life told me that he had thought about me; he had not forgotten.

I admit I remember little more of that conversation. I needed time to take everything in.

We spoke again and he told me that, after the war, he had tried to contact Eve, but without much luck. And he knew that Eve was not about to leave England for the killing fields of Kemper County.

As a family, we were ecstatic and we vowed to visit our long lost family in the United States. After we had talked on the phone I wrote to Clarence...

THE LETTER TO MY FATHER

Unit 4 / 6 Isabella Street
West Geelong
Victoria 3218
Australia
May 1983

Dear Clarence Lee,

I'm not sure where to begin. I remember just after the war receiving parcels of chewing gum and peanuts, and a rice paper calendar from Japan I think.

I do know however that when I heard your voice the other day I was the happiest man alive. I hope you are well and in good health and that life has been good to you.

But most of all I want you to understand that I know and understand too about the war, love and emotion and being black or white, and that I want to know who my father is.

I hold no grudges and only look forward to the day when we might meet.

I never went without much, Mum and Gran Stacey kept their eye on me! I did all the things little boys do. Mum had a photograph of you in uniform and I remember I cried the day I could not find it anymore. I kept writing to Electric Mills, a PO box number for some years, but could not get a reply. Strangely none of the letters came back. It wasn't until later I found out, that Electric Mills was in Mississippi not Missouri! Mum married in1950. Ted's a kindly man and never did me any harm, but never went out of his way to be a father either. I have four stepbrothers and sisters, Kenny, Vanessa Mandy and Melanie.

Granddad Stacey died in1948 or 1949 (1950 actually) Gran Stacey in 1970 and Mums sisters Mavis, Beryl and Edie have all gone too.

Mum moved across town about the same time I won a scholarship to Grammar School. Most of these years were spent between Mum's place and Gran.

Edie and Beryl influenced me greatly then. Mum too used to tell me stories about yourself, Bob Ashe, Louis Edmonds and Ray de la Zouche! Two I remember, knocking down the cow, and trying to get my pram up the kerb sideways.

I'm not sure what happened then. I guess I was growing up, long summers and playing football and the questions passed from my mind. I often used to wonder.

I had an awful shock. Mum was sent a cutting from a paper that showed, a man jumping from a bridge in either Washington or New York. The headline said it was you.

(Clarence Sims jumps to his death.)

Naturally we wrote everywhere but couldn't get a scrap of information. Mum said it wasn't you, but I didn't believe her. So for years I went on believing you were dead. That was until two years ago... the kids were watching 'ROOTS'. They just wouldn't stop. Where's your dad? What was he like? So we sat down and went through the whole story. We tried the Red Cross, Veterans Association, Newspapers. One day we met a lady who was an adoptee. She gave us a few addresses stateside to write to, and luckily Edith Smith tried to track you down and succeeded.

I was sorry to hear about Auntie Curry. I guess from what Mum told me she may have been the lady who wanted to adopt me? (This was actually Auntie Annie in Little Rock). I have a million questions to ask you, but perhaps I'll just content myself with a few bits and pieces until I can get my thoughts together.

Dot my wife has been married to me for twenty years! I love her very much. We were just kids but we went ahead anyway. Your two granddaughters are Michele Lee we didn't forget you (Mum had said that Clarence was named Clarence Lee but this was conjecture) and Natalie Jayne. Michele is nineteen and Natalie is seventeen.

They are very aware and proud of their black background. Always asking questions. Always reading books. I think you would be proud of them. I met Dot when we were fifteen. She went through the identity crisis with me. The "I'm alone and nobody loves me thing." She's stuck by me through thick and thin and drove me to reopen the search, when I had looked for years, with no results.

How did we get to Australia? Well I played pro football for years and we came for a two-year holiday and stayed. I graduated from College and went to work for the government. To cut a long story short, I'm applying for a job in Canberra. I've enclosed an application. It sort of tells you what I'm about. Also there are a few newspaper clippings regarding soccer. Mum came from England last year and stayed for six weeks. She encouraged me to keep writing and searching. I think she would like to settle here but it would be a big wrench.

I'm rambling on. I'd like to know what happened to you over the years. I hope you'll be honest with me. Dot, the kids and myself feel we've missed half a family somewhere along the line.

I know it's a bit premature but I'll ask anyway. I really would like you to consider coming to Australia to visit us sometime. I'd be happy to provide a ticket for you. I hope it's something you will consider. In the meantime I'll close by saying that you really have made a big difference to our lives and thank God we found you.

Kind regards

Stephen

(Brackets are my notes and were not in the letter)

FINDING MY ROOTS

I n 1992, Dot and I bit the bullet. We had established contact with the 'Americans' and Clarence had visited us, now it was our turn.

We turned it into a widespread visit. I was to meet some of my old time school friends on the way, in New Zealand and New York. We were going to pass Hawaii, so why not spend a few days there, so we did! We did the same in Los Angeles. Who knew when we would be back?

Dot and I had been in the 'Big Apple' for almost a week. I was about to do what, in my heart, I had wanted most my whole life. I was going to visit my roots, Mississippi. I was apprehensive, excited and curious, all at once.

Dot declined the trip. She felt that Clarence and I should share this between us. She did not want to interfere, although in our conversations I tried to explain to her that she would gain an understanding of what black America and the Deep South was all about. She held firm and I must say I understood exactly where she was coming from.

These were personal matters that father and son would need space to discuss.

The Delta Airlines flight from La Guardia was half empty. We flew way down the east coast, past the Appalachian Mountains and on into New Orleans. We hadn't booked a hotel. The plan was to push on immediately by bus or train. The train proved a no go, but the bus would get us into Meridian early the next morning. Clarence made a couple of phone calls after we had checked the bus timetable.

He had old friends in Meridian we could catch a coffee with, and his schoolboy friend Tommy Reed would drive down from Scooba to pick us up in the morning.

We had hours to kill. We took a cab and instructed the driver to take us to a 'nice bar'. The chosen spot was off the beaten track, on a back street. A husband and wife team ran the bar and they were friendly and wore cheerful smiles.

Clarence did most of the talking over a couple of Millers, and then a couple more.

The man and woman were captivated with my Bristolian accent. I resisted the temptation to give them the real Pirate spiel, but we did the story about father and son and had another beer.

Clarence was getting restless. I thought it a lovely spot and although the place was real quiet, a few drifted in and a couple drifted out, I realised we would have to move.

We called a cab.

"Need some life," said Clarence to the driver.

"Know just the place," said the cab driver.

He dropped us off outside a bright and lively joint, and as we entered, the difference was immediately apparent. Here there was music, lights, people, noise and girls. Clarence pulled up his chair at the bar. He looked relaxed and at home.

"Two Millers."

"Yes, suh."

I pulled up my stool and took it in. There was definitely some action going on.

"Hello, my man," boomed a voice.

"No thanks."

"Hi honey."

"No thanks."

"Sailors?"

"No!"

"Are we staying?" I asked

"It's 20 minutes back to the other place. See it out."

"Whatever you say, Pa."

Another cab took us to the bus station. The driver asked if we were new in town, and then added, "You boys certainly went to the action place! Man, they got everything there, drugs, fancy women and the occasional shooting." Suddenly I felt relieved we had got out alive.

We boarded the bus for Meridian. The driver wanted to talk, so we talked. At a place called Laurel we took a break. The coke machine took my money but wouldn't give me a can of coke. That frustrated me. I fronted the store man who, without a flicker of discontent, handed over the coke. My mood changed and I thought that Mississippi couldn't be all that bad after all.

Clarence had rung Tommy and we had to wait for him for a while. The taxi that took us to the café would wait for us so that we could move on to the meeting point with Tommy without any delay. We had breakfast and coffee.

In the meantime, we had to visit Clarence's long-time friend Horace. Horace was dying. The poor guy was lying in bed and all I could hear was his deep rasping breaths, like every one could be his last. His wife did us some eggs, but Clarence said nothing.

Tommy arrived and off we went north to Scooba. Along the way, Clarence wanted to stop to grab some beer. It was a small grocery store. A man and lady who I presumed were the owners attended the store, and with them was a small girl eight or nine perhaps. The family were all white.

We walked in, had a look round for the beer, and took a cold case. We put the money on the counter and took the change, which was also deposited on the counter. I picked up the beer and we both walked out.

No one had spoken a word. No one had made eye contact except the little girl playing on the floor of the shop. I thought it strange. Wasn't the (American Civil) war over?

On the way we passed through Electric Mills. I asked Tommy to stop the car and Clarence took a picture of me hanging on to the sign.

I briefly contemplated what the name Electric Mills had meant to me over the years.

The birthplace of my father and his family, in a land far, far away. The place where I first learned that blacks and whites were no longer, or ever had been, equal. My mother's telling of stories where long lost relations were to be found.

The end of a long, long search at Electric Mills, Mississippi. Hmmm.

We arrived at Scooba and Aunt Curry and Aunt Julia were a revelation. Julia, with her curled black wig, and Curry, with her greying hair, welcomed me like a long lost son. The house was set back on a large block, some 50 acres or so, I was told. Empty except for the house, a single story weatherboard construction. There was some water on the back of the block. It was tranquil, peaceful, and silent. It felt as if it was a place waiting to be asked questions. Questions like what had happened here over the years?

I was now in 'Bloody' Kemper County, a killing ground of black African-Americans. It was almost as if you could hear the screams through the trees as they rustled. There was so much history here, but a history rarely spoken of. My imagination started to run away with me as I wondered whether the ghosts of all those that died wandered the groves at night.

We were sat down one evening for tea. Aunt Curry had promised me southern fried chicken and black-eyed peas, and did the lady deliver. She sat there and, as we talked, her face suddenly went taut and she screamed, "White man! White man is coming, oh lord a white man…"

I personally have never, in all my life, ever been so moved.

The fear, the memories, the stories and sadly the truth of all that had happened down here in Kemper County, Mississippi, became clear. Aunt Curry had taken me back 50 years in a way that not even a time machine could match. 'Old Timers' disease was how Aunt Julia explained the sudden outburst. But what kind of experience would trigger an outburst such as this? Where in your youth had this come from, Aunt Curry, to last half a century?

I had headed to Mississippi to seek answers to my history, my fears and my hopes, and to get to know Clarence, my father, at the age of forty. If there is a single memory that is important to me, about my search for identity, it came when Clarence took me for a walk.

We had eaten breakfast, and we walked out on a pleasant Mississippi morning. I was alone with my father on a day that boasted blue skies and a light, chilly breeze. Our walk took us out of the little white weatherboard house, down a short dusty path, past trees and scrubs to a red dirt road in Kemper County, Mississippi.

We turned onto the red dirt road. Clarence led the way and I followed. We crossed the road. The red dirt was a stark contrast to the blue sky and the green fields. This is my chance, I told myself, my chance to ask this man, why he left my mother and I. Why he never came back. Now I would ask him about his childhood. How did he suffer? How did he bear the pain of being black? I wanted to hear some of the atrocities that took place in Mississippi. I wanted to know if he had any brothers and sisters, uncles and aunts. If I did, and where were they now? I wanted to know if he had ever sat in the front of the bus, and argued with a white man. Most of all I wanted to know that he loved my mother, and that he had thought of me.

On we walked, past a hedge and a line of trees on one side of the road, on the other an open field stretching into the distance. The road curved gently to the right, and in the distance far ahead of us, a spread of tall trees broke the line of the horizon between earth and sky. A gunshot rang out. Clarence did not flinch; he said, "Deer season," and kept walking.

Clarence offered nothing of his own free will. I realised that I would have to ask questions if I wanted answers. Do I hint and hope he opens up? Do I interrogate, ask politely, or demand the truth? How do you ask a man you hardly know to give you all the answers you need to know, that you have waited a lifetime for an answer? Ahhh, Steve, courage mate.

Behind the tall hedge was a house. It was a short walk down the road from Julia and Curry's place, a distance, a country-neighbour distance, vastly different from a town-neighbour distance. I ventured across to the other side of the road, to the driveway. The short path led to a house like the one I had just left. It was different, individual but similar. Old, yet was carefully tended. The front porch was home to a rocking chair and a man was gently rocking. A dog barked.

The man in the rocking chair looked up. His foot never moved off the cushions that they rested on. Our eyes met over a distance of 20, maybe fewer, yards. He wore military fatigue greens. He stroked the dog with one hand and raised a bottle, slightly, gently, not emphasised, with the other. He never spoke, neither did his expression change, neither did he stop looking at Clarence or I. Five, maybe ten, seconds passed, I wanted to talk. I looked briefly at Clarence, for permission, but he turned to go. I raised my hand to the man in the rocking chair, fingers open, and palm facing him. He smiled, raised the bottle one more time, stroked the dog, eased back into the chair, and adjusted his feet.

"Veteran," said Clarence, "Vietnam."

We walked on. Yet still I did not ask. I had this dilemma. I didn't want to spoil this meeting with my father by turning it into an interrogation. I feared that he might curl up into a hole and tell me nothing. I had already concluded that he wasn't a forthright man. I knew dragging answers out of him was going to be difficult. I had imagined this man my whole life, and now I was with him, I did not want to lose him by asking the wrong question.

Finding and meeting Clarence was a story in itself. I had known him for only a few brief moments in my life, six weeks or so. Knowing is a misnomer. I had been in his presence for six weeks is a better way of putting it. He was spared the inquisition I had given Eve. He was different. I had known my mother. I barely knew Clarence.

We had one brief serious conversation, or shall I say a conversation that moved only briefly away from the comfort zone.

A four-wheel drive approached and screeched to a halt on the red dirt road, sending up clouds of dust. A white man got out, dressed in a full camouflage uniform.

"Want a lift? Can I take you anywhere?" He asked.

"No thanks."

We were walking in the opposite direction.

"Sure about that?" He asked. Then he went to the back of the vehicle and picked up a rifle, from an assortment of rifles.

"Got me a couple today." I'm hoping it was deer. He works the bolt several times.

"Sure?"

"Sure."

He jumped back into the cab and drove off in a billowing cloud of dust, spinning his wheels as he went.

Clarence walked in silence for some minutes, and then he spoke. "You know, Steve, ten years ago he would have just run all over us. That was Ol' Miss then."

I can't help but ponder on this incident, it gives me a view into

Clarence's life and allows me a glimpse of what it must have been like when he was a young boy.

As we walked on I waited to talk about life in Mississippi, and Scooba in particular. I didn't probe, I let him talk. Talk about King, Kennedy, the Black Panthers and Malcolm X. About being black, and being black in America, in Mississippi and in New York. Even what it was like being black in Bristol, too, but there was not much forthcoming.

Electric Mills is just up the road from Meridian. Meridian is just a little east of Jackson. Meridian is the town where the trial of the killers of the young civil rights workers, Michael Schwerner, Andrew Goodman and James Chaney was finally held, in 1967. The injustice of these murders was portrayed in the film 'Mississippi Burning'.

Chaney was a black lad, Schwerner and Goodman white, murdered by the Klan for attempting to organise black Americans to vote.

Clarence took me to the spot where the young boys had been murdered and dumped by the Klan. It was a lonely, solitary, chilling place. It's no place to end your life.

It made me want to know more about what it was like for my father growing up in a state with many of its occupants clearly racist. Where black people's lives were cheaper than a loaf of bread, or a quart of milk. Where to simply look at a white person could get you killed. I could not imagine what it was like to live in fear from the moment of waking until the sunset, and beyond.

Then to have to fight a war, which you knew nothing about, and for a cause that you knew even less about. You fall in love with a white woman, and for her to have your child. These two actions alone were a 'crime' in Mississippi, a crime that would most likely get you hanged. Maybe even both of you hanged.

What must it have felt like to be suddenly thought of as an equal?

To be accepted into the bosom of Eve's family. For her sisters and her parents to welcome you, to appreciate the war that you fought and the deeds that you did. To be valued and treated as an equal. How that young man must have loved the sense of freedom and respect that had been endowed upon him.

I felt sure that this would have been something he took home with him after the war, that he would have told his parents and his family. We don't have to live like this. In England, we're all free. I can sit next to ten white men in a coffee shop or a pub and be admired.

On the way home, we passed a place which had flashing lights and the faint sound of music.

"Well I'll be," says Clarence, "don't know this place. Let's have a look."

In we go. On the floor as we enter on the left is a midget, a very small person, and he's smashed. He was frothing at the mouth and muttering some unintelligible words. At the bar are a few of, I assume, the locals, male and female. We squeeze in between two ladies.

"Two beers," says Clarence.

The bar lady leans over and says. "What kind of beer do you want?"

"Millers," says Clarence, "two."

She went to the fridge and brought back two beers. They weren't Millers.

Clarence looked at me. I looked at him. No words were exchanged. Clarence paid for the beers. He didn't get any change.

"Hi honey." The 'girl' on my left says. The husky voice can't be hidden.

Not again, I thought. We took the beers with us. We didn't talk much, Clarence and I. I mean deep, meaningful conversations. Was he shy? Maybe guilt. Perhaps he was afraid of being read the wrong way in all he said, did, and perhaps his comments being misinterpreted. I didn't know how to take all of this. Maybe it was a reminder that I didn't fit in to black America at all. Getting close was difficult.

Every question I asked was dismissed: "Don't know that one". Umm, really? Dragging Eve and I, Gran and the girls and his relationship out of him was, well, impossible. He didn't want to talk.

But he did say to me one day, "You know, Steve, you're black outside, but inside, you're all white".

I know, Clarence, I've felt this on the football fields of Europe.

Two football teams and a crowd of double digit thousands and you the only black man, ummm.

I never knew Clarence, I only knew of him.

Children of mixed race have a foot in two worlds. Some fit into both, some fit into only one and some fit into neither. That is why I hold out my hand to anyone, anywhere, anytime, who needs help, aid or assistance to fight racial abuse.

It was funny after that comment by my father. I remembered when my two daughters were growing up and were both in primary school. There had been some discussion in their classes about heritage and background. We were at home discussing these issues over tea, and in particular the amount of the bloodline from each culture. I had just finished crunching the numbers for Michele and Natalie. There was a pause before Michele piped up and said, "Dad we're kind of like mongrels aren't we?"

"Yes, my love," I replied. "But doesn't it make you proud?"

BLACK PIONEER?

When I made my debut for Wrexham, I was simply happy to be playing in the first team and fulfilling my lifelong dream.

I was not aware, when I ran onto the pitch one day at Southport, in the old Fourth Division, that I was the first African-American to have played professional football in the English Football League.

When I made my debut for Ipswich in the old First Division, I became the first African-American to play in the highest league in England.

The most prominent of the black players around the time I was playing was probably Albert Johanneson, a South African who played for Leeds United at outside left. He was the first black player and the first player of African heritage to feature in an English FA Cup final.

His life in South Africa, at the height of the apartheid era, where football was the black man's sport, and rugby belonged to the whites, had left him a little shy and apprehensive of himself in front of white folks. Legend has it that when Albert seemed a little unsure of getting in the bath with all these white players, the lads got up and threw him in.

What I do know is this; the view is that if you are good enough to pull on a jersey, to represent the club, then you are good enough to get in the bath with us.

When you represent the club, everything that you do is under the microscope. Your life belongs to your contract. You disgrace yourself, you disgrace the club, more importantly you disgrace the playing group.

I believe that ability on the football field negates colour. Believe me, if you walk into a football club and the colour of your skin is a rainbow, you ask for a game, and you show you can play to the required standard, then you're in. Good enough to play professional football is the only criteria.

Your teammates become your friends, those close personal relationships that cannot be had with anyone else. No matter who your friends are, you can't create the intimacy, perhaps the brutality, of that late sliding tackle that saved the game in front of 3,000 or 30,000 frenzied fans on a cold wet February afternoon.

Moments shared on and off the field, such as this, melt into one. These moments transcend race, age and gender.

Your personal life does not belong to you anymore. It belongs to the manager, the coach and the board. So, too, do the good things that you do. Whatever it is that was good, very good, brilliant, magnificent, exemplary, extraordinary, or has never been done before, it was all a product of a club policy, youth development, training, coaching, the coach, and/or marketing. If it hadn't been you, it would have been someone else.

Professional sports people, in my experience, don't care whether you are blue, black, white or red. They care mostly about your ability to deliver on your skill level under the most trying of circumstances.

I can tell you right now that when you're sat in that dressing room, the only thing that you worry about is how your afternoon is going to pan out. It's a credit to my fellow professionals that while I was playing, I do not recall any incident of racial abuse levelled against me. A few of the incidents mentioned could have happened to anyone and I have no proof that the colour of my skin had anything to do with any of them.

If you are a minority, and you are given an opportunity, then you are starting with a bucket of goodwill. People obviously respect your ability to give you a chance. It's up to you whether they respect you as a person.

In 1948, the mass emigration from the Caribbean to the UK began. What also began was a new era in British football. The transition of black athletic achievement started with that migration.

Viv Anderson became the first black player to represent England at Wembley on November 29, 1978. Paul Ince became the first black player to captain England in a full international in1993. Earlier in the same year, Ugo Ehiogu had captained the England Under 21 side. There are close to 100 black players who hold the distinction of having pulled on the England shirt. This has happened in 40 short years.

This is a powerful message. Consider how the views of many people have changed over the years. A black man playing for England was unimaginable in the 1960s. A black man captaining the last bastion of the Empire was simply preposterous.

If attitudes and values and perceptions are changing, are they changing for the better? Is it all about sport or are there other considerations?

We are talking about massive exposure; 240 million people in 200 countries play football, so to understand and know that the captain of your country is a minority black player gives other minorities reason for hope.

It is interesting that one rarely considers distinguishing players along racial or ethnic lines when discussing sports clubs. We don't refer to the white part of Arsenal or Liverpool, or the catholic or protestant players at a club. We don't leave the 'ethnics' out when the club plays golf or tennis, or hosts the awards night or dines at the finest restaurants, or meets the politicians.

We talk about the club and everyone, regardless of race, colour, religion or social status, is included.

If the Australian team was captained by an Indigenous player, what pride would one feel if a black man led Australia onto a world stage? Mark Ella has captained the Wallabies in rugby union, but few other Aboriginals have been afforded the honour of leading their country.

In Australia, the Indigenous community languishes at the lower end of the statistics of education, health, justice and other social issues, with never an upward trend in sight. If sport is a part of the road out, keeps people healthy, gets kids to stay at school longer, and keeps them off the streets, and out of jail, then let's broaden the road, and turn it into a six lane freeway.

Where would I have ended up without sport? Given my early teenage track record, I don't want to contemplate that. If I hadn't signed that piece of paper all those years ago in Fred Ford's office, where would this little coloured lad have ended up in the hurly burly world of labour and work statistics?

Would I have stayed in the travel industry back in the UK?

Would I have found it easy to find a job of my choice, being a different colour, if Bristol City hadn't given me a chance?

Enoch Powell's 'Rivers of Blood' speech in 1968 wouldn't have helped the cause.

Australia would have been but a distant dream.

Dream on, young man. Cherish the dawn. Be grateful for who you are and what you have achieved.